Mastering Spring Boot 2.0

Build modern, cloud-native, and distributed systems using
Spring Boot

Dinesh Rajput

BIRMINGHAM - MUMBAI

Mastering Spring Boot 2.0

Commissioning Editor: Merint Mathew
Acquisition Editor: Karan Sadawana
Content Development Editor: Akshada Iyer
Technical Editor: Supriya Thabe
Copy Editor: Safis Editing
Project Coordinator: Prajakta Naik
Proofreader: Safis Editing
Indexer: Aishwarya Gangawane
Graphics: Jisha Chirayil
Production Coordinator: Shraddha Falebhai

First published: May 2018

Production reference: 1300518

Published by Packt Publishing Ltd.
Livery Place
35 Livery Street
Birmingham
B3 2PB, UK.

ISBN 978-1-78712-756-2

www.packtpub.com

First, I want to dedicate this book to all the soldiers of the Indian Army.

To my parents, my lovely wife, and my kids, Arnav and Rushika.

Specially dedicated to my grandfather, the late Mr. Arjun Singh, and my maternal grandfather, the late Mr. Durjan Lal Rajput.

`mapt.io`

Mapt is an online digital library that gives you full access to over 5,000 books and videos, as well as industry leading tools to help you plan your personal development and advance your career. For more information, please visit our website.

Why subscribe?

- Spend less time learning and more time coding with practical eBooks and Videos from over 4,000 industry professionals

- Improve your learning with Skill Plans built especially for you

- Get a free eBook or video every month

- Mapt is fully searchable

- Copy and paste, print, and bookmark content

PacktPub.com

Did you know that Packt offers eBook versions of every book published, with PDF and ePub files available? You can upgrade to the eBook version at `www.PacktPub.com` and as a print book customer, you are entitled to a discount on the eBook copy. Get in touch with us at `service@packtpub.com` for more details.

At `www.PacktPub.com`, you can also read a collection of free technical articles, sign up for a range of free newsletters, and receive exclusive discounts and offers on Packt books and eBooks.

Contributors

About the author

Dinesh Rajput is the founder of *Dineshonjava*, a blog for Spring and Java techies. He is a Spring enthusiast and a Pivotal Certified Spring Professional. He has written a bestselling book, Spring 5 Design Patterns. He has more than 10 years of experience with different aspects of Spring and cloud-native development, such as REST APIs and microservices architecture.

He is currently working as an architect at a leading product. He worked as a tech lead at Bennett, Coleman & Co. Ltd and Paytm.

He completed his master's degree in computer engineering at JSS Noida, and he lives in Noida, India.

Technically, I authored this book, but it was not possible without the unconditional support of my wife, Anamika, who helped me focus on this book. Thanks to my kids, Arnav and Rushika. I have taken away a lot of time that I'd spend playing with them to write this book.

A huge thanks go to my father, Shrikrashan Rajput, and mother, Indira Rajput, and Surendra Singh who encouraged me to do work that they can feel proud of.

About the reviewers

Samer ABDELKAFI has 13 years of experience as a software architect and engineer, a major in open source technologies. He has contributed to numerous and diverse projects in different sectors such as banking, insurance, education, public services, and utility billing. In 2016, he created DEVACT, a company specializing in information technology consulting. He has also reviewed two books related to Spring projects titled, *Spring MVC Blueprints* and *Mastering Spring Cloud*. In addition to this, he shares his experience on his blog and writes articles related to Java and web technologies.

Yogendra Sharma is a developer with experience of the architecture, design, and development of scalable and distributed applications. He was awarded a bachelor's degree from Rajasthan Technical University in computer science. With a core interest in microservices and Spring, he also has hands-on experience in technologies such as AWS Cloud, Python, J2EE, NodeJS, JavaScript, Angular, MongoDB, and Docker. Currently, he works as an IoT and cloud architect at Intelizign Engineering Services Pune.

Packt is searching for authors like you

If you're interested in becoming an author for Packt, please visit `authors.packtpub.com` and apply today. We have worked with thousands of developers and tech professionals, just like you, to help them share their insight with the global tech community. You can make a general application, apply for a specific hot topic that we are recruiting an author for, or submit your own idea.

Table of Contents

Preface

Mastering Spring Boot 2.0 is for all Java developers who want to learn Spring Boot and Spring Cloud as enterprise-distributed cloud-based applications. Therefore, enterprise Java and Spring developers will find this book particularly useful in helping them understand cloud-native design patterns using the microservices architecture used by Spring Boot 2.0 and Spring Cloud, how the microservices architecture solves the common design problems of the cloud-native infrastructure in distributed applications, and they will appreciate the examples presented in this book. Before reading this book, readers should have basic knowledge of the basics of Core Java, Spring Core Framework, and Spring Boot. You can read my other book, *Spring 5 Design Patterns* to learn more about Spring Framework.

Spring Boot 2.0 has been newly launched by Pivotal with the reactive programming and the cloud. Spring Boot 2.0 introduces many new features and enhancements we will discuss in this book. *Mastering Spring Boot 2.0* is a mastering book that will give you in-depth insight into the Spring Boot and cloud microservices architecture.

The great part of today's Spring Boot is that many companies have already adopted it as a primary framework for the development of the enterprise applications, especially for the REST APIs using the microservices architecture. For Spring Boot, no external enterprise servers are needed to start working with them.

The goal of writing this book is to discuss the common designs used behind cloud-native applications and how they are implemented in the Spring Cloud module of the Spring Boot 2.0. Here, the author has also outlined some best practices that should be used during logging of the distributed design and development of the application.

The book contains 15 chapters, which cover everything from the development of microservices-based cloud applications to the deployment of microservices by either using virtual machines or containers such as Docker.

Mastering Spring Boot 2.0 is divided into four parts. The first part introduces you to the essentials of Spring Boot 2.0, Spring Boot CLI, and Spring Cloud. Part 2 steps behind the interservice communication in the microservices architecture using Rest Template, Spring Cloud Netflix Feign. Part 3 expands on that by explaining how to build an event-driven resilient system with Spring Cloud Stream and Kafka. This part also shows you how to monitor using Hystrix and Turbine. Finally, part 4 explains how to test and build APIs, and deploy to containers such as Docker, and also to clouds, such as AWS.

Who this book is for

Mastering Spring Boot 2.0 is for all Java developers who want to learn Spring Boot and Spring Cloud in the enterprise-distributed cloud-based applications. Therefore, enterprise Java and Spring developers will find it particularly useful in understanding cloud-native design patterns using the microservices architecture used by Spring Boot 2.0 and Spring Cloud, how microservices architecture solves common design problems of the cloud-native infrastructure in the distributed application, and they will most fully appreciate the examples presented in this book. Before reading this book, readers should have basic knowledge of Core Java, Spring Core Framework, and Spring Boot basics.

What this book covers

Chapter 1, *Getting Started with Spring Boot 2.0*, will give you an overview of Spring Boot 2.0 and all its new features, including some essential key components. You'll also get an overview of the greater the Spring Boot.

Chapter 2, *Customizing Auto-Configuration in Spring Boot Application*, will give an overview of the Spring Boot auto-configuration feature and explains how you can override the default autoconfiguration.

Chapter 3, *Getting Started with Spring CLI and Actuator*, will show you several ways to create Spring Boot applications using Spring Boot's web-based interface, the STS IDE, and Spring Boot CLI. In this chapter, we will discuss Spring Boot CLI deeply and will also see how to install it on your machine and how to use it to create Spring Boot applications. Also, you'll see Spring Boot's production-ready features using the Actuator.

Chapter 4, *Getting Started with Spring Cloud and Configuration*, will explore how to create a configuration server to provide a set of configuration files from a Git repository to client applications. In this chapter, the reader will also learn about Spring Cloud configuration service and how to build and consume the configuration service.

Chapter 5, *Spring Cloud Netflix and Service Discovery*, will explore Spring Cloud Netflix and Service Discovery with Eureka.

Chapter 6, *Building Spring Boot RESTful Microservice*, will build a RESTful atomic microservice that performs CRUD operations on an in-memory database, either HSQL or H2, using Spring Cloud and Spring Data, enable the service for service discovery registration to the Eureka server.

Chapter 7, *Creating API Gateway with Netflix Zuul Proxy*, will explore the need of the API gateway pattern for microservices communication, either from UI components or from inter service calls. We will implement an API gateway using the Netflix API Zuul. We will see how to set up a Zuul proxy in your application.

Chapter 8, *Simplify HTTP API with Feign Client*, will explore what Feign is and how it works. It gives a detailed explanation of how Feign can be extended/customized for business needs, with a reference implementation for a custom encoder, decoder, Hystrix, and exception handling with unit testing.

Chapter 9, *Building Event-Driven and Asynchronous Reactive Systems*, will provide a detailed overview of how to use event-driven architectures to build event-driven microservices as cloud-native applications. We will look at some of the important concepts and themes behind handling data consistency in distributed systems.

Chapter 10, *Building Resilient Systems Using Hystrix and Turbine*, will explore the circuit breaker pattern with a reference implementation using the Netflix Hystrix library, touching base on configuring the Turbine dashboard to aggregate hystrix streams from multiple services.

Chapter 11, *Testing Spring Boot Application*, will explore unit testing Spring Boot Services using JUnit and Mockito. All our reference implementation will have unit testing done, so this chapter is more of an aggregation of the different testing mechanisms available for microservices.

Chapter 12, *Containerizing Microservice*, will provide an introduction to containers, dockerizing the services built in the previous chapter, writing a Dockerfile, orchestrating the containers using docker-compose, and providing an orchestration example in Kubernetes.

Chapter 13, *API Management*, will explore the need for an API manager in distributed systems, setting up KONG open source API manager, configuring the API endpoints built in the previous chapters in the KONG API Manager, introducing Swagger for API standards, and finally closing with demonstrating rate limiting and logging using KONG.

Chapter 14, *Deploying in Cloud (AWS)*, will explore deploying microservices in AWS EC2 instances manually and using cloudformation scripts. You will learn how to run a Docker-enabled Spring Boot microservice application on Amazon EC2 instances.

Chapter 15, *Production Ready Service Monitoring and Best Practices*, will elaborate on some of the best practices in building distributed systems and also will elaborate on performance monitoring for production ready services. We will introduce log aggregation using the ELK(Elasticsearch/Logstash/Kibana) stack for a distributed application.

To get the most out of this book

This book can be read without a computer or laptop at hand, in which case you need nothing more than the book itself. However, to follow the examples in the book, you need Java 8, which you can download from `http://www.oracle.com/technetwork/java/javase/downloads/jdk8-downloads-2133151.html`, and you will also need your favorite IDE. I have used the Software Spring Tool Suite; download the latest version of Spring Tool Suite (STS) from `https://spring.io/tools/sts/all` according to your OS. Java 8 and STS work on a variety of platforms—Windows, macOS, and Linux.

Download the example code files

You can download the example code files for this book from your account at `www.packtpub.com`. If you purchased this book elsewhere, you can visit `www.packtpub.com/support` and register to have the files emailed directly to you.

You can download the code files by following these steps:

1. Log in or register at `www.packtpub.com`.
2. Select the **SUPPORT** tab.
3. Click on **Code Downloads & Errata**.
4. Enter the name of the book in the **Search** box and follow the onscreen instructions.

Once the file is downloaded, please make sure that you unzip or extract the folder using the latest version of:

- WinRAR/7-Zip for Windows
- Zipeg/iZip/UnRarX for Mac
- 7-Zip/PeaZip for Linux

The code bundle for the book is also hosted on GitHub at `https://github.com/PacktPublishing/Mastering-Spring-Boot-2.0`. In case there's an update to the code, it will be updated on the existing GitHub repository.

We also have other code bundles from our rich catalog of books and videos available at `https://github.com/PacktPublishing/`. Check them out!

Conventions used

There are a number of text conventions used throughout this book.

`CodeInText`: Indicates code words in the text, database table names, folder names, filenames, file extensions, pathnames, dummy URLs, user input, and Twitter handles. Here is an example: "Let's configure Zuul properties in our application using the `application.yml` configuration file."

A block of code is set as follows:

```
@RestController
class HelloController {
  @GetMapping("/")
  String hello() {
    "Hello World!!!"
  }
}
```

When we wish to draw your attention to a particular part of a code block, the relevant lines or items are set in bold:

```
<dependencies>
    <dependency>
      <groupId>org.springframework.boot</groupId>
      <artifactId>spring-boot-starter-web</artifactId>
    </dependency>
</dependencies>
```

Any command-line input or output is written as follows:

```
$ Spring run HelloController.groovy
```

Bold: Indicates a new term, an important word, or words that you see onscreen. For example, words in menus or dialog boxes appear in the text like this. Here is an example: "Click the **Generate Project** button, and we have a ready-to-run application."

 Warnings or important notes appear like this.

Tips and tricks appear like this.

Get in touch

Feedback from our readers is always welcome.

General feedback: Email feedback@packtpub.com and mention the book title in the subject of your message. If you have questions about any aspect of this book, please email us at questions@packtpub.com.

Errata: Although we have taken every care to ensure the accuracy of our content, mistakes do happen. If you have found a mistake in this book, we would be grateful if you would report this to us. Please visit www.packtpub.com/submit-errata, selecting your book, clicking on the Errata Submission Form link, and entering the details.

Piracy: If you come across any illegal copies of our works in any form on the Internet, we would be grateful if you would provide us with the location address or website name. Please contact us at copyright@packtpub.com with a link to the material.

If you are interested in becoming an author: If there is a topic that you have expertise in and you are interested in either writing or contributing to a book, please visit authors.packtpub.com.

Reviews

Please leave a review. Once you have read and used this book, why not leave a review on the site that you purchased it from? Potential readers can then see and use your unbiased opinion to make purchase decisions, we at Packt can understand what you think about our products, and our authors can see your feedback on their book. Thank you!

For more information about Packt, please visit packtpub.com.

Getting Started with Spring Boot 2.0 {.chapter-number}

1

Getting Started with Spring Boot 2.0

As we know, the Spring Framework makes development very easy for both core and enterprise Java applications. Spring has settled, and is now a very popular framework. The Spring team is continuously inventing something new to enhance software development and they are focused on making software development easy. The Spring team released one of its major projects for the Spring Framework in 2013, Spring Boot.

This project from the Spring team makes software development with Java easy. Spring Boot is built on top of the existing Spring Framework. So basically, Spring Boot is not a separate framework, but it is similar. It's a collection of ready-made things to just pick and use without taking any overhead configuration.

The Spring team is introducing many exciting things to the Spring ecosystem to sustain it in the market. There are many new things such as cloud computing, big data, schemaless data persistence, and reactive programming. But one of the most exciting and game changing features has come with Spring Boot in the past year. Spring Boot is a great invention for the Spring Framework by the Spring team. That is why Spring has settled for a long time and is winning major laurels.

Spring Boot is a tricky framework to understand. This chapter will help you to understand Spring Boot 2.0 and the underlying important concepts—starter projects, auto-configuration, and starter parents. You will also understand how Spring Boot makes software development easy. As a bonus, I will discuss the story behind the success of Spring Boot. This chapter will cover a demo application with Spring Boot and create a REST service.

At the end of this chapter, you will understand how Spring Boot develops Spring applications with agility and provides an already prepared menu for creating a REST service. You will learn how Spring Boot solves common problems at the configuration level of an enterprise application by using auto-configure.

This chapter will cover the following points:

- Introducing Spring Boot
- Simplifying Spring application development using Spring Boot
- The essential key components of Spring Boot
    - Spring Boot Starter projects
    - Auto-configuration
    - Spring Boot CLI
    - Spring Boot Actuator
- Setting up a Spring Boot workspace
- Developing your first Spring Boot application
- New features in Spring Boot 2.0

Let's look at these topics in detail.

Introducing Spring Boot

In my opinion, Spring Boot is like a cooked meal waiting to be eaten. In terms of Spring application development, Spring applications typically require a lot of setup. Suppose you are working with JPA. You need `DataSource`, `TransactionManager`, `EntityManagerFactory`, and so on. If you are working with a web MVC application, you need `WebApplicationInitializer`/`web.xml`, `ContextLoaderListener`, and `DispatcherServlet`. If you are working on an MVC application using JPA, you would need all of these. But much of this is predictable. Spring Boot can do most of this setup for you.

Spring Boot provides a new strategy for application development with the Spring Framework, with minimal fuss. It enables you to focus only on the application's functionality rather than Spring metaconfiguration. Spring Boot requires either minimal or zero configuration in the Spring application.

According to the Spring Boot documentation:

> *"Spring Boot makes it easy to create stand-alone, production-grade Spring based Applications that you can "just run.""*

Spring Boot has changed the way Spring applications are being developed. If you look at the initial versions of the Spring Framework, Spring was a very lightweight and POJO-oriented framework. That means it was decoupled and had less component code, with configurations being set up using XML. As of Spring version 2.5, annotations were introduced, which reduced the XML configurations by using component-scanning. Spring 3.0 came with Java configuration; do note that there was still no escape from configuration. Eventually, with the latest Spring version, component-scanning reduced configuration and Java configuration made it less time-consuming, but Spring still required a lot of configuration.

All these configurations in the Spring application affect the development of actual business functionality. It works as a source of friction in Spring application development. There is no doubt the Spring Framework does much more for us in the area of application development using Java. But if a mistake happened in the configuration level, it required a lot of time to debug and solve it.

Another point of friction is project dependency management. Adding dependencies is very hectic work that gives developers headaches when it comes to deciding what libraries need to be part of the project build. It is even more challenging to identify the versions of depending libraries.

Overall, you can see that configurations, dependency management, and deciding versions of depending libraries consume a lot of the development time of the software engineer. Finally, it reduces the productivity of developers.

Spring Boot has changed all of that, but remember it is not a code generator or an IDE plugin.

Spring Boot has an opinionated view of the Spring application. An opinionated runtime for Spring Projects supports different project types, such as Web and Batch, and it handles most low-level, predictable setup for you.

What is an opinionated runtime? Spring Boot uses sensible defaults, *opinions*, mostly based on the classpath contents. For example, it sets up a JPA Entity Manager Factory if a JPA implementation is on the classpath. Spring Boot uses a default Spring MVC setup if Spring MVC is on the classpath. Still, everything can be overridden easily, but most of the time there is no need to override anything.

Let's see how Spring Boot simplifies Spring application development.

Simplifying Spring application development using Spring Boot

As we have discussed in the previous section, the Spring Framework provides lot of flexibility to configure beans in the Spring application in multiple ways such as XML, annotation, and Java configuration. But remember, if the number of modules and features increases in the Spring application, it also increases the complexity in the configuration. After a point, your Spring application tends to become tedious and error-prone.

Here, Spring Boot comes into the picture to address the complexity of the configuration of your Spring application.

Spring Boot does exactly what you are looking for. It will do things automatically for you but allows you to override the defaults if required. (Remember the point about it being an opinionated framework?)

Spring Boot is not a separate framework, but it is Spring at heart. It is built on top of the Spring Framework to remove tedious work from the developer end and allow developers to focus on the business code with minimal or zero configurations.

See the following diagram that shows what Spring Boot is exactly:

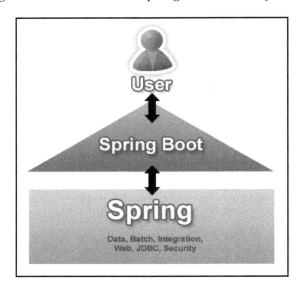

In the preceding diagram, you can see that **Spring Boot** is the surface layer over the **Spring Framework**, with all of the modules such as **Web** (MVC), **JDBC**, **Security**, **Batch**, and so on. It presents a small surface area for **User** to approach and extract value from the rest of **Spring**.

Suppose you are working with a task, a `Hello World` web application. If you are choosing to develop with the Spring Framework, what would you need to do?

The following are the bare minimum configurations required for a small web application:

- Creating a project structure either by using Maven or Gradle and defining required dependencies such as Spring MVC and the Servlet API dependencies for your case.
- A deployment descriptor file, that is, `web.xml`. In the case of Java configuration, you require the `WebApplicationInitializer` implementation class that declares Spring's `DispatcherServlet`.
- The Spring MVC configuration class to enable the Spring MVC module for your `Hello World` application.
- You have to create a controller class that will respond to your request.
- You require a web application server such as Tomcat.

Of these points, most are generic boilerplate code and common configuration for a Spring web application, except writing application-specific controllers. So, Spring Boot provides all common configurations and boilerplate code based on the available library of the classpath. You don't need to take responsibility for writing this common and generic code.

Let's create the same `Hello World` application using Spring Boot. Suppose for a moment we are using a `Groovy-based controller` class as follows:

```
@RestController
class HelloController {
    @GetMapping("/")
    String hello() {
        "Hello World!!!"
    }
}
```

This code is a complete Spring web application, with nothing required to configure. No `web.xml` file, no build specification, and not even an application server. This is the entire application. We can run this application using Spring Boot CLI with the following command:

```
$ Spring run HelloController.groovy
```

So, you can see how Spring Boot simplifies Spring application development. We will also see the same application using Java in the next section of this chapter.

 Spring Boot does not compete with the Spring or Spring MVC Framework. It makes it easy to use them in the Spring application.

The essential key components of Spring Boot

You have seen how Spring Boot simplifies Spring application development. But how does Spring Boot make it possible? What is the magic behind it? Spring Boot brings this magic to Spring application development. The following are essential key components of Spring Boot:

- Spring Boot Starters
- Automatic configuration
- Spring Boot CLI
- Spring Boot Actuator

These four core key components are the reason behind Spring Boot's magic. These components make Spring application development easy. Let's see these components in detail.

Spring Boot Starters

Starter is like a small Spring project for each module such as web MVC, JDBC, ORM, and so on. For your Spring application, you just add the starters of the respective module in the classpath, and Spring Boot will ensure that the necessary libraries are added to the build by using Maven or Gradle. As a developer, you don't need to worry about the module libraries and dependent versions of libraries, that is, transitive dependencies.

 Spring Boot documentation says Starters are a set of convenient dependency descriptors that you can include in your application. You get a one-stop-shop for all the Spring and related technologies that you need, without having to hunt through sample code and copy-paste loads of dependency descriptors.

Suppose you want to create a web application or an application to expose RESTful services using the Spring web MVC module to your Spring application; just include the `spring-boot-starter-web` dependency in your project, and you are good to go.

Let's see what it would look like in the Spring application:

```
<dependencies>
   <dependency>
         <groupId>org.springframework.boot</groupId>
         <artifactId>spring-boot-starter-web</artifactId>
   </dependency>
</dependencies>
```

This starter dependency resolves the following transitive dependencies:

- `spring-web-*.jar`
- `spring-webmvc-*.jar`
- `tomcat-*.jar`
- `jackson-databind-*.jar`

See the following diagram about **spring-boot-starter-web**:

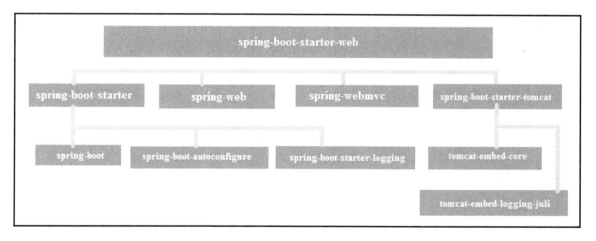

The **spring-boot-starter** not only reduces the build dependency count, but also adds specific functionality to your build. In your case, you added the web starter to your Spring application, so it provides web functionality that your application needs. Similarly, if your application will use ORM, then you can add the `orm` starter. If it needs security, you can add the `security` starter.

Spring Boot provides a wide range of Starter projects. Spring Boot provides the following application Starters under the `org.springframework.boot` group:

- `spring-boot-starter-web-services`: For building applications exposing SOAP web services
- `spring-boot-starter-web`: Build web applications and RESTful applications
- `spring-boot-starter-test`: Write great unit and integration tests
- `spring-boot-starter-jdbc`: Traditional JDBC applications
- `spring-boot-starter-hateoas`: Make your services more RESTful by adding HATEOAS features
- `spring-boot-starter-security`: Authentication and authorization using Spring Security
- `spring-boot-starter-data-jpa`: Spring Data JPA with Hibernate
- `spring-boot-starter-cache`: Enabling the Spring Framework's caching support
- `spring-boot-starter-data-rest`: Expose simple REST services using Spring Data REST

Spring Boot Starter Parent POM

The Starter Parent POM defines key versions of dependencies and Maven plugins. It typically uses `spring-boot-starter-parent` as the parent in the `pom.xml` file:

```
<parent>
    <groupId>org.springframework.boot</groupId>
    <artifactId>spring-boot-starter-parent</artifactId>
    <version>2.0.2.RELEASE</version>
    <relativePath/> <!-- lookup parent from repository -->
</parent>
```

Spring Boot Starter Parent POM allows us to manage the following things for multiple child projects and modules:

- **Configuration**: Java version and other properties
- **Dependency management**: Version of dependencies
- **Default plugin configuration**: This includes configurations such as build plugins

It is an easy way to bring in multiple coordinated dependencies including *transitive* dependencies.

Let's see the Spring Boot auto-configuration.

Spring Boot auto-configuration

Spring Boot can automatically provide configuration for application functionality, which is common to many Spring applications. Auto-configuration works by analyzing the classpath as follows:

- If you forget a dependency, Spring Boot can't configure it
- A dependency management tool is recommended
- Spring Boot Parent and Starters make it much easier
- Spring Boot works with Maven, Gradle, and Ant/Ivy

Spring Boot offers auto-configuration of those modules in your Spring application based on the JAR dependencies that you have added. Suppose you added the JPA starter dependency (`spring-boot-starter-data-jpa`) in your Spring application classpath; Spring Boot attempts to automatically configure JPA to your Spring application. Now, you have not manually configured any database connection beans related to JPA. Similarly, if you want to add an in-memory database such as HSQLDB, just add it (`org.hsqldb`) in the classpath of your Spring application, and it will auto-configure an in-memory database.

Spring Boot provides the auto-configuration feature in the following ways:

- First, Spring Boot looks for frameworks available on the classpath
- After that, it checks existing configuration for the application

Based on these points, Spring Boot provides the basic configuration needed to configure the application with these frameworks. This is called **auto-configuration**.

In another book, *Spring 5 Design Patterns*, I have written an application related to the backend that accesses a relational database by using JDBC. As we know that the Spring Framework provides `JdbcTemplate`, we have to register this `JdbcTemplate` as a bean in the application context of our application as follows:

```
@Bean
public JdbcTemplate jdbcTemplate(DataSource dataSource) {
    return new JdbcTemplate(dataSource);
}
```

This configuration creates an instance of `JdbcTemplate` and injects it with another bean dependency, `DataSource`. So, also we have to register this `DataSource` bean to be met. Let's see in the following configuration how the `HSQL` database is configured with a `DataSource` bean:

```
@Bean
public DataSource dataSource() {
    return new EmbeddedDatabaseBuilder()
        .setType(EmbeddedDatabaseType.HSQL)
        .addScripts('schema.sql', 'data.sql')
        .build();
}
```

This configuration creates an instance of `DataSource` specifying the SQL scripts `schema.sql` and `data.sql` with the `HSQL` embedded database.

You can see that the two bean methods are not too complex to define, but are also not part of the application logic. This represents just a fraction of application configuration. If you add the Spring MVC module to the same application, then you have to register another corresponding bean method. These methods will be the same for each Spring application where you want to use the same modules. We can say that this is boilerplate configuration code in each Spring application.

In short, the configuration, whatever we have defined, is a common configuration for each application. Ideally, we should not have to write it for each application.

Spring Boot addresses this problem of common configuration. It can automatically configure these common configuration bean methods. Spring Boot provides this auto-configuration based on the available library in your application's classpath. So, if we have to add the HSQL database library in your application's classpath, then it will automatically configure an embedded HSQL database.

If a Spring JDBC-related library is in the classpath of your Spring application, then it will also configure a `JdbcTemplate` bean for your application. There is no need to configure these beans manually in your Spring application. These beans will be automatically configured for you; just use them for business logic. Spring Boot reduces such boilerplate code configuration at the developer's end.

Enabling Spring Boot auto-configuration

Spring Boot provides the @EnableAutoConfiguration annotation that is responsible for enabling the auto-configuration feature. This annotation is used in the main application file of the Spring Boot application. The @EnableAutoConfiguration annotation on a Spring Java configuration class causes Spring Boot to automatically create beans it thinks you need, usually based on classpath contents, that it can easily override.

Let's see the following code that represents the main application launcher class in the Spring Boot application:

```
@Configuration
@EnableAutoConfiguration
public class MyAppConfig {
    public static void main(String[] args) {
    SpringApplication.run(MyAppConfig.class, args);
    }
}
```

But, Spring Boot also provides a shortcut for this configuration file by using another annotation, @SpringBootApplication.

It is very common to use @EnableAutoConfiguration, @Configuration, and @ComponentScan together. Let's see the following updated code:

```
@SpringBootApplication
public class MyAppConfig {
    public static void main(String[] args) {
    SpringApplication.run(MyAppConfig.class, args);
    }
}
```

In this code, @ComponentScan, with no arguments, scans the current package and its sub-packages.

@SpringBootApplication has been available since Spring Boot 1.2.

Let's see the following diagram to explain it better than the code:

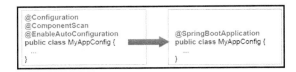

In this diagram, we can say that the @SpringBootApplication annotation has composed functionality from three annotations—@EnableAutoConfiguration, @ComponentScan, and @Configuration.

Spring Boot Starter reduces a build's dependencies and Spring Boot auto-configuration reduces the Spring configuration.

If you want to exclude auto-configuration for some of the modules, then you use the exclude property of @SpringBootAnnotation. Let's look at the following code:

```
@SpringBootApplication(exclude = {DataSourceAutoConfiguration.class,
HibernateJpaAutoConfiguration.class})
public class MyAppConfig {
    ...
}
```

As you can see in the code, this Spring Boot application will consider DataSourceAutoConfiguration.class and HibernateJpaAutoConfiguration.class for the auto-configuration.

Let's see the following diagram that explains all about the Spring Boot auto-configuration feature:

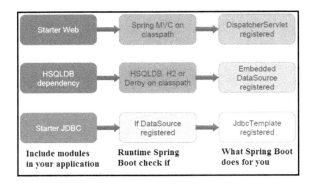

As you can see in the diagram, you just include the required modules in your Spring application. At runtime, Spring Boot checks libraries at the classpath of your application. If the required libraries are available on the classpath of your application, then Spring Boot configures the required beans and other configuration for your application. You don't need to worry about the configuration of the modules in the Spring Boot application.

Let's discuss another key component, Spring Boot CLI, in the next section.

Spring Boot CLI

Spring Boot also provides a command-line tool that can be used to quickly write Spring applications. You can run Groovy scripts with Spring Boot CLI. Groovy code has almost zero boilerplate code compared with Java.

The Spring Boot documentation says:

> *"You don't need to use the CLI to work with Spring Boot but it's definitely the quickest way to get a Spring application off the ground."*

Spring Boot's CLI gives you more free time from having to add starter dependencies and auto-configuration to let you focus only on writing your application-specific code. We have seen this in this chapter in the Groovy script `HelloController`. We can run this Groovy script with Spring Boot CLI.

Spring Boot CLI is a smart tool, because in the Groovy script, if you noticed, there are no import lines. But, Spring Boot CLI allows us to run it. What about dependent libraries, you ask? We don't have Maven or Gradle here. CLI is smart; it detects classes being used in your application and it also knows which Starter dependencies should be used for these classes; accordingly, Spring Boot CLI adds dependencies to the classpath to make it work.

As Spring Boot CLI adds dependencies, a series of auto-configuration kicks in and adds the required bean method configuration so that your application is able to respond to HTTP requests.

CLI is an optional feature of Spring Boot; it just allows you to write a complete application with your application code only as, it doesn't need to build a traditional project. CLI provides tremendous power and simplicity for Spring development. In Chapter 2, *Customizing Auto-Configuration in Spring Boot Application*, we will see how to set up Spring Boot CLI.

Let's move to another key component of Spring Boot's building blocks. This is Spring Boot Actuator, which gives us insight about running a Spring Boot application.

Spring Boot Actuator

There are a lot of frameworks that provide tools for application development. But Spring Boot doesn't only provide application development-specific features; it also provides a post-production grade feature. This allows you to monitor your Spring application during production using HTTP endpoints or with JMX.

Spring Boot Actuator is the final key component of its building blocks. Other parts of Spring Boot's building blocks simplify Spring development; the Actuator instead offers the ability to inspect the internals of your application at runtime. The Actuator provides data on auditing, metrics, and the health of your Spring Boot application using HTTP endpoints or with JMX. It helps to you manage your application when it's pushed to production.

The Actuator installed in a Spring Boot application provides the following benefits:

- It provides details of all beans configured in the Spring application context
- Actuator also provides details about Spring Boot's auto-configuration
- It also ensures all environment variables, system properties, configuration properties, and command-line arguments are available to your application
- The Actuator gives various metrics pertaining to memory usage, garbage collection, web requests, and data source usage
- It provides a trace of recent HTTP requests handled by your application
- It also gives information about the current state of the threads in the Spring Boot application

Spring Boot Actuator provides the listed information in two ways:

- You could use web endpoints
- Or you could use it via a shell interface

We'll explore Spring Boot Actuator's capabilities in detail when we get to `Chapter 3`, *Getting Started with Spring CLI and Actuator*.

We have seen all the building blocks of Spring Boot. These blocks serve to simplify Spring application development in its own way.

Now, let's move to the next section of this chapter, and see how to set up a Spring Boot workspace to develop your first Spring Boot application.

Setting up a Spring Boot workspace

Let's see how to set up a Spring Boot workspace to create a Spring Boot application. No special tool integration is required to set up a Spring Boot application. You can use any IDE or text editor. But, Spring Boot 2.0's minimum system requirements are as follows:

- Java SDK v1.8 or higher
- Spring Framework 5.0.0.RELEASE or above
- Maven (3.2+) and Gradle 4
- Tomcat 8.5, that is, a Servlet 3.0+ compatible container

Let's see the following ways to set up the workspace for the Spring Boot application:

- Set up Spring Boot with Maven
- Set up Spring Boot with Gradle

Now, we will explore how to set up a Spring Boot application with Maven and Gradle in detail.

Setting up Spring Boot with Maven

Spring Boot is compatible with Apache Maven 3.2 or above. If your machine doesn't already have Java 8 or above, first download Java 8 or above from Oracle's official website:

```
http://www.oracle.com/technetwork/java/javase/downloads/jdk8-downloads-2133151.
html
```

And if you don't already have Maven, first download it from `https://maven.apache.org/`; Ubuntu users can run `sudo apt-get install maven`. Let's see the following Spring Boot dependencies with the `org.springframework.boot` groupId:

```xml
<?xml version="1.0" encoding="UTF-8"?>
<project xmlns="http://maven.apache.org/POM/4.0.0"
xmlns:xsi="http://www.w3.org/2001/XMLSchema-instance"
    xsi:schemaLocation="http://maven.apache.org/POM/4.0.0
http://maven.apache.org/xsd/maven-4.0.0.xsd">
    <modelVersion>4.0.0</modelVersion>

    <parent>            <groupId>org.springframework.boot</groupId>
<artifactId>spring-boot-starter-parent</artifactId>
<version>2.0.2.RELEASE</version>        <relativePath/> <!-- lookup parent
from repository -->    </parent>
```

```
    <dependencies>
        <dependency>
<groupId>org.springframework.boot</groupId>                    <artifactId>spring-
boot-starter-web</artifactId>
    </dependency>

    </dependencies>
    ...
    ...
</project>
```

This `.pom` file is the minimum requirement for the Spring Boot 2.0 application.

Let's see the Gradle setup for the Spring Boot application.

Setting up Spring Boot with Gradle

We have seen that Java 8 is the minimum requirement for Spring Boot 2.0, both with Maven and Gradle. However, if you want to use Gradle, then first install Gradle 4 or above in your machine from www.gradle.org/.

Now, see the following Gradle Spring Boot dependencies file with `org.springframework.boot` groupId. Here's what the `build.gradle` file should look like:

```
buildscript {
    repositories {
        jcenter()
        maven { url 'http://repo.spring.io/snapshot' }
        maven { url 'http://repo.spring.io/milestone' }
    }
    dependencies {
        classpath 'org.springframework.boot:spring-boot-gradle-
plugin:2.0.0.M7'
    }
}
apply plugin: 'java'
apply plugin: 'org.springframework.boot'
apply plugin: 'io.spring.dependency-management'

jar {
    baseName = 'HelloWorld'
    version =  '0.0.1-SNAPSHOT'
}
```

```
repositories {
    jcenter()
    maven { url "http://repo.spring.io/snapshot" }
    maven { url "http://repo.spring.io/milestone" }
}

dependencies {
    compile("org.springframework.boot:spring-boot-starter-web")
    testCompile("org.springframework.boot:spring-boot-starter-test")
}
```

The preceding Gradle file has minimum requirements for the Spring Boot application. You could use either Maven or Gradle since the process is the same. Spring Boot creates an application using the same process.

Let's create your first Spring Boot application and see how to set up the project's structure using Spring Boot Initializr.

Developing your first Spring Boot application

Let's create a Hello World REST application in Java, and create a simple REST service that returns the Hello World message on request. In this application, we will use Maven to build this project.

You would have noticed that whenever you create a simple project structure, you face some difficulties to create it. Where will you place configuration files, properties files, and so on, and build files with dependencies? Traditionally, to resolve this problem and find an easy solution for the project structure, you would have to go to Google and search multiple blogs. I have spent quite some time doing this!

However, things have changed because the Spring Boot team has provided a solution for the project structure. This is the Spring Boot Initializr.

The Spring Boot Initializr provides solutions to all these problems related to setup work, and it creates a more traditional Java project structure.

The Spring Boot Initializr is nothing but a web application that can create a Spring Boot project structure for you. It generates a basic project structure, either a Maven or Gradle build specification; it depends on you what you choose from the menu. But remember, it doesn't generate any application code. You can use this Spring Initializr in several ways:

- Spring Boot Initializr through a web-based interface (`https://start.spring.io`)
- You can also use it through an IDE such as **Spring Tool Suite** (**STS**) and IntelliJ IDEA
- Using the Spring Boot CLI

We will explore Spring Initializr with Spring Boot CLI in `Chapter 3`, *Getting Started with Spring CLI and Actuator*. Let's check the other two ways of using Spring Initializr and start with the web-based interface.

Using a web interface for Spring Initializr

The Spring team provides a web application hosted at: `https://start.spring.io`. It is the most simple way to create a Spring Boot application and the most straightforward way to use the Spring Initializr. It has all the menu options for you, just choose them and use them in your application.

Let's see the following screenshot of what the home page look like:

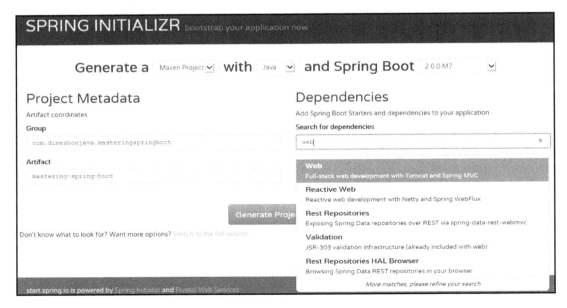

As you can see, there are a number of options you need to fill in. They are:

- **Project type**: Maven or Gradle
- **Language**: Java, Kotlin, or Groovy
- Spring Boot version

On the **SPRING INITIALZR** home page, on the left side of the form, it asks to specify minimum project metadata, so you must provide the project's **Group** and **Artifact**.

You can enter minimal details for whatever **SPRING INITIALZR** asks about your application, pick your build system, favorite language, and version of Spring Boot you wish to use, whatever you want. After that, choose your application's dependencies from the menu and also provide your project's **Group** and **Artifact**. Click the **Generate Project** button, and we have a ready-to-run application.

Here, I have selected the **Spring Boot 2.0.2, Maven** build from the drop-down menu and **Java** as the language from the drop-down menu. Next, I have given my project's **Group** and **Artifact** as follows:

- **Group**: `com.dineshonjava.masteringspringboot`
- **Artifact**: `mastering-spring-boot`

Let's see another interesting thing about the web-based interface. Once you click the **Switch to the full version** link at the bottom of the web interface, it expands to provide more options. It lets you pick the ingredients for your application, like picking off a delicious menu. And also, you can specify additional metadata such as version and base package name.

As you can see in the previous screenshot, I have added some more ingredients such as project description, package name, packaging style (either JAR or WAR), and you could also choose a Java version as well. Let's click on the **Generate Project** button on the form to have Spring Initializr generate a project for you.

Spring Initializr presents this project to you as a ZIP file, named as the value in the **Artifact** field, that is downloaded by your browser. In our case, this ZIP file is named `mastering-spring-boot.zip`.

Let's unzip this file and you will have a project structure as follows:

As you can see, there's very little code in this project and it also creates a couple of empty directories. The generated project contains the following:

- pom.xml: A Maven build specification
- MasteringSpringBootApplication.java: A class with a main() method to bootstrap the application
- MasteringSpringBootApplicationTests.java: An empty JUnit test class instrumented to load a Spring application context using Spring Boot auto-configuration
- application.properties: An empty properties file for you to add configuration properties to as you see fit
- static directory: Here, you can put any static content (JavaScript, style sheets, images, and so on) to be served from the web application
- templates directory: Here, you can put templates that render model data

Finally, import this project to your favorite IDE. If you are using the Spring Tool Suite IDE, it supports creating Spring Boot applications, so you don't need to go to the web-based interface.

Let's have a look at how to create a Spring Boot project by using the STS IDE.

Creating a Spring Boot project using the STS IDE

Spring Tool Suite is one of most popular IDEs for Java developers to develop Spring-based applications. If you don't have STS in your machine, first download the latest version of STS from the following link:

```
http://spring.io/tools/sts
```

Let's create a new Spring Boot application in the STS by selecting the **New | Spring Starter Project** menu item from the **File** menu. Let's see the following screenshot; STS will present you with a dialog box:

As you can see in the screenshot, this dialog box asks for the same information as the web-based Spring Initializr. So, let's fill it in with the same information, whatever we filled in the web-based Spring Initializr with.

Let's click the **Next** button. It will present us with a second dialog box like the one shown in the following screenshot:

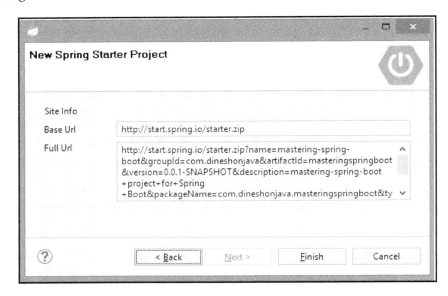

Let's click on the **Finish** button. It will present the project structure in your workspace with the same directory structure and default file as the web-based approach presented to you in the ZIP file.

You must be connected to the internet in order for it to work, because STS internally delegates to the Spring Initializr at `http://start.spring.io` to produce the project.

Now that the project has been imported into your workspace, let's create your application files, such as controllers.

Implementing the REST service

Let's start by creating a simple REST controller as follows:

```
package com.dineshonjava.masteringspringboot.controller;

import org.springframework.web.bind.annotation.GetMapping;
import org.springframework.web.bind.annotation.RestController;

@RestController
public class HelloController {

    @GetMapping("/hello")
    String sayHello(){
        return "Hello World!!!";
    }
}
```

Let's see this small REST controller (`HelloController`) in detail:

- `@RestController` annotation: It indicates that this is the controller class and its result writes into the response body and doesn't want to render view
- `@GetMapping` annotation: It indicates a request handler method and it is a shorthand annotation for `@RequestMapping(method = RequestMethod.GET)`
- `sayHello()` method: It returns a greeting message

In the STS IDE, you could run your application as a Spring Boot application with an embedded server by selecting **Run As | Spring Boot Application** from the **Run** menu as follows:

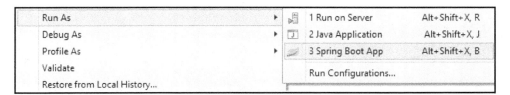

Spring Initialzr creates the `main` application launcher class as follows:

```
package com.dineshonjava.masteringspringboot;

import org.springframework.boot.SpringApplication;
import org.springframework.boot.autoconfigure.SpringBootApplication;

@SpringBootApplication
```

```
public class MasteringSpringBootApplication {

    public static void main(String[] args) {
        SpringApplication.run(MasteringSpringBootApplication.class, args);
    }
}
```

This tiny class is actually a fully operational web application! Let's see some details:

- `@SpringBootApplication`: This annotation tells Spring Boot, when launched, to scan recursively for Spring components inside this package and register them. It also tells Spring Boot to enable auto-configuration, a process where beans are automatically created based on classpath settings, property settings, and other factors.
- `main()` method: It is a simple `public static void main()` method to run the application.
- `SpringApplication.run()`: The `SpringApplication` class is responsible for creating the Spring application's context, and the `run()` method initializes the application's context in your Spring application.

Let's run your Spring Boot application and observe the logs on the console as follows:

```
Console ⊠   Progress   Problems
mastering-spring-boot - MasteringSpringBootApplication [Spring Boot App] C:\Program Files\Java\jre1.8.0_151\bin\javaw.exe (19-Feb-2018, 10:55:31


  .   ____          _            __ _ _
 /\\ / ___'_ __ _ _(_)_ __  __ _ \ \ \ \
( ( )\___ | '_ | '_| | '_ \/ _` | \ \ \ \
 \\/  ___)| |_)| | | | | || (_| |  ) ) ) )
  '  |____| .__|_| |_|_| |_\__, | / / / /
 =========|_|==============|___/=/_/_/_/
 :: Spring Boot ::        (v2.0.0.M7)

2018-02-19 22:55:36.225  INFO 11820 --- [           main] c.d.m.MasteringSpringBootApplication
2018-02-19 22:55:36.225  INFO 11820 --- [           main] c.d.m.MasteringSpringBootApplication
2018-02-19 22:55:36.392  INFO 11820 --- [           main] ConfigServletWebServerApplicationContext
2018-02-19 22:55:39.483  INFO 11820 --- [           main] o.h.v.i.engine.ValidatorFactoryImpl
2018-02-19 22:55:40.069  INFO 11820 --- [           main] o.s.b.w.embedded.tomcat.TomcatWebServer
2018-02-19 22:55:40.097  INFO 11820 --- [           main] o.apache.catalina.core.StandardService
2018-02-19 22:55:40.101  INFO 11820 --- [           main] org.apache.catalina.core.StandardEngine
2018-02-19 22:55:40.137  INFO 11820 --- [ost-startStop-1] o.a.catalina.core.AprLifecycleListener
2018-02-19 22:55:40.367  INFO 11820 --- [ost-startStop-1] o.a.c.c.C.[Tomcat].[localhost].[/]
2018-02-19 22:55:40.367  INFO 11820 --- [ost-startStop-1] o.s.web.context.ContextLoader
2018-02-19 22:55:41.054  INFO 11820 --- [ost-startStop-1] s.w.s.m.m.a.RequestMappingHandlerMapping
2018-02-19 22:55:41.061  INFO 11820 --- [ost-startStop-1] s.w.s.m.m.a.RequestMappingHandlerMapping
2018-02-19 22:55:41.065  INFO 11820 --- [ost-startStop-1] s.w.s.m.m.a.RequestMappingHandlerMapping
2018-02-19 22:55:41.185  INFO 11820 --- [ost-startStop-1] o.s.w.s.handler.SimpleUrlHandlerMapping
2018-02-19 22:55:41.185  INFO 11820 --- [ost-startStop-1] o.s.w.s.handler.SimpleUrlHandlerMapping
2018-02-19 22:55:41.219  INFO 11820 --- [ost-startStop-1] o.s.w.s.handler.SimpleUrlHandlerMapping
```

As you can see in the console logs, you can observe several things:

- Logs have the Spring Boot banner at the top of the logs and Spring Boot version. You can also add your own ASCII banner by creating `banner.txt` or `banner.png` and putting it into the `src/main/resources/` folder.
- There is an embedded Tomcat server with the server port `8080`; it is the default port, but you can customize it by adding the `server.port` property to the `application.properties` file as follows:

      server.port= 8181

- Logs also shows all possible request mappings of your application as follows:

```
Mapped "{[/hello],methods=[GET]}" onto java.lang.String com.dineshonjava.masteringspringboot.controller.HelloController.sayHello()
Mapped "{[/error]}" onto public org.springframework.http.ResponseEntity<java.util.Map<java.lang.String, java.lang.Object>> org.springframework.boot.
Mapped "{[/error],produces=[text/html]}" onto public org.springframework.web.servlet.ModelAndView org.springframework.boot.autoconfigure.web.servlet
```

As you can see, your application is running on the default embedded Tomcat server with the default server port, `8080`. Let's verify it on the system browser, where it will look as follows:

In this chapter, we have created a very simple `Hello World` REST application and run this application on the embedded Tomcat server of Spring Boot.

Let's see what new features and enhancements have been added to the new version of Spring Boot, 2.0.

New features in Spring Boot 2.0

Spring Boot was first released four years ago in 2014. In 2018, a newer version of Spring Boot was released. There are many new features and updates in Spring Boot 2.0. Here are some of the most important changes:

- There are many new packages and Starters that help with dependency management.

- Spring Boot 2.0 also supports auto-configuration. This helps in reducing the configuration that was needed in previous Spring apps.
- It has introduced better longing through features like Actuator.
- Software quality testing and utilities have been enhanced. This helps in a better user experience. With `spring-boot-devtools`, you can have much more enhanced feedback loops.
- Spring Boot 2.0 supports Java version 8 and greater only. It is one of the few options available where you can use the latest Java 9.
- The Gradle plugin is replaced by BootJar and BootWar.
- The dependency management plugin is no longer activated automatically.
- It's far more secure.
- Reactive models have new starters of different types, such as WebFlux.
- Actuator has been upgraded with huge changes. Earlier, only Spring MVC could be supported by Actuator, but with version 2.0, Actuator is independent.

You can see that a lot of exciting new features and enhancements can be found in Spring Boot 2.0. So in this book, we will look at many of these new features with examples.

Summary

This chapter has given you a quick overview of what Spring Boot has to offer. In this chapter, we have learned how Spring Boot simplified Spring application development. Spring Boot made this magic possible by using its key components such as Spring Boot auto-configuration, Starters, Spring Boot CLI, and Spring Boot Actuator. You can take advantage of Spring Boot Starter dependencies and auto-configuration; you can do rapid development of the Spring application by just focusing only on the application logic, rather than configurations and build dependencies, libraries, and version management. Meanwhile, auto-configuration frees you from boilerplate configuration.

We have also created a very simple `Hello World` REST application by using the web-based Spring Initializr and Spring Tool Suite IDE, and we have run this application, where we used the embedded Tomcat container.

In `Chapter 2`, *Customizing Auto-Configuration in Spring Boot Application*, we'll dive deeper into Spring Boot auto-configuration and its customization in the Spring Boot application.

2
Customizing Auto-Configuration in Spring Boot Application

Spring Boot gives us a free hand when it comes to overriding auto-configurations in each module. It doesn't force us to use default configurations. It is very opinionated about the configurations. In this chapter, we will explore how to override auto-configurations using properties and YML files.

Some days ago, one of my friends purchased a car. You know that car companies also provide full control of exterior decoration to make it look like a sports car. You could change the color combination, headlights, wheels, door LEDs, and so on. The car can be changed according to your precise specifications.

But on the other hand, most models of car can't be overridden. You have to purchase them with auto-configuration. Some car companies offer a form of auto-configuration so, you don't have to explicitly specify the colors of the external and internal body. Either the companies already applied the color customization within offers, or they will not give you a hand when choosing the body color.

Most of the cars or car companies will let you customize your car, so that you can purchase a pre-configured car with default configuration. Similarly, if you are working with a traditional Spring configuration, you have full control over what goes into your Spring configuration, much like purchasing a car and explicitly specifying all of the features you want.

On the other hand, Spring Boot auto-configuration is like purchasing a car on offer. It's easier to let Spring Boot handle the details than to declare each and every bean in the application's context. Fortunately, Spring Boot auto-configuration is flexible. Spring Boot will let you step in and influence how it applies auto-configuration.

At the end of this chapter, you will understand how Spring Boot provides flexibility to override auto-configuration by using explicit configuration overrides and fine-grained configuration with properties.

This chapter will cover the following points:

- Understanding auto-configuration
- Customizing Spring Boot
    - Overriding the auto-configuration of Spring Boot
- Externalizing configuration with properties
- Fine-tuning with logging
- Using YAML for configuration
- Customizing application error pages

Let's see these topics in detail.

Understanding auto-configuration

Spring Boot auto-configuration provides automatic configuration to your Spring application based on the modules and associated library dependencies of those modules that you have added. For instance, if you have added the embedded in-memory database H2 in your classpath, you are not required to manually configure any bean related to the database such as `DataSource`, `JdbcTemplate`, and so on. Spring Boot provides your H2 database with auto-configuration after adding dependency on the H2 database in your application's classpath.

Spring Boot provides the magic of autoconfiguration by extensive use of pre-written `@Configuration` classes for each module of Spring Framework. But these auto-configurations are activated based on:

- The contents of the classpath of your Spring application
- Properties you have set in the application
- Beans already defined in your application

The `@Profile` annotation of Spring Framework is an example of conditional configuration. Spring Boot takes this idea to the next level and provides a layer of auto-configuration on top of the traditional Spring Framework. That is why Spring Boot is not a separate framework by heart; it is Spring Framework.

`@Profile` is a special case of `@Conditional`.

Learning how auto-configuration works

Let's see what the `@Conditional` annotation does:

- It allows conditional bean creation. It only creates a bean if other beans exist (or don't exist) as follows:

```
@Bean
@ConditionalOnBean(name={"dataSource"})
public JdbcTemplate jdbcTemplate(DataSource dataSource) {
    return new JdbcTemplate(dataSource);
}
```

- Or `@Conditional` annotations allow us to create the bean by checking the type of other classes:

```
@Bean
@ConditionalOnBean(type={DataSource.class})
public JdbcTemplate jdbcTemplate(DataSource dataSource) {
    return new JdbcTemplate(dataSource);
}
```

- There are many other options available under `@Conditional` annotation, as follows:
    - `@ConditionalOnClass`
    - `@ConditionalOnProperty`
    - `@ConditionalOnMissingBean`
    - `@ConditionalOnMissingClass`

Let's see what the auto-configuration class looks like in Spring Boot.

It is a pre-written Spring configuration in the `org.springframework.boot.autoconfigure` package in the `spring-boot-autoconfigure` JAR file:

```
@Configuration
public class DataSourceAutoConfiguration implements EnvironmentAware {
    ...
```

```
@Conditional(...)
@ConditionalOnMissingBean(DataSource.class)
@Import(...)
protected static class EmbeddedConfiguration { ... }
        ...
}
```

Spring Boot defines many of these configuration classes. They are activated in response to dependencies on the classpath of your Spring application.

Let's see how to customize Spring Boot auto-configuration in your Spring application in the next section.

Customizing Spring Boot

Spring Boot offers you full control over auto-configuration. You can control what Spring Boot does. There are several options for customizing Spring Boot configuration. They are as follows:

- You can customize by setting some of **Spring Boot's properties** in the properties or YAML files
- Also, you can **define certain beans** yourself so Spring Boot won't use the default
- You can **disable some autoconfiguration explicitly**
- Change **dependencies**

Let's see these four points in detail, and how to use them to customize Spring Boot auto-configuration in your Spring application.

Customizing using Spring Boot properties

Spring Boot allows you to customize your application configurations and you can use the same application code in different environments such as staging, production, and so on. Spring Boot provides several methods for this customization—you can use properties files, YAML files, environment variables, and command-line arguments to externalize configuration.

Spring Boot gives you a free hand to override auto-configuration using a lot of Spring Boot properties. So that you can easily override these properties. Let's see how to override the values of these Spring Boot properties using the `application.properties` file. By default, Spring Boot looks for `application.properties` in these locations (in this order):

- The `/config` sub-directory of the working directory
- The working directory
- The `config` package in the `classpath`
- The `classpath` root

You can create a `PropertySource` based on these files. There are many, many configuration properties available in Spring Boot.

Let's see the following configuration example of the `DataSource` bean. In this example, we will see how to control or override Spring Boot's default configuration of the `DataSource` bean in the Spring application. There are the following typical customizations:

- Use the predefined properties
- Change the underlying data source connection pool implementation
- Define your own `DataSource` bean

Let's see the following common properties configurable from the properties file; first, we have to override the `DataSource` bean configuration:

```
# Connection settings

spring.datasource.url=
spring.datasource.username=
spring.datasource.password=
spring.datasource.driver-class-name=

# SQL scripts to execute

spring.datasource.schema=
spring.datasource.data=

# Connection pool settings

spring.datasource.initial-size=
spring.datasource.max-active=
spring.datasource.max-idle=
spring.datasource.min-idle=
```

As you can see, you have to define your setting for the `DataSource` bean definition, such as `Connection settings`, `SQL scripts to execute`, and `Connection pool settings`. But Spring Boot creates a pooled `DataSource` bean by default if a known pool dependency is available. The `spring-boot-starter-jdbc` or `spring-boot-starter-jpa` Starter pulls in the `tomcat-jdbc` connection pool by default. But you can override this to use alternatives—Tomcat, HikariCP, and Commons DBCP 1 and 2.

Let's see another example for web container configuration using Spring Boot properties. Here's the configuration code:

```
server.port=9000
server.address=192.168.11.21
server.session-timeout=1800
server.context-path=/accounts
server.servlet-path=/admin
```

Let's see how to override auto-configuration in the Spring Boot application by replacing generated beans in the next section.

Replacing generated beans

You can also customize Spring Boot auto-configuration by defining certain beans yourself in your Spring application, so Spring Boot won't use default configuration for those beans.

Normally, beans you declare explicitly disable any auto-created ones. Let's see the following example:

```
@Bean
public DataSource dataSource() {
    return new EmbeddedDatabaseBuilder().
        setName("AccountDB").build();
}
```

In the preceding code, we have explicitly defined a `DataSource` bean; your `DataSource` bean configuration stops Spring Boot from creating a default `DataSource`. Bean names are often not important. It works with XML-based configuration, annotation, and/or Java-based configuration.

Let's see another way of customizing Spring Boot autoconfiguration.

Disabling specific auto-configuration classes

At any point in time, if you don't want to use some of the specific auto-configuration classes or if they don't suit your needs, you can disable those auto-configuration classes. For this, you can use the `exclude` attribute of the `@EnableAutoConfiguration` annotation. Let's see the following example:

```
@EnableAutoConfiguration(exclude=DataSourceAutoConfiguration.class)
public class ApplicationConfiguration {
    ...
}
```

As per the code snippet, we have used the `@EnableAutoConfiguration` annotation with the `exclude` attribute. The `DataSourceAutoConfiguration` class will be excluded from the auto-configuration. Similarly, we can define a list of auto-configuration classes that need to be excluded.

 You can define exclusions both at the annotation level and by using the property.

Let's move to another point of customizing auto-configuration in the Spring Boot application.

Changing a library's dependencies

Spring Boot includes auto-configuration based on the starter's JAR, which is available on the classpath of the Spring application. Spring Boot POMs has dependencies on the Starters, so you can override dependency versions by setting the appropriate Maven property in your `pom.xml` like this:

```
<properties>
    <spring.version>5.0.0.RELEASE</spring.version>
</properties>
```

There are good reasons to override dependency version sometimes, such as a bug in the given version, or your company policies. Ideally, you should avoid changing a dependency version because it makes your life more complicated as you won't be able to manage the version's transitive dependencies in your application.

If some libraries don't suit your Spring application, you could exclude them from the classpath of the Spring application. Let's see the following example:

```
<dependency>
    <groupId>org.springframework.boot</groupId>
    <artifactId>spring-boot-starter-websocket</artifactId>
    <exclusions>
        <exclusion>
            <groupId>ch.qos.logback</groupId>
            <artifactId>logback-classic</artifactId>
        </exclusion>
    </exclusions>
</dependency>

<dependency>
    <groupId>org.slf4j</groupId>
    <artifactId>slf4j-log4j12</artifactId>
</dependency>
```

As you can see, I have excluded the default `logback` library from the `spring-boot-starter-websocket` starter and added the `log4j` library for application logging.

Let's move to another section about customizing configuration of Spring Boot.

Externalizing configuration with properties

Spring Boot offers you more than 1,000 properties for fine-tuning. Spring Boot documentation (`https://docs.spring.io/spring-boot/docs/2.0.2.RELEASE/reference/htmlsingle/#common-application-properties`) gives an exhaustive list of these properties. You can use these properties to adjust the settings of your Spring application. You can specify these properties via environment variables, Java system properties, JNDI, command line arguments, or property files. But Spring Boot has an order of overriding these properties in case you define same properties on all of them. Let's see the order of evaluation of the properties in the next section.

Order of evaluation for overridden properties

Let's see the following order of evaluation for overridden properties:

1. Defined properties for the Devtools global settings in your home directory
2. Defined properties for `@TestPropertySource` annotations on your tests

3. Properties as command-line arguments
4. Defined properties from `SPRING_APPLICATION_JSON`
5. The properties with `ServletConfig init` parameters
6. The properties with `ServletContext init` parameters
7. JNDI attributes from `java:comp/env`
8. Java system properties
9. OS environment variables
10. Property file(s)—including `application.properties` and its YAML variant

This preceding list is in order of precedence. That means if you set any property from a source higher in the list, Spring will override the same property defined in the source lower in the list. The test environment and command-line arguments override properties from any other property source.

Let's see the following order of evolution of the properties file and YAML variants:

1. A `RandomValuePropertySource` class that injects properties with random value into configuration file define as `random.*`
2. Profile-specific application properties outside of your packaged JAR, that is, in the `/config` subdirectory of the directory from which the application is run (`application-{profile}.properties` and YAML variants)

 Select a profile by executing the JAR with param `Dspring.profiles.active=dev` or setting the property `spring.profiles.active=dev`.

3. Profile-specific application properties outside of your packaged JAR but in a directory from which the application is run (`application-{profile}.properties` and YAML variants)
4. Profile-specific application properties packaged inside your JAR but in a package named config (`application-{profile}.properties` and YAML variants)
5. Profile-specific application properties packaged inside your JAR but at the root of the classpath (`application-{profile}.properties` and YAML variants)
6. Application properties outside of your packaged JAR, that is, in the `/config` subdirectory of the directory from which the application is run (`application.properties` and YAML variants)
7. Application properties outside of your packaged JAR but in a directory from which the application is run (`application.properties` and YAML variants)

8. Application properties packaged inside your JAR but in a package named config (`application.properties` and YAML variants)

9. Application properties packaged inside your JAR but at the root of the classpath (`application.properties` and YAML variants)

10. `@PropertySource` annotations on your `@Configuration` classes

11. Default properties (specified using `SpringApplication.setDefaultProperties`)

According to the order of precedence, if you set any properties in a profile-specific `application-{profile}.properties` will override the same properties set in an `application.properties` file at the same location as the `application-{profile}.properties` file.

Again, this list is in order of precedence. That is, an `application.properties` file in a `/config` subdirectory will override the same properties set in a `application.properties` file in the application's *classpath*.

Let's see how to customize the name of the application property file (`application.properties`).

Renaming application.properties in the Spring application

Spring Boot doesn't force us to use only one properties file with the name `application.properties` or `application.yml`. It allows you to override the name of this file. For example, you could use `myapp.properties` as follows:

```
package com.dineshonjava.masteringspringboot;

import org.springframework.boot.SpringApplication;
import org.springframework.boot.autoconfigure.SpringBootApplication;

@SpringBootApplication
public class MasteringSpringBootApplication {

    public static void main(String[] args) {
        System.setProperty("spring.config.name", "myapp");
        SpringApplication.run(MasteringSpringBootApplication.class, args);
    }
}
```

The property filename must be defined as `myapp`, not `myapp.properties`; if we use `myapp.properties`, the file would get named as `myapp.properties.properties`.

As you can see in the code snippet, here, I am using the `myapp.properties` file instead of using the `application.properties` file.

Let's see how to create external application properties by using beans and how to register with the Spring application as a property file.

Externally configuring application properties

Spring Boot allows you to create your own customized configuration of application properties with beans. You can register these beans as properties with Spring Boot by using the `@ConfigurationProperties` annotation, and after this, you can set these properties by using either the `application.properties` or `application.yml` file.

Spring Boot provides alternative ways of working with properties that allow you to strongly type safe beans and validate the configuration of your application. Let's see the use of the `@ConfigurationProperties` annotation for a dedicated container bean:

- This `@ConfigurationProperties` annotation will hold the externalized properties
- It avoids repeating the prefix
- Data members automatically set from corresponding properties

Let's see the following example:

```
@Component
@ConfigurationProperties(prefix="accounts.client")
public class ConnectionSettings {
    private String host;
    private int port;
    private String logdir;
    private int timeout;
    ...
    // getters/setters
    ...
}
```

This POJO defines the following properties in the `application.properties` file:

```
accounts.client.host=192.168.10.21
accounts.client.port=8181
accounts.client.logdir=/logs
accounts.client.timeout=4000
```

You could set these properties as environment variables, or you could specify these properties as command-line arguments, or you can add these in any of the other places where configuration properties can be set.

Don't forget to add `@EnableConfigurationProperties` in one of your Spring configuration classes because the `@ConfigurationProperties` annotation won't work unless you have enabled it by adding the `@EnableConfigurationProperties` annotation.

Using the @EnableConfigurationProperties annotation

The `@EnableConfigurationProperties` annotation in the configuration class specifies and auto-injects the container bean. Let's see the following configuration class file:

```
@Configuration
@EnableConfigurationProperties(ConnectionSettings.class)
public class AccountsClientConfiguration {
    // Spring initialized this automatically
    @Autowired
    ConnectionSettings connectionSettings;

    @Bean
    public AccountClient accountClient() {
        return new AccountClient(
                connectionSettings.getHost(),
                connectionSettings.getPort(),
                ...
        );
    }
}
```

This is often unnecessary, however, because all of the configuration classes behind Spring Boot auto-configuration are already annotated with `@EnableConfigurationProperties`.

Fine-tuning with logging

Logging is very important in each application to debug and analyze the application's bugs during runtime. If you are working with the old-fashioned Spring Framework, then you have to configure the logging framework explicitly in your application. But Spring Boot provides support for several logging frameworks and also allows you to customize and fine-tune logging in to your Spring application. Spring Boot includes, by default:

- **SLF4J**: Logging facade
- **Logback**: SLF4J implementation

But as a best practice, stick to default logging in your application and use the SLF4J abstraction in the application code. Spring Boot also supports other logging frameworks such as Java Util Logging, Log4J, and Log4J2. You can use another logging frameworks by just adding a dependency, as follows:

```xml
<dependency>
    <groupId>org.springframework.boot</groupId>
    <artifactId>spring-boot-starter-websocket</artifactId>
    <exclusions>
        <exclusion>
            <groupId>ch.qos.logback</groupId>
            <artifactId>logback-classic</artifactId>
        </exclusion>
    </exclusions>
</dependency>
<dependency>
    <groupId>org.slf4j</groupId>
    <artifactId>slf4j-log4j12</artifactId>
</dependency>
```

According to this code, we are using log4j12 instead of the logback logging framework. Let's see how to configure logging output in a Spring application.

Logging output

Spring Boot logs, by default, to the console, but you can also log to rotating files. You can specify a file or path in `application.properties`. Let's see the following configuration:

```
# Use only one of the following properties

# absolute or relative file to the current directory
logging.file=accounts.log

# will write to a spring.log file
logging.path=/var/log/accounts
```

 Spring Boot can also configure logging by using the appropriate configuration file of the underlying logging framework.

As you have seen how we can customize the logging activity in a Spring Boot application, let's move to the next section and see an alternative to the properties file.

Using YAML for configuration

In a Spring Boot application, the `SpringApplication` class automatically supports YAML as an alternative to properties. YAML isn't a markup language. It is an alternative to `.properties` files and it allows you to define properties in the hierarchical configuration. The Java parser for YAML is called **SnakeYAML**. It must be in the classpath, but it is automatically added to the classpath by `spring-boot-starters`.

YAML for properties

Spring Boot supports YAML for properties as an alternative to properties files. YAML is convenient for hierarchical configuration data. Spring Boot properties are organized in groups, for example, server, database, and so on.

Let's see the following properties:

- In `application.properties`:

  ```
  database.host = localhost
  database.user = admin
  ```

- In `application.yml`:

```
database:
    host: localhost
    user: admin
```

Let's see, in the following section, how to define multiple profiles in a single YAML file.

Multiple profiles inside a single YAML file

A YAML file can contain configuration for multiple profiles. You can define multiple profile-specific configurations in a single YAML file. Spring Boot provides a `spring.profiles` key to indicate when the document applies. Let's see the following example of how to define multiple profile-specific configurations in a single YAML file:

```
#Used for all profiles

logging.level:
org.springframework: INFO

#'dev' profile only
---

spring.profiles: dev
database:
    host: localhost
    user: dev

#'prod' profile only

---

spring.profiles: prod
database:
    host: 192.168.200.109
    user: admin
```

In this `application.yml` file, we have defined database settings according to two profiles, `dev` and `prod`, by using a spring.profile key. In the file, `'---'` implies a separation between profiles.

Also, I've found that if you have both `application.properties` and `application.yml` side by side at the same level of precedence, properties in `application.yml` will override those in `application.properties`.

Let's see how to customize the error page in the Spring web application.

Customizing application error pages

Every application has a chance of encountering an error, even if it is an extremely robust application. So, designing custom error pages is important for any enterprise application. Spring Boot applications provide a default error page. You can see one in the following screenshot:

But if you want to use a custom error page for a given status code, you can add a file to the `/error` folder. You can create a custom error page by using static HTML, FreeMarker, Velocity, Thymeleaf, JSP, and so on. The name of the file should be the exact status code or a series mask.

Let's see the following image to map `404` to a static HTML file; your folder structure would be as follows:

```
src/
+- main/
    +- java/
    |    + <source code>
    +- resources/
        +- public/
            +- error/
            |    +- 404.html
            +- <other public assets>
```

As you can see, I have added a custom `404` error page (static error page `404.html`) under the `/resource/public/error` directory; see the following output from the error page:

As you can see, Spring Boot now displays a custom error page instead of the default WhiteLabel error page as part of auto-configuration.

Summary

Spring Boot takes care of the boilerplate configuration that's often required in Spring applications. Auto-configuration can be overridden or disabled, and framework versions can be overridden too. Spring Boot enhances Spring configuration externalization mechanisms by using properties/YAML files, which are it's easier to override Spring auto-configuration by using Properties and YAML file.

Spring Boot provides fine-tuning with logging frameworks, and you can exclude some default frameworks from your application. Spring Boot also auto-configures a simple whitelabel error page for you.

In the next chapter, we'll understand Spring Cloud and Spring CLI installation.

Getting Started with Spring CLI and Actuator
3

In the previous chapters, we have seen several ways to create a Spring Boot application using the Spring Boot web-based interface, STS IDE, and Spring Boot CLI. In this chapter, we will discuss Spring Boot CLI a bit deeper and will also see how to install CLI in your machine and how to create a Spring Boot application using the CLI interface.

By the end of this chapter, you will understand how to install and use Spring Boot CLI to develop Spring applications with more simplicity and understand how you can run this application using the CLI. Also, you will get understanding of Spring Boot's production-ready feature, the Actuator. The Spring Boot Actuator provides many endpoints to look at what's going on with your application in production.

This chapter will cover the following points:

- Getting started with using Spring Boot CLI:
    - Installing the Spring Boot CLI
- Using the Initializr with the Spring Boot CLI
- Spring Boot Actuator:
    - Taking Application's Insights
    - Enabling Spring Boot's Actuator in your application
    - Analyzing the Actuator's endpoints
    - Exposing configuration details
    - Exposing metrics endpoints
    - Exposing application information
    - Shutting down your application
    - Customizing your Actuator endpoints
- Securing the Actuator endpoints
- The Actuator with Spring Boot 2.X

Let's look at these topics in detail.

Getting started with using Spring Boot CLI

Spring Boot provides two interfaces, Spring Boot `ApplicationRunner` and Spring Boot `CommandLineRunner`. Let's dig a bit deeper into Spring Boot CLI.

Spring Boot CLI, as the name suggests, is another command-line prototyping tool. It's famous for being super fast and easy. Spring, however, is a Java application framework. It is a popular framework in the Java community, used by any Java application and for building web applications.

Spring Boot makes it easier to create Spring-powered applications and services with less hassle. And Spring Boot CLI assists in executing the applications and services created by Spring Boot. Spring Boot CLI is not necessarily used with Spring Boot IDE, but it is quicker to execute Spring applications if both are used together. The Spring Boot CLI is self-sufficient and doesn't require any additional platforms to run.

As we discussed earlier, the Spring Boot CLI offers an interesting, albeit unconventional, approach to developing Spring applications. Let's look at how to install the Spring Boot CLI so that you can run the code we looked at in `Chapter 1`, *Getting Started with Spring Boot 2.0*.

Installing the Spring Boot CLI

The Spring community provides several ways to install the Spring Boot CLI. Let's see the following ways:

- Manually installing from a downloaded distribution
- Installation with SDKMAN!
- Installing with OSX Homebrew
- MacPorts installation
- Command-line completion

Let's look at each installation option. But we'll start with how you can install the Spring Boot CLI manually from a distribution.

Manually installing from a downloaded distribution

Spring Boot CLI can be downloaded from the official site of Spring Framework:

- https://repo.spring.io/snapshot/org/springframework/boot/spring-boot-cli/2.0.0.BUILD-SNAPSHOT/spring-boot-cli-2.0.0.BUILD-SNAPSHOT-bin.zip
- https://repo.spring.io/snapshot/org/springframework/boot/spring-boot-cli/2.0.0.BUILD-SNAPSHOT/spring-boot-cli-2.0.0.BUILD-SNAPSHOT-bin.tar.gz

These sites offer manual installation through CLI distributions from the Spring software repository. Once you've downloaded the distribution from the site, there is a text file in it by the name of INSTALL.txt. It contains instructions on how to install the Spring Boot CLI. In short, there is a Spring script in bin/directory which is to be executed. Spring.bat for Windows users a Spring script for Unix.

Spring Boot CLI requires Java JDK v1.8 or above in order to run. No specific environment variables are required to run the CLI; however, you may want to set SPRING_HOME to point to a specific installation. You should also add SPRING_HOME/bin to your PATH environment variable.

To test if you have successfully installed the CLI, you can run the following command:

```
spring --version
```

Let's see the following screenshot:

```
C:\Users\Dinesh.Rajput>spring --version
Spring CLI v2.0.0.BUILD-SNAPSHOT
C:\Users\Dinesh.Rajput>
```

It has displayed the Spring Boot CLI version on the Command Prompt.

It is a very simple, manual way to install Spring Boot CLI, so it doesn't require more configuration. But the Spring community offers other ways of installing it. Let's see another way of installing the Spring Boot CLI.

Installation with SDKMAN!

The second option provided is via the **Software Development Kit Manager** (**SDKMAN!**). It is utilized when you have to handle many versions of SDKs that are binary, such as Groovy. You can get SDKMAN! from sdkman.io and then install Spring Boot CLI with the commands in the first link provided, under this section.

For Linux machines, use the following command:

```
$ curl -s get.sdkman.io | bash
```

Once SDKMAN! is installed, you can install Spring Boot's CLI as follows:

```
$ sdk install springboot
$ spring --version
```

Installing with OSX Homebrew

Another installation option is for a Mac users who use Homebrew. It is a package management system for macOS:

```
$ brew tap pivotal/tap
$ brew install springboot
```

Homebrew installs Spring to `/usr/local/bin` path.

MacPorts installation

If you have Mac machine, then you can set Spring Boot CLI to use MacPorts, one of the popular installers for macOS X. First, install MacPorts according to your Mac version from `https://www.macports.org/`. Once you have MacPorts installed, you can install the Spring Boot CLI at the command-line as follows:

```
$ sudo port install spring-boot-cli
```

MacPorts will install the Spring Boot CLI to `/opt/local/share/java/spring-boot-cli` and put a symbolic link to the binary in `/opt/local/bin`, which should already be in your system path from installing MacPorts. You can verify the installation by checking the version that was installed:

```
$ spring -version
```

This command displays the version of Spring Boot.

Command-line completion

For users of Linux operating systems, a command-line completion method is provided. The script named Spring which is initialization bash (system wide) has to be sourced. In a Debian system, these scripts are found in the `/shell-completion/bash` directory; also, all the scripts in this directory can be used when one shell is initialized.

Using the Initializr with the Spring Boot CLI

You can also use Spring Initializr from the Spring Boot CLI. It offers some commands that can be used to kick-start development. The Spring Boot CLI provides an `init` command to create a Spring Boot application structure and acts as a client interface to the Spring Initializr. Let's see how to use the `init` command to create a Spring Boot project as follows:

```
$ spring init
```

Let's see the following output of the `init` command:

```
D:\packt-book-workspace>spring init
Using service at https://start.spring.io
Content saved to 'demo.zip'
D:\packt-book-workspace>_
```

As you can see in the preceding screenshot, a `demo.zip` file is created and saved to the workspace. If you unzip this project, you'll find a typical project structure with a Maven `pom.xml` build specification. Download the project with very minimal configuration with the Maven specification, and test it.

But actually, if you want to create a web application using Spring MVC that uses JPA for data persistence, let's see the following command that includes all the required dependencies for your application:

```
$ spring init -dweb, jpa
```

 You can specify those initial dependencies with either `--dependencies` or `-d`.

The preceding command also creates the same file, named `demo.zip`, with same project structure, but with Spring Boot's Web and JPA Starters expressed as dependencies in `pom.xml`:

```
D:\packt-spring-boot-ws>spring init -dweb,jpa
Using service at https://start.spring.io
Content saved to 'demo.zip'
D:\packt-spring-boot-ws>
```

It's important to not type a space between -d and the dependencies.

As shown, I didn't define any build specification; by default, it includes the Maven build specification but if you want to specify the Gradle build specification, you have to use the following command:

```
spring init -dweb,jpa --build gradle
```

We specify Gradle as the build type with the --build parameter:

```
D:\packt-spring-boot-ws>spring init -dweb,jpa --build gradle
Using service at https://start.spring.io
Content saved to 'demo.zip'
D:\packt-spring-boot-ws>_
```

Now, the demo.zip file is saved in the working directory with the Gradle build specification instead of Maven. And one more thing, by default, a demo.zip project with either Maven or Gradle build specification will produce an executable JAR file. If you want to create WAR instead of JAR, then you can specify one more parameter in the following command:

```
$ spring init -dweb,jpa --build gradle -p war
```

You can specify this with the --packaging or -p parameter.

```
D:\packt-spring-boot-ws>spring init -dweb,jpa --build gradle -p war
Using service at https://start.spring.io
Content saved to 'demo.zip'
D:\packt-spring-boot-ws>
```

You can find other parameters by using the following command:

```
$ spring help init
```

```
usage: spring init [options] [location]

Option                 Description
_____                 _____
-a, --artifactId       Project coordinates; infer archive
                         name (for example 'test')
-b, --boot-version     Spring Boot version (for example
                         '1.2.0.RELEASE')
--build                Build system to use (for example
                         'maven' or 'gradle') (default: maven)
-d, --dependencies     Comma-separated list of dependency
                         identifiers to include in the
                         generated project
--description          Project description
-f, --force            Force overwrite of existing files
--format               Format of the generated content (for
                         example 'build' for a build file,
                         'project' for a project archive)
                         (default: project)
-g, --groupId          Project coordinates (for example 'org.
                         test')
-j, --java-version     Language level (for example '1.8')
-l, --language         Programming language  (for example
                         'java')
-n, --name             Project name; infer application name
-p, --packaging        Project packaging (for example 'jar')
--package-name         Package name
-t, --type             Project type. Not normally needed if
                         you use --build and/or --format.
                         Check the capabilities of the
                         service (--list) for more details
--target               URL of the service to use (default:
                         https://start.spring.io)
-v, --version          Project version (for example '0.0.1-
                         SNAPSHOT')
-x, --extract          Extract the project archive. Inferred
                         if a location is specified without
                         an extension

examples:

    To list all the capabilities of the service:
        $ spring init --list

    To creates a default project:
        $ spring init

    To create a web my-app.zip:
        $ spring init -d=web my-app.zip

    To create a web/data-jpa gradle project unpacked:
        $ spring init -d=web,jpa --build=gradle my-dir
```

You can use the following command to find out what choices are available for those parameters by using the `--list` parameter with the `init` command:

```
$ spring init -list
```

You have seen the Spring Boot CLI `init` command for creating your Spring project. The Spring community offers a web-based interface, Spring Tool Suite, or Spring Boot CLI to initialize your Spring Boot project.

Spring Boot CLI has no need to specify the build specification. CLI gets hits from the code and resolves dependencies accordingly and produces deployment artifacts. Spring Boot CLI produces an almost friction-free development experience and eliminates all code noise.

After your installation is complete, you can also run a simple application, whatever we have created in Chapter 1, *Getting Started with Spring Boot 2.0*. To do so, you will have to use the same web application, by the name of app.groovy, as follows:

```
@RestController
class HelloController {
    @GetMapping("/")
    String hello() {
        return "Hello World!!!"
    }
}
```

Save this file as app.groovy in a directory and let's run the application from a shell by using the following command:

```
$ spring run app.groovy
```

Open http://localhost:8080/ from the browser. If the output shows you **Hello World** or whatever you might have asked your application to do—the installation was successful.

Let's see the following console after running the preceding command at the Spring Boot CLI. The first line in the console is resolving dependencies, but in this application we didn't define the dependencies. Spring Boot CLI automatically resolves the dependencies based on the classes we have written for the application. But, you can define explicit library dependencies by using the @Grab annotation. Let's see the following @Grab annotation for the HSQL database in your application. Let's run this application using Spring Boot CLI as follows:

```
@Grab("HSQL")
```

Let's see the following screenshot of the output in the browser:

As you can see, the Spring Boot CLI provides the quickest way of developing without any code friction.

Let's discuss another important feature and key component of Spring Boot.

Spring Boot Actuator – taking Application's Insights

Have you ever thought to look at what's going on with your Spring application in production? How many objects have been created? How much free or used memory is left? Let's consider, if any framework can allow you to watch all these insights, you can manage your application very well during production by using HTTP endpoints or with JMX. You can find out how your application is behaving and check on its health.

Here, I am going to explain a key component of Spring Boot, Actuator. The Spring Boot Actuator allows you to monitor production-ready features, such as metrics and the health of the Spring application.

Spring Boot Actuator is a sub-project of Spring Boot, with a lot more functionalities at your disposal. You can control the sensitivity and security of your application more effectively with Spring Boot Actuator. Monitoring the metrics, incoming traffic, and state of a database in your applications becomes very easy when Actuator is enabled. The main advantage is that these production-grade tools are available to you, without you having to implement these features.

Let's see how to enable these production-ready features in your Spring application.

Enabling Spring Boot's Actuator in your application

To enable Spring Boot Actuator in your application, you will have to add Spring Boot Actuator dependency in your package manager. This is the simplest way to enable the production-ready features in your Spring application, by adding a Starter dependency, `spring-boot-starter-actuator`.

Let's add the Actuator to a Maven-based project as follows in your Spring Boot project:

```
<dependencies>
    <dependency>
            <groupId>org.springframework.boot</groupId>
            <artifactId>spring-boot-starter-actuator</artifactId>
    </dependency>
</dependencies>
```

The preceding Maven script will enable the production-ready features that are Spring Boot's Actuator. Now let's see how to enable the Actuator with a Gradle-based project.

Let's use the following declaration:

```
dependencies {
    compile("org.springframework.boot:spring-boot-starter-actuator")
}
```

The preceding "Gradle script will enable the production-ready features in your Spring application.

After enabling the production-ready features, let's see what all the endpoints are that Spring Boot's Actuator provides.

Analyzing the Actuator's endpoints

Spring Boot's Actuator offers you several web endpoints; these let you monitor your running Spring application and you can view the internals of your application in production. It provides you a number of predefined endpoints for your Spring application, but you can also add your own custom endpoint for monitoring your application in production.

For example, the health endpoint provides basic application health information and you can also find out how beans are wired together in the Spring application context, determine what environment properties are available to your application, get a snapshot of runtime metrics, and more.

You can easily make use of your application and optimize it by invoking HTTP endpoints if your application is configured with Spring Boot Actuator. There is a wide range of HTTP endpoints that Spring Boot Actuator can support. Some of these are:

- Bean details
- Logger details

- Configuration details
- Health details
- Version details

With these built-in endpoints in Spring Boot Actuator, it also allows you to add your own endpoint or customize an existing one. Spring Boot sets the sensitive default to some HTTP endpoints, which cannot be exposed publicly. These endpoints require a password or a username.

The Spring Boot's Actuator exposes a number of endpoints in multiple ways, but these depend on the technology you are using. Once Spring Boot Actuator is configured into your application, it provides you several Actuator REST endpoints. If you are choosing HTTP web endpoints, then you can see the following endpoints:

REST endpoints	Description
/actuator	It gives a discovery platform in place of a page for other endpoints. To enable Actuator, you have to put Spring HATEOS on the classpath. Actuators are sensitive by default and hence require username and password, or they can be disabled due to disabled web security.
/auditevents	All information on audit and events is contained in this endpoint.
/autoconfig	It provides an auto-configuration report of all the auto-configurations applied in the application.
/beans	It shows all the beans configured in the application. Beans are super important for applications configured in Spring. It is an object that is initialized, assembled, and managed in Spring IoC container.
/configprops	It shows you the details of config properties.
/dump	This is for dumping a thread.
/env	It shows different properties of all configurable environments in Spring.
/flyway	This helps when you want to see database migrations.
/health	This displays the health information of an application. Health information includes security, authentication of connections made, and message details of authentications for an application.
/info	This is the arbitrary application information.
/loggers	You can use it if you want to show or change the config of different loggers in your application.
/liquibase	This is in case you want to see migrations of liquibase.
/metrics	This shows metric information for an application.

`/mappings`	This shows a queue of the entire request mapping paths in the application.
`/shutdown`	It is enabled to allow the application a graceful shutdown. Spring Boot Actuator does not enable it by default. You will have to enable it should you require it.
`/trace`	Shows trace data (timestamp, headers, and so on) which is the 100 latest HTTP requests.

The preceding table has several web endpoints. You can organize these endpoints into the following three categories:

- Configuration endpoints
- Metrics endpoints
- Application information endpoints

Let's take a look at how to expose these endpoints that provide insight into the configuration of your application. Since endpoints may contain sensitive information, careful consideration should be given about when to expose them. Out of the box, Spring Boot will expose all enabled endpoints over JMX, but only the health and info endpoints over HTTP.

Exposing configuration details

Spring Boot Actuator provides some endpoints that expose the configuration details of your Spring application. These endpoints provide you all configured bean details and also provide insight into the decisions that auto-configuration made when populating the Spring application context. Let's see the most essential endpoint for exploring an application's Spring context, which is the `/beans` endpoint. This endpoint returns information in the form of JSON as follows:

```
[
{
context: "application",
parent: null,
beans:
[
{
bean: "springBootActuatorApplication",
scope: "singleton",
type:
"com.dineshonjava.sba.SpringBootActuatorApplication$$EnhancerBySpringCGLIB$
```

```
$ee8dc6d9",
resource: "null",
dependencies: [ ]
},
{
bean:
"org.springframework.boot.autoconfigure.internalCachingMetadataReaderFactor
y",
scope: "singleton",
type:
"org.springframework.core.type.classreading.CachingMetadataReaderFactory",
resource: "null",
dependencies: [ ]
},
{
bean: "loginService",
scope: "singleton",
type: "com.dineshonjava.sba.LoginService",
resource: "file [D:/packt-spring-boot-
ws/SpringBootActuator/target/classes/com/dineshonjava/sba/LoginService.clas
s]",
dependencies:
[
"counterService"
]
},
{
bean: "myCustomEndpoint",
scope: "singleton",
type: "com.dineshonjava.sba.MyCustomEndpoint",
resource: "file [D:/packt-spring-boot-
ws/SpringBootActuator/target/classes/com/dineshonjava/sba/MyCustomEndpoint.
class]",
dependencies: [ ]
},.....
```

As you can see in the preceding JSON data of the `/beans` endpoint, all configured beans in the application have the following information about the bean:

- **Bean**: A bean is a name or ID of the configured bean in your Spring application
- **Dependencies**: The dependency is a list of bean IDs that this bean is injected with
- **Scope**: It exposes the bean's scope
- **Type**: The bean's Java type

The `/beans` shows all the beans configured in the application. Beans are super important for applications configured on Spring. It is an object that is initialized, assembled, and managed at Spring IoC container. The `/autoconfig` endpoint provides an auto-configuration report of all the auto-configurations applied in the application. Spring Boot auto-configuration is built upon Spring conditional configuration. Spring Boot provides multiple configuration classes with `@Conditional` annotations. This `@Conditional` annotation decides whether beans should be automatically configured. Let's see the following JSON data that the `/autoconfig` endpoint provides:

```
{
positiveMatches:
{
AuditAutoConfiguration#auditListener:
[
{
condition: "OnBeanCondition",
message: "@ConditionalOnMissingBean (types:
org.springframework.boot.actuate.audit.listener.AbstractAuditListener;
SearchStrategy: all) found no beans"
}
],
AuditAutoConfiguration#authenticationAuditListener:
[
{
condition: "OnClassCondition",
message: "@ConditionalOnClass classes found:
org.springframework.security.authentication.event.AbstractAuthenticationEve
nt"
},
{
condition: "OnBeanCondition",
message: "@ConditionalOnMissingBean (types:
org.springframework.boot.actuate.security.AbstractAuthenticationAuditListen
er; SearchStrategy: all) found no beans"
}
. . . . . . . . . .
],
negativeMatches:
{
CacheStatisticsAutoConfiguration:
[
{
condition: "OnBeanCondition",
message: "@ConditionalOnBean (types:
org.springframework.cache.CacheManager; SearchStrategy: all) found no
beans"
```

```
}
],
CacheStatisticsAutoConfiguration.CaffeineCacheStatisticsProviderConfigurati
on:
[
{
condition: "OnClassCondition",
message: "required @ConditionalOnClass classes not found:
com.github.benmanes.caffeine.cache.Caffeine,org.springframework.cache.caffe
ine.CaffeineCacheManager"
},
{
condition: "ConditionEvaluationReport.AncestorsMatchedCondition",
message: "Ancestor
'org.springframework.boot.actuate.autoconfigure.CacheStatisticsAutoConfigur
ation' did not match"
}
],.....
}
```

The preceding JSON is the output of the /autoconfig endpoint. This JSON is divided into
two parts—positiveMatches and negativeMatches. Data under negativeMatches
means there's a condition that decides whether to configure a bean. And
positiveMatches means you'll find a condition used to decide whether Spring Boot
should auto-configure a bean.

Let's look at another configuration endpoint, /env; it shows different properties of all
configurable environments in Spring:

```
{
profiles: [ ],
server.ports: {
local.server.port: 8080
},
commandLineArgs: {
spring.output.ansi.enabled: "always"
},
servletContextInitParams: { },
systemProperties: {
.....
sun.boot.library.path: "C:Program FilesJavajre1.8.0_151bin",
java.vm.version: "25.151-b12",
java.vm.vendor: "Oracle Corporation",
java.vendor.url: "http://java.oracle.com/",
java.rmi.server.randomIDs: "true",
path.separator: ";",
java.vm.name: "Java HotSpot(TM) 64-Bit Server VM",
```

```
file.encoding.pkg: "sun.io",
user.name: "Dinesh.Rajput",
com.sun.management.jmxremote: "",
java.vm.specification.version: "1.8",
sun.java.command: "com.dineshonjava.sba.SpringBootActuatorApplication --
spring.output.ansi.enabled=always",
java.home: "C:Program FilesJavajre1.8.0_151",
sun.arch.data.model: "64",
sun.desktop: "windows",
sun.cpu.isalist: "amd64"
},
systemEnvironment: {
.....
LOCALAPPDATA: "C:UsersDinesh.RajputAppDataLocal",
PROCESSOR_LEVEL: "6",
FP_NO_HOST_CHECK: "NO",
USERDOMAIN: "TIMESGROUP",
LOGONSERVER: "\TGNOIFCTYDC01",
JAVA_HOME: "C:Program FilesJavajdk1.8.0_121",
SESSIONNAME: "Console",
APPDATA: "C:UsersDinesh.RajputAppDataRoaming",
USERNAME: "Dinesh.Rajput",
ProgramFiles(x86): "C:Program Files (x86)",
VBOX_MSI_INSTALL_PATH: "C:Program FilesOracleVirtualBox",
CommonProgramFiles: "C:Program FilesCommon Files",
.....
},
applicationConfig: [classpath:/application.properties]: {
endpoints.health.enabled: "true",
endpoints.health.id: "health",
management.port: "8080",
info.app.description: "This is my first Working Spring Actuator Examples",
info.app.version: "0.0.1-SNAPSHOT",
endpoints.info.id: "info",
endpoints.metrics.id: "metrics",
endpoints.metrics.sensitive: "false",
endpoints.metrics.enabled: "true",
security.user.name: "admin",
management.security.enabled: "true",
security.user.password: "******",
management.context-path: "/",
info.app.name: "Spring Boot Actuator Application",
endpoints.health.sensitive: "false",
security.basic.enabled: "true",
endpoints.info.enabled: "true",
endpoints.info.sensitive: "false"
}
}
```

Now let's see how the endpoint exposes the metric of your application.

Exposing metrics endpoints

Spring Boot Actuator allows you to inspect some interesting parameters of your running application, such as application memory circumstances (available versus free). The following listing shows a sample of what the /metrics endpoint might give you:

```
{
mem: 308564,
mem.free: 219799,
processors: 4,
instance.uptime: 3912392,
uptime: 3918108,
systemload.average: -1,
heap.committed: 254976,
heap.init: 131072,
heap.used: 35176,
heap: 1847808,
nonheap.committed: 54952,
nonheap.init: 2496,
nonheap.used: 53578,
nonheap: 0,
threads.peak: 25,
threads.daemon: 23,
threads.totalStarted: 29,
threads: 25,
classes: 6793,
classes.loaded: 6793,
classes.unloaded: 0,
gc.ps_scavenge.count: 8,
gc.ps_scavenge.time: 136,
gc.ps_marksweep.count: 2,
gc.ps_marksweep.time: 208,
httpsessions.max: -1,
httpsessions.active: 0,
gauge.response.beans: 20,
gauge.response.env: 16,
gauge.response.autoconfig: 14,
gauge.response.unmapped: 1,
counter.status.200.beans: 2,
counter.login.failure: 2,
```

```
counter.login.success: 10,
counter.status.200.autoconfig: 2,
counter.status.401.unmapped: 3,
counter.status.200.env: 2
}
```

As you can see, a lot of information is provided by the `/metrics` endpoint.

Now let's check the health of the application by using the `/health` endpoint:

```
{
   status: "UP",
   diskSpace:
   {
      status: "UP",
      total: 290391584768,
      free: 209372835840,
      threshold: 10485760
   }
}
```

As you can see, the preceding information is about the health of your Spring application. Along with the basic health status, you're also given information regarding the amount of available disk space and the status of the database that the application is using.

Let's see how to expose application information by using `/info` endpoints.

Exposing application information

In Spring Boot, Actuator also provides arbitrary application information by using the `/info` endpoint. If you make a GET request call to the `/info` endpoint, by default it will return empty JSON, {}.

The empty JSON means Spring Boot doesn't provide default information for your application. The `/info` endpoint provides any information for your Spring application that you want to expose to your client or the public. You can add any information about your application to this endpoint in `application.properties` or `application.yml` as follows:

application.properties

```
info.app.name=Spring Boot Actuator Application
info.app.description=This is my first Working Spring Actuator Examples
info.app.version=0.0.1-SNAPSHOT
```

```
info.helpline.email=admin@dineshonjava.com
info.helpline.phone=0120-000001100
application.yml
info:
   app:
        name: Spring Boot Actuator Application
        description: This is my first Working Spring Actuator Examples
        version: 0.0.1-SNAPSHOT
   helpline:
        email: admin@dineshonjava.com
        phone: 0120-000001100
```

In the preceding examples, you can see that we want to provide some information about our application such as application name, description, version, email, and helpline number in the /info endpoint response. Now let's request the /info endpoint; you'll get the following response:

```
{
  helpline:
  {
    email: "admin@dineshonjava.com",
    phone: "0120-00000110"
  },
  app:
  {
    description: "This is my first Working Spring Actuator Examples",
    version: "0.0.1-SNAPSHOT",
     name: "Spring Boot Actuator Application"
  }
}
```

As shown, the Spring Boot Actuator /info endpoint exposes information about your application to the outside of your application. This information might be useful for callers.

Let's see in the next section how to kill your application using an Actuator's endpoint.

Shutting down your application

You can also shut down your application by using the /shutdown endpoint. But by default, this endpoint is disabled, so first, you have to enable the /shutdown endpoint, and then you can use it as follows:

```
endpoints.shutdown.enabled=true
```

Let's enable it by using the `application.yml` file:

```
endpoints:
    shutdown:
          enabled: true
```

Let's invoke the `/shutdown` endpoint and see what happens:

```
POST http://localhost:8080/shutdown
```

The preceding is a `POST` request. It returns the following response:

```
{
    "message": "Shutting down, bye..."
}
```

This `/shutdown` endpoint can kill your application, so you have to take care with this endpoint.

Spring Boot's Actuator provides most of the insight you require concerning your running application in production, but sometimes it is not enough for your needs. That is why Spring Boot also allows you to customize the Actuator endpoints.

Let's see in the next section how to customize the endpoints of Spring Boot's Actuator.

Customizing your Actuator endpoints

You can also customize your Actuator endpoints by using Spring properties. Endpoints can be customized in the following ways:

- Enabling/disabling endpoints
- Sensitivity
- Changing endpoint IDs
- Writing custom health indicators
- Creating custom endpoint
- Many more customizations

To customize the properties in your application, you can enable or disable an endpoint, make its sensitivity true or false, and customize its ID. You can also customize all endpoints globally, and also create exceptions for the ones you want to. Let's see how to customize the Actuator.

Enabling or disabling endpoints

By default in Spring Boot, all endpoints are enabled except /shutdown, but you can disable some of them. You can also enable the /shutdown endpoint.

In the application.properties file, it would look like this:

```
endpoints.shutdown.enabled=true
```

In the application.yml file, it would look like this:

```
endpoints:
    shutdown:
        enabled: true
```

Similarly, you can also disable any of the other endpoints as follows:

```
endpoints._endpoint-id.enabled = false
```

In the application.yml file, it would look like this:

```
endpoints:
    _endpoint-id:
        enabled: false
```

Let's suppose you want to disable the /health endpoint. Then in the application.properties file, you have to set the following property:

```
endpoints.health.enabled=true
```

In application.yml, it would look like this:

```
endpoints:
    health:
        enabled: false
```

You can also disable all endpoints at once by setting the following property to false in the application.properties file:

```
endpoints.enabled=false
```

In the application.yml file, it would look like this:

```
endpoints:
    enabled: false
```

As you can see, all endpoints will be disabled, so you can enable specific endpoints if you want to enable then by setting `endpoints._endpoint-id.enabled = true`.

Changing endpoint IDs

As you have seen in the table of all Actuator endpoints, each of the Actuator endpoints has an ID that is used to call that endpoint as a REST service. For example `/health`, `/metrics`, and `/beans` endpoints have health, metrics, and beans, respectively, as their IDs. But you can change this endpoint ID and set what you want for your application as follows:

```
endpoints.endpoint-id.id=new_id
```

For example, let's customize the ID of the `/health` endpoint. Now I want to change it to `GET` requests sent to `/status`. In the `application.properties` file, it looks like this:

```
health.id = status
```

In the `application.yml` file, it looks like this:

```
health:
    id: status
```

Now you can check the health of your application by using the `/status` custom endpoint. It will work the same as the `/health` endpoint.

Changing the sensitivity of the Actuator's endpoints

By default, many of the Actuator's endpoints are sensitive. All default endpoints in Spring Boot Actuator are automatically sensitive. Hence the endpoints can be secured by using default properties for fault security. These include username, password, and role, within the properties file of your application. But you can also mark sensitive as `false` if the endpoint doesn't expose sensitive information, as follows:

```
endpoints._endpoint-id.sensitive = false
```

In the `application.yml` file, it would look like the following:

```
endpoints:
    _endpoint-id:
          sensitive: false
```

You can also set it to true if all endpoints expose sensitive information.

For example, let's set the `/health` endpoint's sensitive value to `false`:

```
endpoints.health.sensitive=false
```

Or in `application.yml` file:

```
endpoints:
   health:
          sensitive: false
```

Now you can access the `/health` endpoint without any authentication security.

Spring Boot Actuators also allows you to create your own endpoint, with your own configurations and implementations. To do so, all you have to do is implement the endpoint interface and override its method.

Writing custom health indicators

Spring Boot's Actuator allows you to write a custom health indicator for your application. The Actuator's default `/health` endpoint provides information about your application status and disk space as follows:

```
{
    status: "UP",
    diskSpace: {
          status: "UP",
          total: 290391584768,
          free: 209125543936,
          threshold: 10485760
    }
}
```

As you can see in the preceding JSON, the `/health` endpoint returns default health indicator data for common needs such as reporting the health of a disk or database. But you can also provide custom health information—you can register Spring Beans that implement the `HealthIndicator` interface. You need to provide an implementation of the `health()` method and return a `Health` response. The `Health` response should include a status and can optionally include additional details to be displayed. The following code shows a sample `HealthIndicator` implementation:

```
package com.dineshonjava.sba;

import org.springframework.boot.actuate.health.Health;
import org.springframework.boot.actuate.health.HealthIndicator;
```

```
import org.springframework.stereotype.Component;
import org.springframework.web.client.RestTemplate;

@Component
public class DineshonjavaHealth implements HealthIndicator{

    @Override
    public Health health() {
        try {
            RestTemplate rest = new RestTemplate();
            rest.getForObject("https://www.dineshonjava.com",
            String.class);
            return Health.up().build();
        } catch (Exception e) {
            return Health.down().build();
        }
    }
}
```

As you can see in the preceding code, we are going to plug in a custom health indicator that will check the health of the linking application website https://www.dineshonjava.com and it will return a response with the health status of this website as follows:

```
{
    status: "UP",
    dineshonjavaHealth: {
        status: "UP"
    },
    diskSpace: {
        status: "UP",
        total: 290391584768,
        free: 209125003264,
        threshold: 10485760
    }
}
```

The DineshonjavaHealth class overrides the health() method of the HealthIndicator interface and simply uses Spring's RestTemplate to perform a GET request to the https://www.dineshonjava.com page. If it works, it returns a Health object indicating that Dineshonjava is UP. Otherwise, it will throw an exception and returns a Health object indicating that Dineshonjava is DOWN. Let's see what the following response will return if https://www.dineshonjava.com is down:

```
{
    status: "DOWN",
    dineshonjavaHealth: {
```

```
            status: "DOWN"
    },
    diskSpace: {
            status: "UP",
            total: 290391584768,
            free: 209124999168,
            threshold: 10485760
    }
}
```

As you can see, the status is DOWN but you can also add more details about its failure to access this website by using the withDetail() method on the Health builder as follows:

```
return Health.down().withDetail("reason", e.getMessage()).build();

Let's see the response of the /health endpoint again.
  {
    status: "DOWN",
    dineshonjavaHealth: {
            status: "DOWN",
            reason: "I/O error on GET request for
"https://www.dineshonjava.com": www.dineshonjava.com; nested exception is
java.net.UnknownHostException: www.dineshonjava.com"
    },
    diskSpace: {
            status: "UP",
            total: 290391584768,
            free: 209124995072,
            threshold: 10485760
    }
}
```

As shown in the preceding example you can add additional details, whatever you want, with success or failure, by calling the withDetail() method of the Health builder class.

Now let's see how to create a custom endpoint.

Creating a custom endpoint

We have seen that the Actuator provides several endpoints for your application. But Spring Boot's Actuator also allows you to create a custom endpoint by implementing the EndPoint interface. Let's see the following example:

```
package com.dineshonjava.sba;
```

```java
import java.util.ArrayList;
import java.util.List;

import org.springframework.boot.actuate.endpoint.Endpoint;
import org.springframework.stereotype.Component;
@Component
public class MyCustomEndpoint implements Endpoint<List<String>>{

    @Override
    public String getId() {
        return "myCustomEndpoint";
    }

    @Override
    public List<String> invoke() {
        // Custom logic to build the output
        List<String> list = new ArrayList<>();
        list.add("App message 1");
        list.add("App message 2");
        list.add("App message 3");
        list.add("App message 4");
        return list;
    }
    @Override
    public boolean isEnabled() {
        return true;
    }

    @Override
    public boolean isSensitive() {
        return true;
    }
}
```

As you can see, the `MyCustomEndpoint` class implemented the `EndPoint` interface and it overrode four methods, `getId()`, `invoke()`, `isSensitive()`, and `isEnabled()`. The `getId()` method returns endpoint ID or name, and by using it you can access /myCustomEndpoint for now. Let's see what the following response returns:

```
[
"App message 1",
"App message 2",
"App message 3",
"App message 4"
]
```

The `invoke()` method returns an application message—whatever you want to expose from this custom endpoint. The `isEnabled()` and `isSensitive()` methods are used for enabling this endpoint for your application and setting the sensitivity of this endpoint respectively.

There are many more ways of customizing Spring Boot's Actuator. Spring Boot allows us to customize all of the Actuator. That is why Spring Boot is opinionated.

Many of the Actuator endpoints expose sensitive data, so you have to protect these endpoints from any unwanted activity. Spring Boot allows you to secure these Actuator endpoints. In the next section, let's see how to make these Actuator endpoints secure.

Securing the Actuator endpoints

The Actuator's endpoints provide many insights into your Spring application to callers, but some of that information might be unsafe if you expose it to the caller. For example, the `/shutdown` endpoint can kill your application in production. So the `/shutdown` endpoint can be very dangerous for your application if you expose it publicly. Similarly, many endpoints in Spring Boot's Actuator expose information that might be very sensitive. So, you have to secure those Actuator endpoints and make them only available to authorized callers. You can use Spring Security to make secure the Actuator endpoints.

Although Spring Boot will not apply any security on your behalf, it does provide some convenient `RequestMatchers` that can be used in combination with Spring Security. In a Spring Boot application, this means adding the Security Starter as a build dependency and letting security auto-configuration take care of locking down the application, including the Actuator endpoints.

Let's add the following Starter dependency for Spring Security:

```
<dependency>
    <groupId>org.springframework.boot</groupId>
    <artifactId>spring-boot-starter-security</artifactId>
</dependency>
```

It will secure all Actuator endpoints, but you can disable basic security as follows:

In the `application.properties` file:

```
security.basic.enabled=false
```

In the `application.yml` file, it looks like this:

```
basic:
      enabled: false
```

The preceding configuration change leaves only the sensitive Actuator endpoints secured and leaves the rest open for access.

Now you can secure sensitive endpoints by defining the default security properties, such username, password, and role, in the `application.properties` file:

```
security.user.name=admin
security.user.password=secret
management.security.role=SUPERUSER
```

The preceding configuration will secure the Actuator endpoints. If any call reaches these endpoints, then it asks for `username` and `password`. That means no one can access these Actuator endpoints without authentication.

This Spring Security configuration is provided by the auto-configuration of the Spring Boot. You can also customize the Spring Security configuration to lock some of the more dangerous Actuator endpoints such as `/shutdown` or provide this Actuator endpoint for a very specific role.

Let's see what changes are introduced with Spring Boot 2.0.

The Actuator with Spring Boot 2.X

The new version of Spring Boot Actuator—2.x Actuator, has been introduced with a simplified model, extended capabilities, and better incorporated defaults. In this version, the security model is integrated with the application for simplification. Some more HTTP requests and responses, and Java APIs, have also been added. The newest version also supports CRUD against the model of read-write it had before.

Actuator 2.x defines the extensible model, which is also pluggable and does not depend on MVC. Hence, you can utilize MVC and Web Flux. In the new version, endpoints also come disabled by default. Should you want to turn them all on, you can use the following:

```
management.endpoints.web.expose = *.
```

Or if you do not want to enable all the endpoints, you can simply list the ones you want to enable and let others be. All Actuator endpoints are now also set under `/actuator` path by default.

Spring Boot 2.x Actuator has also introduced some more built-in endpoints:

- `/conditions`: This is simply auto-config renamed
- `/Prometheus`: This is also the same as metrics, but it supports a Prometheus server
- `Scheduledtasks`: This endpoint provides details of every scheduled task in the application
- `/sessions`: This is a list of HTTP sessions using Spring Sessions
- `/threaddump`: This endpoint dumps the thread information

Spring Boot 2.x Actuator allows you to manipulate the endpoints in similar ways to previous versions. You can customize them; however, there have been a few changes introduced to the method of customization. This is mostly because 2.x Actuator supports CRUD operations instead of just read and write. And you can also add new endpoints to existing ones, with your own configurations and implementations.

Spring Boot Actuator allows you to manipulate and manage your application very easily.

Summary

In this chapter, we have learned about the Spring Boot CLI and how to install it in your machine. The Spring Boot CLI offers you a very simple and fast way of developing the Spring Boot application. You can run the Spring Boot application with the Groovy language using the CLI; it makes it possible to develop the Spring application with minimal code noise and reduces all code friction. The Spring Boot CLI is also able to automatically resolve several dependency libraries. You can also take advantage of the Gradle `@Grab` annotation to explicitly declare dependencies; no need to define a build specification, either using Maven or Gradle.

We have also run a very simple `Hello World` REST application by using the web-based Spring Boot CLI.

You have seen in this chapter how to find out about your Spring application in production. Spring Boot provides you a production-ready feature, Spring Boot Actuator. The Actuator provides many endpoints and you can monitor these endpoints using the web-based REST services, remote shell, and JMX client. But in this chapter, I have explained only web-based REST endpoints. You can also customize these Actuator endpoints.

In `Chapter 4`, *Getting Started with Spring Cloud and Configuration*, we'll start to understand Spring Cloud and configurations.

4
Getting Started with Spring Cloud and Configuration

In the previous chapter, we discussed the Spring Boot CLI installation as well as application creation and execution using the CLI. Spring Boot provides the CLI for quick application implementation with zero code friction. We also looked at Spring Boot's production-ready feature—the Actuator. The Actuator provides all the production Ops metrics and the application's health status in production. Spring Boot provides several extraordinary features.

In this chapter, we will explore another extension from Spring Boot, Spring Cloud. So what is Spring Cloud? What is it used for? How does Spring Cloud provide solutions for building robust cloud-native applications and solve common problems faced when moving to a distributed environment?

At the end of this chapter, you will have answers to these questions. And you will understand how to configure the Spring Cloud server and client for your distributed application.

This chapter will cover the following points:

- Cloud-native application architecture
- Microservices architecture:
    - Benefits
    - Challenges
- Introduction to Spring Cloud
- Usages of Spring Cloud
- Projects under Spring Cloud

- Getting started with Spring Cloud:
    - Mastering Spring Cloud Configuration management
    - Implementing the Spring Cloud Config Server
    - Implementing the Spring Cloud Config Client

Let's look at these topics in detail.

Cloud-native application architecture

Many top companies are moving ahead very rapidly due to a lot of innovations in business and innovations in the software they are using. As *Mark Andreessen* said, *Software is eating the world*. So software is also one of the main pillars for each business. Top companies are innovating the following common features:

- Software speed
- Availability of services
- Software scalability
- Software user experiences for all devices, such as computer and mobile

So moving to the cloud is one of the major evolutions in software innovations; providing cloud-native solutions and architecture to software is one of the major innovations taken by many top companies. Cloud provides on-demand storage resources and networking solutions elastically. Such services include Amazon Web Services, Google Cloud, and Microsoft Azure.

Using cloud-native application architecture gives you several benefits and addresses the common problems of scalability, durability, and availability. Here are some common motivations for the cloud-native application architecture:

- Speed of the application
- Safety and security
- Software scalability
- Monitoring the application
- Fault isolation and tolerance

So, as you can see, your application must follow cloud-native patterns because it is based on the distributed nature and easily scalable. The application must be designed as horizontally scalable rather than vertically scalability. Microservices architecture is one of the examples of horizontally scalable application architectures. You could create a number of small applications or services based on the bounded context instead of creating a single large application. The cloud-native pattern provides optimal resource utilization; if your application needs resources, it provides the resource elastically on demand. Suppose your application doesn't need more resources, then it must release these zero utilization resources. The elasticity of the cloud demands ephemerality.

 Horizontally scalable means we can add resources on demand to the existing application without making any changes in the application. In the case of vertical scalability, we have to change the application architecture.

If you want to create applications, then at the initial level of design you have to focus on some key characteristics of the cloud-native application architecture. The following are key characteristics of the cloud-native application:

- **Twelve-Factor applications**: A set of patterns for an optimized application to improve application design for speed, safety, and scale.
- **Microservices**: An architecture pattern. According to this pattern, we create individual and independent services such as deploying these without impacting other business services. It allows each capability to move independently and autonomously, and in turn faster and safer.
- **Self-service agile infrastructure**: It is related to the cloud platforms and infrastructure that enable development teams to operate at an application and service-abstraction level.
- **API-based collaboration**: It defines service-to-service interaction between several microservices.
- **Antifragility**: It is related to responsiveness, which means that as we increase load on the system using sudden traffic or speed and scale, the system improves its ability to respond, increasing safety.

The preceding points are the best practices for any cloud-based application. Spring Cloud facilitates these styles of development. So let's move to the next section and explore one of the characteristics of the cloud-native application—the microservices architecture.

Microservices architecture

Microservices is not a new word, the term was coined in 2005 by *Dr Peter Rodgers*. It was first called *micro web services* and based on SOAP. The term *microservice* is meant to convert large software into a number of pieces. Each piece focuses on a particular point of business. It is just like a little service with a microscopic scope for a specific target, compared to existing monolithic applications where the scope is very broad.

So, it divides the monolithic application into smaller microservices and manages and deploys these services as a single business goal; communication across these distributed services is a difficult task for developers. Use Spring Cloud to simplify integration between these distributed services.

Nowadays, industries are working on new functionality implementations and innovations every day or every week, constantly growing the application to a large size. A lot of complexity and coupling between various systems makes it difficult to change anything in the application. So various modules' teams must take care regarding impact on various parts of the application, either for large changes or the tiniest changes.

Let's look at the following diagram of a monolithic application without the microservices architecture:

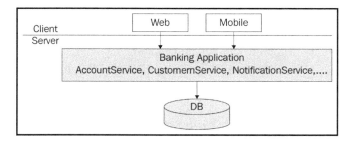

As you can see, the preceding diagram shows, the **Banking Application** using a monolithic architecture without microservices. It's an all-in-one application, which means all modules, such as **AccountService**, **CustomerService**, and **Notification Service**, are in a single application.

Suppose you change CustomerService, you have to ensure the functionality of other modules' notification and account services is not impacted by the style of the architecture.

Let's divide this monolithic application into separate pieces according to the modules, and create with the microservice architecture. See the following diagram:

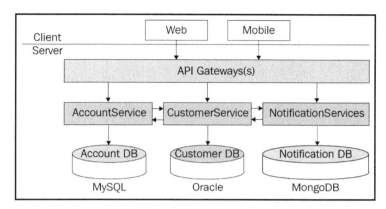

As you can see, we've now created the Banking Application with the microservices-based architecture. Here, the main application has been divided in a set of sub-applications, called microservices.

As core Spring concepts are applied to application architecture, Spring enables a separation of concerns between the application components, such as loose coupling, which means the effect of the change is isolated, and tight cohesion, which means the code performs a single, well-defined task. Similarly, microservices exhibit the same strengths, that is, loose coupling between the collaborating services of the application, and you can change these services independently. Another strength is tight cohesion, which means an application service that deals with a single view of data; it also known as **Bounded Contexts** or **Domain-driven design (DDD)**.

Let's look at the following benefits of the microservice architecture.

Microservice benefits

These are following benefits if you are using the microservice architecture in your application:

- Smaller code bases are easy to maintain
- Easy to scale means you can scale individual components
- Technology diversity means you can use mix libraries, frameworks, data storage, and languages

- Fault isolation means component failure should not bring the whole system down
- Better support for smaller, parallel teams
- Independent deployment
- Reduced team size also reduces the overhead associated with keeping a team focused and moving in one direction

There are several benefits to the microservices architecture approach; most of these benefits focus on reliability and agility. It also has some challenges, which we will discuss in the next section.

Microservice challenges

Even though we have a lot of benefits with the microservices, it also has some challenges. Let's see:

- Difficulty to achieve strong consistency across services, such as maintaining ACID transactions within multiple processes
- Because of distributed system, it's harder to debug/trace
- Greater need for end-to-end testing
- How applications are developed and deployed
- Communication across services and service-to-service calls

There are numerous challenges related to the microservice infrastructure. There are multiple processes working together as a single business unit. Because of this distributing nature, the following issues arise:

Difficulty	Solution
How do multiple microservices find each other?	It is service discovery.
How do we decide which instance of a service to use?	It is client-side load balancing.
What happens if a particular microservice is not responding?	It is a fault tolerance.
How do we control the access of a microservice, such as providing security and rate limits?	It is service security.
How do multiple microservices communicate with each other?	It is messaging.

So far, we have seen that there are several challenges with microservices and distributed systems. But Spring Boot makes microservices-based approaches easy to use. And Spring Cloud comes into the picture to provide the solution to all these challenges. Spring Cloud makes the development of distributed microservices quite practical by using leverage capabilities of the auto-configuration.

Spring Boot makes for easy development with the microservices:

- You can create numerous services by using Spring Boot
- You can expose resources via `RestController`
- You can also consume these remote services using `RestTemplate`

Spring Cloud leverages capabilities for continuous deployment, rolling upgrades of new versions of code, quick rollback in case of defects, and running multiple versions of the same service at the same time. And more, which we'll discuss in the next section.

Introduction to Spring Cloud

The Spring team provided Spring Boot on top of the Spring Framework to make Spring application development easy, by using a lot of auto-configuration for most of all modules. As Spring Boot is an extension of the Spring Core Framework, Spring Cloud is also an extension of Spring Boot, which provides various libraries and focuses on several cloud-native patterns. Spring Cloud expands on Spring Boot by giving us a bundle of libraries that improve the working of an application when added to classpath. You can exploit the basic default behavior to begin rapidly and, after that, you can design or stretch out to make a custom code.

Spring Cloud is an umbrella project of the Spring team; Spring Cloud has multiple sub-projects under it. It is the collection of the Spring sub-projects that provide solutions for cloud-native problems. These problems come into the picture when your application grows in size and traffic and also whenever you move to a mobile platform. As we have discussed in the previous section about the cloud-native application architecture, the microservices architecture is one of the solutions for cloud-native problems.

Spring Cloud gives room for coders to rapidly assemble a portion of the regular patterns in distributed systems (for example, configuration administration, circuit breakers, routing, micro-proxy, and control bus). By using Spring Cloud, coders can easily, and in no time, set applications and configurations using distributed systems. They will function great in a distributed environment, including the coder's own particular workstation, uncovered metal servers, and other platforms such as Cloud Foundry.

Building blocks of the cloud and microservice applications

Spring Cloud is a building block for the cloud and microservice based on the application's architecture. It provides platform support for the Spring-based cloud-native application: microservices. Let's look at the building blocks required for the cloud-native services:

- **Platform support and IaaS**: Access platform-specific information and services available for Cloud Foundry, AWS, and Heroku.
- **Microservices infrastructure**: It provides useful services such as service discovery, configuration server, and monitoring. There are several based on other open source projects such as Netfilx OSS and HashiCorp's Consul.
- **Dynamic Cloud reconfiguration**: You can create distributed configuration for the services. Spring Cloud Config provides a client and server approach for creating and serving distributed configurations across multiple applications and environments.
- **Cloud utilities**: There are several cloud utilities provided by the Spring Cloud, such as Spring Cloud Security, CLI, and Cloud Stream. Spring Cloud Security is required for securing services and controlling access. And Spring Cloud Stream is required for messaging and event-based cloud applications. Spring Cloud CLI is being used to create applications rapidly in Groovy.
- **Data ingestion**: This building block of the Spring Cloud is used for the data flow of microservices-based information pipelines. For example, Spring Cloud Data Flow and Spring Cloud Modules.
- **Uses Spring Boot style Starters**: Spring Cloud is an extension of Spring Boot. So, the cloud-native application requires Spring Boot to work.

Let's look at the following diagram, which has all the building blocks of cloud and the microservice application:

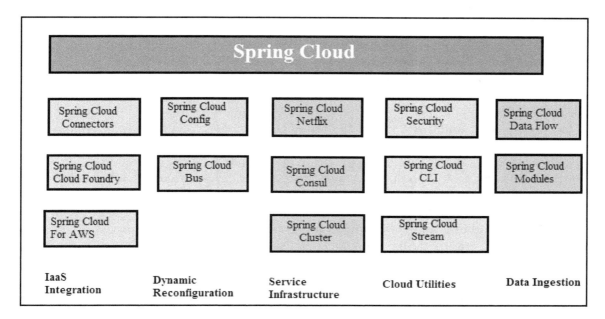

As you can see in the preceding diagram, there are several sub-projects associated with Spring Cloud. Spring Cloud provides a solution for each cloud-native problem. Let's look at all the associated main projects of Spring Cloud:

- **Spring Cloud Config**: External configuration management that is centralized and upheld by a Git repository. The configuration assets delineate to the Spring environment, however they could be utilized by non-Spring applications if you wanted.
- **Spring Cloud Bus**: An event bus for connecting service instances and services together with distributed messaging. Helpful for spreading state changes over a group (for example: config change events).
- **Spring Cloud Netflix**: Integrated and mixed with different Netflix OSS segments (Eureka, Hystrix, Zuul, Archaius, and so on).
- **Spring Cloud Cluster**: It has stateful patterns and leadership election with an abstraction and usage for Zookeeper, Redis, Hazelcast, and Consul.
- **Spring Cloud Consul**: Service disclosure and design administration with Hashicorp Consul.
- **Cloud Foundry**: Incorporates your application with Cloud Foundry. Gives an implementation of a service, and makes it simple to execute SSO and OAuth2-secured assets, as well as to make a service of the Cloud Foundry broker.

- **Spring Cloud Foundry Service Broker**: Gives a beginning stage to build a broker service that deals with a Cloud Foundry administrated service.
- **Spring Cloud Connectors**: Makes it simple for PaaS applications in an assortment of stages to associate with backend running services such as databases and the message broker (the venture previously known as **Spring Cloud**).
- **Spring Cloud for Amazon Web Services**: Simple mix with a host facilitated by Amazon Web Services. It gives a helpful method to collaborate with AWS' given services utilizing understood Spring idioms and APIs, for example, the messaging API. Coders can fabricate their application around the facilitated services without caring about foundation or support.
- **Spring Cloud Security**: Offers help for stack-adjusted OAuth2 REST customer and authentication or confirmation header transfers in a Zuul proxy.
- **Spring Cloud Sleuth**: Spring Cloud applications' distributed tracing, perfect with Zipkin, HTrace, and log-based (for example: ELK) following.
- **Spring Cloud Data Flow**: A cloud-native arrangement service for microservice applications on present-day runtimes. Simple-to-utilize DSL, intuitive GUI, and REST-APIs together disentangle the general organization of microservice-based information pipelines.
- **Spring Cloud Stream**: A small-size event-based microservices structure to rapidly assemble applications that can associate with outside frameworks. Basic revelatory model to send and get messages between Spring Boot applications utilizing Apache Kafka or RabbitMQ.
- **Stream App Starters in Spring Cloud**: These are the Spring Boot Starters where S=starters. These are enhanced when used with external frameworks.
- **Spring Cloud Task**: A fleeting microservices framework to rapidly fabricate applications that perform limited measures of information processing. Basic decisive for including both useful and non-useful highlights to Spring Boot applications.
- **Spring Cloud Zookeeper**: Apache Zookeeper's service discovery and also configuration.
- **Spring Cloud Starters**: Spring Boot-style Starter activities to simplify reliance administration for customers of Spring Cloud. (Ceased as an undertaking and converged with alternate ventures after Angel.SR2.)
- **Spring Cloud CLI**: A plugin for Spring Boot for making Spring Cloud applications quickly in Groovy.

- **Spring Cloud Contract**: It solves issues for developers where they need to have a customer-driven contracts method.
- **Spring Cloud Gateway**: Spring Cloud Gateway is a keen and programmable switch in light of Project Reactor.

Usages of Spring Cloud

As we have seen, Spring Cloud has many several modules depending on the usages. There are many use cases supported by Spring Cloud, such as cloud integration, dynamic reconfiguration, service discovery, security, and data ingestion. We will talk more about microservices support, such as service discovery, and client-side load balancing.

Let's see the following typical use cases of the Spring Cloud and also give you an extensible system:

- Distributed configuration
- Service registration
- Service discovery
- Intelligent routing
- Distributed messaging
- Load balancing
- Circuit breakers
- Leadership election and cluster state
- Global locks
- Service-to-service calls

Now we will explore some configurations for Spring Cloud. Let's see how to configure a distributed system using the Spring Cloud Config.

Configuring the Spring Cloud application

One of the major issues of the cloud-native application is maintaining and distributing configuration across the distributed services; developers spend lot of time configuring each environment-specific configuration. But at the time of scaling our service horizontally, we have to again reconfigure our services. Spring Cloud provides a module or sub-project for this cloud-native problem. This module is known as a **Spring Cloud Config**.

Spring Cloud Config is a sub-project of the Spring Cloud ecosystem. It provides a server and client approach to store and sever distributed configurations across several environments and distributed systems.

External configuration management is centralized and upheld by a Git repository. The configuration assets delineate to the Spring environment, but could be utilized by non-Spring applications if we wanted. We can create an external configuration and we can use the existing configuration on the central place, such Git version control. Spring Cloud Config provides support for both creating and using the configuration:

- Spring Cloud Config Server
- Spring Cloud Config Client

This configuration fits very well in the Spring application and you use it through `Environment`, `PropertySource` or `@Value` for any environment with any programming language. In the **Continuous Deployment** (**CD**) pipeline, a Spring application moves from deployment to test and then test to production; you can easily manage the configurations in all environments. It also ensures that the Spring application has every resource at every place, which is required for running at the time of its migration.

By default, the Spring Cloud Config Server uses Git implementation. It also easily supports labelled versions of configuration environments. But you can easily add alternative implementations and plug them in with Spring configuration.

Let's solve this configuration problem, and accumulate all of our configurations into a single Git repository and connect that to one application that manages a configuration for all our applications. We are going to be setting up a very simple implementation.

Creating the configuration producer Spring Cloud Config Server

Here, we'll explore an example of how to set up a Git-backed Config Server and use it in a simple REST application server.

Let's go to `http://start.spring.io`, select **Maven and Spring Boot 2.0.2.RELEASE**, and set the **Artifact** to **cloud-config-app**. Also select dependencies for **Config Server** and add that module. Then generate the application and you will be able to download a ZIP file with a preconfigured project.

Project setup and dependencies

The following dependencies will be shared between all the projects:

```xml
<parent>
    <groupId>org.springframework.boot</groupId>
    <artifactId>spring-boot-starter-parent</artifactId>
    <version>2.0.2.RELEASE</version>
    <relativePath/> <!-- lookup parent from repository -->
</parent>

<properties>
    <project.build.sourceEncoding>UTF-8</project.build.sourceEncoding>
<project.reporting.outputEncoding>UTF-8</project.reporting.outputEncoding>
    <java.version>1.8</java.version>
    <spring-cloud.version>Finchley.BUILD-SNAPSHOT</spring-cloud.version>
</properties>

<dependencies>
    <dependency>
        <groupId>org.springframework.cloud</groupId>
        <artifactId>spring-cloud-config-server</artifactId>
    </dependency>
</dependencies>

<dependencyManagement>
    <dependencies>
        <dependency>
            <groupId>org.springframework.cloud</groupId>
            <artifactId>spring-cloud-dependencies</artifactId>
            <version>${spring-cloud.version}</version>
            <type>pom</type>
            <scope>import</scope>
        </dependency>
    </dependencies>
</dependencyManagement>
```

In the preceding Maven POM configuration file, you can see that we are using the Finchley.BUILD-SNAPSHOT version of the Spring Cloud release train. This release train manages the dependencies for all associated modules as you can see in the <dependencyManagement> tag. We added a spring-cloud-config-server module for our cloud-config-app application. After setup dependencies management, let's implement Cloud Config Server.

Implementing Cloud Config Server

Let's implement an application main class that has more special annotations.
Here, `@SpringBootApplication` will pull all the default and required configurations, and
another annotation, `@EnableConfigServer`, will turn our application into a configuration
server:

```
package com.dineshonjava.cloudconfigapp;

import org.springframework.boot.SpringApplication;
import org.springframework.boot.autoconfigure.SpringBootApplication;
import org.springframework.cloud.config.server.EnableConfigServer;

@SpringBootApplication
@EnableConfigServer
public class CloudConfigApplication {
    public static void main(String[] args) {
            SpringApplication.run(CloudConfigApplication.class, args);
    }
}
```

As you can, this enables the application as a configuration server. But by default, the server
port will be `8080`. We can change this default port configuration, and we have to provide
the Git URI, which provides our version-controlled configuration content. Let's look at the
following `application.properties` file.

Configuring the application.properties file

Let's use the `application.properties` file:

```
server.port=8888
spring.application.name=cloud-config
spring.cloud.config.server.git.uri=file://${user.home}/app-config-repo
```

As you can see, we have configured three properties, `server.port`,
`spring.application.name`, and `spring.cloud.config.server.git.uri`, where
`${user.home}/app-config-repo` is a Git repository containing `YAML` and properties
files.

If you are using a Windows machine, then you need to give an extra `/` as
`file:///` in the file URL. If you using Unix, then use `file://`.

Let's look at how to create a local Git repository on your local machine.

Creating a Git repository as configuration storage

Let's create a Git repository in this example:

```
$ cd $HOME
$ mkdir app-config-repo
$ cd app-config-repo
$ git init .
$ echo 'user.role=Dev' > application-dev.properties
$ echo 'user.role=Admin' > application-prod.properties
$ git add .
$ git commit -m 'Initial commit for application properties'
```

As you can see, you can add multiple configuration files depending on your requirements.

Remember, using the local filesystem for your Git repository is intended for testing only. Use a server to host your configuration repositories in production.

Running your configuration application

Let's run your configuration application by using the command line, type `mvn spring-boot:run`. The Git-backed configuration API provided by our server can be queried using the following paths:

```
/{application}/{profile}[/{label}]
/{application}-{profile}.yml
/{label}/{application}-{profile}.yml
/{application}-{profile}.properties
/{label}/{application}-{profile}.properties
```

Let's understand the following variables for parameterized environment resources:

- The `{application}` variable maps to the `spring.application.name` property's value on the client side
- The `{profile}` variable maps to `spring.profiles.active` property's value on the client side
- The `{label}` refers to a Git branch name, commit ID, and tag

You can find the configuration by using the preceding URI, let's retrieve some of them.

Suppose our Config client is running under the development profile in the branch master via:

```
/{application}/{profile}[/{label}]
```

Let's see the following example of the preceding pattern:

```
http://localhost:8888/cloudconfig/dev/master
```

Let's look at the following screenshot as output:

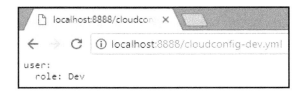

Let's retrieve the configuration as the following URI:

```
/{application}-{profile}.yml
```

Let's see the following example of the preceding pattern:

```
http://localhost:8888/cloudconfig-dev.yml
```

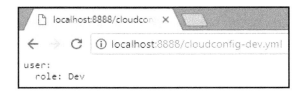

As you can see in the preceding screenshots, we can get these configurations from the cloud configuration application.

Currently we have used the local repository by using the prefix file, so it is a simple and quick way to use the Git repository without a server. In this scenario, our cloud server application operates on the local Git repository without cloning it. But if you want to scale your Cloud Config Server with high availability, then you have to use the central remote Git repository instead of directly using the local Git repository using the ssh—protocol or the HTTP protocol. This shared file system repository can be cloned and you can use it as local working copy as a cache.

The {label} parameter of the HTTP resource represents the mapping for the repository implementation. Here, Git label means commit ID, branch name, or tag, so if the Git branch contains a slash in the name, then the label in the HTTP URL has been resolved by using an underscore ("_") instead of the slash ("/") to remove the ambiguity of URL paths.

Let's configure the Spring Cloud Config Server application using a Git repository URL with placeholders for the {application}:

```
spring.cloud.config.server.git.uri=https://github.com/dineshonjava/{applica
tion}
```

Similarly, here's the configuration in the .yml file:

```
spring:
      cloud:
    config:
        server:
          git:
            uri:
https://github.com/dineshonjava/{application}
```

As you can see, the preceding configuration is based on the *one repo per application* policy.

If you want to use multiple organizations with your Spring Cloud server application, then use the following configuration:

```
spring:
      cloud:
        config:
    server:
      git:
        uri:  https://github.com/{application}
```

So you could use " (_) " within your {application} parameters to configure multiple organizations, such as {application}, which will be provided at request time as dineshonjava(_)application.

Configuring multiple repositories using patterns

Spring Cloud Config also supports configurations for multiple repositories using matching patterns of the application and profile name. The pattern can be configured in multiple ways, such as a comma-separated list of `{application}/{profile}` names with wildcards.

Let's look at the following configuration for the pattern matching multiple repositories configuration:

```
spring:
  cloud:
    config:
      server:
        git:
          uri: https://github.com/dineshonjava/app-config-repo
          repos:
                dev:
                  pattern:
                    - '*/development'
                    - '*/staging'
                  uri:
https://github.com/dineshonjava/development/app-config-repo
                staging:
                  pattern:
                    - '*/qa'
                    - '*/production'
                  uri:
https://github.com/dineshonjava/staging/app-config-repo
```

As you can see, we have configured multiple repositories according to the patterns, such as `'*/development'`, `'*/staging'`, and `'*/qa'`, `'*/production'`. The `https://github.com/dineshonjava/development/app-config-repo` Git URI will be used for the `'*/development'`, `'*/staging'` URL patterns, and the `https://github.com/dineshonjava/staging/app-config-repo` Git URI will be used for the `'*/qa'`, `'*/production'` URL patterns.

By default, the server clones remote repositories when configuration is first requested. You can also configure it to clone the Git repository at startup time by using the `cloneOnStart` property making true:

```
spring:
  cloud:
```

```
config:
  server:
    git:
      uri: https://github.com/dineshonjava/app-config-repo
      repos:
            dev:
              pattern:
                - '*/development'
                - '*/staging'
              cloneOnStart: true
      uri:
https://github.com/dineshonjava/development/app-config-repo
            staging:
              pattern:
                - '*/qa'
                - '*/production'
              cloneOnStart: false
      uri: https://github.com/dineshonjava/staging/app-config-repo
```

In the preceding configuration file, the server clones `dev`'s `app-config-repo` on startup time before it accepts any requests. And other repository staging doesn't clone on startup time, the server clones staging's `app-config-repo` at first request.

Authentication

Suppose your remote repository requires basic authentication to access it, then we have to configure `username` and `password` properties in the configuration file:

```
spring:
  cloud:
    config:
      server:
        git:
      uri: https://github.com/dineshonjava/app-config-repo
        username: arnav
        password: sweety
```

Here, `username` and `password` are for the Git remote repository. As we have seen, Spring Cloud Config Server makes a clone of the remote Git repository to your local copy, but after some time, the local copy of the repository gets dirty due to a lot of testing and development. So, Spring also supports force-pull in the Git repository.

Force-pull property

There is a force-pull property provided and by default it is false. You can make it true to avoid making your local repository dirty. Let's look at the following configuration:

```
spring:
 cloud:
   config:
     server:
       git:
      uri: https://github.com/dineshonjava/app-config-repo
         username: arnav
         password: sweety
         force-pull: true
```

Let's see how to implement the Spring Cloud Config Client application in the next section.

Creating the configuration consumer Spring Cloud Config client

Let's create a Spring Boot application that connects with the Spring Config Server to take advantage of reading external property sources from the central configuration server. So, for the client project, we have to add the following Maven configuration for the spring-cloud-starter-config and spring-boot-starter-web modules:

```
<dependencies>
<dependency>
<groupId>org.springframework.cloud</groupId>
<artifactId>spring-cloud-starter-config</artifactId>
</dependency>
<dependency>
<groupId>org.springframework.boot</groupId>
<artifactId>spring-boot-starter-web</artifactId>
</dependency>
</dependencies>
```

Next, let's create a client class that is a simple REST controller with one GET method mapping:

```
package com.dineshonjava.cloudconfigclient;

import org.springframework.beans.factory.annotation.Value;
import org.springframework.web.bind.annotation.GetMapping;
```

```
import org.springframework.web.bind.annotation.PathVariable;
import org.springframework.web.bind.annotation.RestController;

@RestController
public class ConfigClientController {
    @Value("${user.role}")
     private String role;
    @GetMapping("/profile/{name}")
    public String getActiveProfile(@PathVariable String name){
        return "Hello "+name+"! active profile name is "+role;
    }
}
```

As you can see, the REST controller class has one request handler method and one `role` property. This property is annotated with the `@Value` annotation to populate the value of `${user.role}`. It will be fetched from our Cloud Config Server hosted at `http://localhost:8888/`. But it must be placed in a resource file named `bootstrap.properties`, because this file will be loaded very early while the application starts. Let's see the configuration of the `bootstrap.properties` file:

```
spring.application.name=config-client
spring.profiles.active=dev
spring.cloud.config.uri=http://localhost:8888
```

As you can see, we have set the application name, and also put the active profile and the connection details for the Spring Cloud server application.

Suppose your Spring Cloud Config Server application is configured with security. Then you also have to give `username` and `password` to access the Config Server application. Let's see the `bootstrap.properties` file with the security configuration:

```
spring.application.name=config-client
spring.profiles.active=dev
spring.cloud.config.uri=http://localhost:8888
spring.cloud.config.username=root
spring.cloud.config.password=s3cr3t
```

Now, I have added the security configuration to access the Config Server. Let's run the client application and see the output of the REST service:

```
package com.dineshonjava.cloudconfigclient;

import org.springframework.boot.SpringApplication;
import org.springframework.boot.autoconfigure.SpringBootApplication;

@SpringBootApplication
```

```
public class CloudConfigClientApplication {

    public static void main(String[] args) {
            SpringApplication.run(CloudConfigClientApplication.class, args);
    }
}
```

Let's call the `http://localhost:8080/profile/Dinesh` **REST** service:

As you can see in the preceding screenshot, the role of the user is fetched from the Spring Cloud Config Server.

Summary

In this chapter, we discussed cloud-native application patterns and problems due to the cloud-native architecture. We have also discussed the microservices architecture and learned that it breaks monolithic applications into separate pieces of the application to focus on the bounded context. Spring Cloud addresses and provides solutions for cloud-native problems.

We have created a configuration server to provide a set of configuration files from a Git repository to client applications. In this chapter, we learned about the Spring Cloud configuration service and how to build and consume the configuration service.

In this chapter, we explored the need for the configuration service and the solution, by Spring Cloud Config, to store config in environments and retrieve the config through a simple point-to-point service call.

In the next chapter, we'll look at the Eureka Client and Server for the service discovery.

5
Spring Cloud Netflix and Service Discovery

In this chapter, we will explore Spring Cloud Netflix and Service Discovery with Eureka. In the previous chapter, we discussed the cloud-native application architecture and the problems associated with this cloud-native pattern. We also discussed how Spring Cloud provides solutions for the configuration management of cloud-based applications. Spring Cloud provides the Spring Cloud Config module, which is helpful in managing the configuration for the distributed applications, such as microservices.

We implemented our own Spring Cloud Config server application and also created a consumer for this Cloud Config Server. In this chapter, we will go another step ahead and see how Spring Cloud provides support with regard to communication between multiple distributed services.

The following topics are going to be discussed in this chapter. These topics will give you a better understanding of the Service Discovery with Eureka:

- Introduction to Spring Cloud Netflix
- Need for Service Discovery in microservices architecture
- Implementing Service Discovery—Eureka Server:
    - Enabling Eureka Server as a Discovery Service Server
- Implementing Service Discovery—Eureka Clients:
    - Registering clients with Eureka
    - Consuming the REST service
    - Using `EurekaClient`
    - Using `DiscoveryClient`
    - Client-side load balancing using Netflix Ribbon
    - Using the `registry-aware` client, Spring Cloud Netflix FeignClient

Let's look at these topics in detail.

Introduction to Spring Cloud Netflix

The Spring Cloud Netflix project is one of the key sub-projects of Spring Cloud. This project provides integration between Netflix OSS and the Spring Boot application using the auto-configuration behavior of Spring Boot. You can build a large, distributed application by using some annotations of Spring Cloud; these annotations enable the Netflix components for your distributed systems. Netflix OSS provides multiple components for the distributed applications for several purposes, such as Service Discovery (Eureka), Circuit Breaker (Hystrix), Intelligent Routing (Zuul), and Client-Side Load Balancing (Ribbon). In this chapter, we will explore more about client-side Service Discovery and registering services to the Discovery server via Spring Cloud Netflix Eureka.

As you know, distributed cloud-native systems are built by several services hosted at different commodity servers. Netflix provides the Eureka server for the cloud-based application and it acts as both a Discovery Service server and client. The server-side Service Discovery allows you to register your services to the Eureka cloud server, and the client-side Service Discovery allows services to find and communicate with each other without hardcoding the hostname and port. The registered services have to send a heartbeat signal to the registry to be informed about the presence of these services.

With Netflix Eureka, you can register multiple services and also register multiple instances of a service. These register instances of the service act as a server and replicate its status to the connected peer clients. Netflix Eureka manages these requests to the instances of a service using a load balancing algorithm. The client retrieves a list of all connected instances of a service registry and distributes the loads to these instances using a load-balancing algorithm, what it Client Side Load Balancing (Ribbon) does.

You could also see this process as a drawback, because all clients must implement certain logic to interact with this fixed point of Eureka and it takes an additional network round-trip before the actual request.

Let's implement this server-side service registry (Eureka Server) and also implement a REST service that registers itself at the registry (Eureka Client):

- Implementing Service Discovery—Eureka Server
- Implementing Service Discovery—Eureka Clients

In this chapter, we will concentrate on the microservices support, which is Service Discovery. Let's discuss, what is the need of Service Discovery in your microservices-based project?

The need for Service Discovery in the microservices architecture

As we know, in the microservices architecture, various protocols may be used for connecting services to each other. But how do these services find each other?

And also, one service may have multiple instances. So, what happens if we run multiple instances? Let's look at the following diagram:

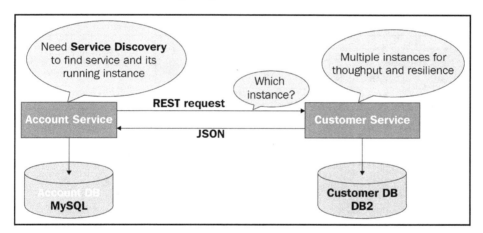

As you can see, there are two services running in this microservices-based application—**Account Service** and **Customer Service**. **Account Service** requests **Customer Service** to fetch records of a customer in JSON format. And both services have their own DB access—**Account DB** and **Customer DB**, respectively. Also, **Customer Service** has multiple running instances due to high availability and throughput, and to make it resilient. But how will **Account Service** call **Customer Service**? Which instance should be called?

To answer these questions, Service Discovery comes into the picture and solves these cloud-native problems. Let's look at the diagram with Discovery Service:

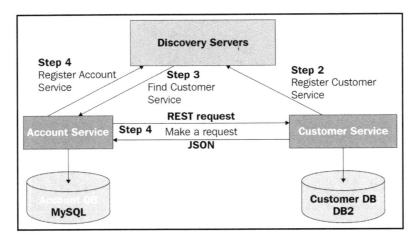

As you can see, the discovery server has been used to register the microservices and consulted to use microservices. Let's see the workflow:

1. **Account Service** registers itself with Eureka Discovery Server
2. **Customer Service** also registers itself with Eureka Discovery Server
3. **Account Service** consults with Discover Server to find Customer Service
4. **Account Service** knows about the Customer Service's instance to be called

As you have seen, Discovery Service solves the cloud-native problems of the microservices-based architecture. Spring Cloud supports several implementations of Service Discovery, such as Netflix Eureka and Hashicorp Consul, Spring Cloud makes it easy to utilize either of those servers while hiding their internal complexity. But, in this chapter, we will discuss the Netflix Eureka Service Discovery and its implementation.

Implementing Service Discovery – Eureka Server

Let's implement Eureka Server for a service registry. It is very easy to implement by adding `spring-cloud-starter-eureka-server` to the dependencies. You can see the following Maven configuration required to create a Eureka server for a service registry.

The Maven build configuration file

Let's see the following configuration in the `pom.xml` file:

```
<parent>
    <groupId>org.springframework.boot</groupId>
    <artifactId>spring-boot-starter-parent</artifactId>
    <version>2.0.2.RELEASE</version>
    <relativePath/> <!-- lookup parent from repository -->
</parent>

<properties>
    <project.build.sourceEncoding>UTF-8</project.build.sourceEncoding>
<project.reporting.outputEncoding>UTF-8</project.reporting.outputEncoding>
    <java.version>1.8</java.version>
    <spring-cloud.version>Finchley.M7</spring-cloud.version>
</properties>

<dependencies>
    <dependency>
        <groupId>org.springframework.cloud</groupId>
        <artifactId>spring-cloud-starter-netflix-eureka-
server</artifactId>
    </dependency>

    <dependency>
        <groupId>org.springframework.boot</groupId>
        <artifactId>spring-boot-starter-test</artifactId>
        <scope>test</scope>
    </dependency>
</dependencies>

<dependencyManagement>
    <dependencies>
        <dependency>
            <groupId>org.springframework.cloud</groupId>
            <artifactId>spring-cloud-dependencies</artifactId>
            <version>${spring-cloud.version}</version>
            <type>pom</type>
            <scope>import</scope>
        </dependency>
    </dependencies>
</dependencyManagement>
```

If the application is a Gradle project then `build.gradle` will be look like as following.

The Gradle build configuration file

See the following configuration:

```
apply plugin: 'java'
apply plugin: 'eclipse'
apply plugin: 'org.springframework.boot'
apply plugin: 'io.spring.dependency-management'

group = 'com.dineshonjava'
version = '0.0.1-SNAPSHOT'
sourceCompatibility = 1.8

repositories {
   mavenCentral()
   maven { url "https://repo.spring.io/snapshot" }
   maven { url "https://repo.spring.io/milestone" }
}


ext {
   springCloudVersion = 'Finchley.M7'
}

dependencies {
   compile('org.springframework.cloud:spring-cloud-starter-netflix-eureka-
server')
   testCompile('org.springframework.boot:spring-boot-starter-test')
}

dependencyManagement {
   imports {
        mavenBom "org.springframework.cloud:spring-cloud-
dependencies:${springCloudVersion}"
   }
}
```

As you can see, with the `pom.xml` Maven configuration file and the `build.gradle` Gradle configuration file, you have added the Starter with the `org.springframework.cloud` group and `spring-cloud-starter-netflix-eureka-server` artifact ID. This starter provides the auto-configuration about Netflix's Eureka server to a service registry.

But, by default, the Eureka server doesn't enable. So you have to enable the Eureka server by using the @EnableEurekaServer annotation in a main Spring Boot application class that is also annotated with the @SpringBootApplication annotation.

Enabling the Eureka server as a Discovery Service server

Let's see the following main Spring Boot application class:

```
package com.dineshonjava.eurekaserver;

import org.springframework.boot.SpringApplication;
import org.springframework.boot.autoconfigure.SpringBootApplication;
import org.springframework.cloud.netflix.eureka.server.EnableEurekaServer;

@SpringBootApplication
@EnableEurekaServer
public class EurekaServerApplication {

    public static void main(String[] args) {
            SpringApplication.run(EurekaServerApplication.class, args);
    }
}
```

If you run this main application class, it will start the Eureka Server. This server has a home page with a UI. This server also has HTTP API endpoints for the normal Eureka functionality under /eureka/*. By default, every Eureka server is also a Eureka client. So you can also disable this default client registry with the Eureka server by setting registerWithEureka to false.

Let's see the following application.yml file for your Eureka server:

```
server:
  port: 8761

eureka:
  instance:
    hostname: localhost
  client:
    registerWithEureka: false
    fetchRegistry: false
    serviceUrl:
      defaultZone:
http://${eureka.instance.hostname}:${server.port}/eureka/
```

As you can see, the `application.yml` file is a configuration file to configure the properties in YAML format. The `server.port` property defines the server port for Eureka; here we are configuring this application port to `8761`, and it is the default one for Eureka servers. We are also configuring the Eureka server instance's hostname to `localhost`. We are telling the built-in Eureka client not to register with itself, because this application should be acting as a server. And the `serviceUrl` is pointing to the same host as the local instance.

Finally, we can point our browser to `http://localhost:8761` to view the Eureka dashboard as follows:

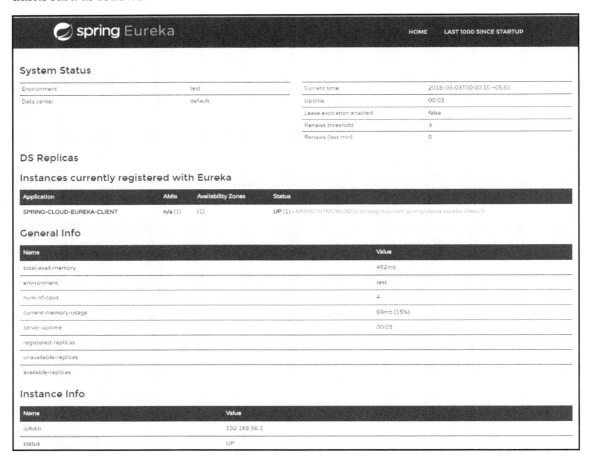

As you can see, currently we don't have any registered service instances. We will discuss this later, but at the moment, we can see basic indicators, such as status and health indicators.

Now, let's move on to the next section to create a Eureka client and also create a REST service that registers itself at the registry server.

Implementing Service Discovery – Eureka clients

Service Discovery is one of the key patterns of a microservice-based architecture. Spring Cloud provides Service Discovery functionality with Netflix OSS's Eureka. Eureka is the Cloud Service Discovery Server and Client. In the previous section, we saw how to implement the Netflix Service Discovery server. Here, I am going to implement the Netflix Service Discovery client.

Adding the Maven dependencies configuration

To implement Eureka Client in your project, include the Spring Cloud Starter with the `org.springframework.cloud` group and the `id spring-cloud-starter-netflix-eureka-client` artifact. Also include `spring-boot-starter-web` in `pom.xml` and implement a REST controller to create a simple REST service to be registered with the Eureka Discovery Server. Let's see the following Maven configuration file:

```
<parent>
    <groupId>org.springframework.boot</groupId>
    <artifactId>spring-boot-starter-parent</artifactId>
    <version>2.0.2.RELEASE</version>
    <relativePath/> <!-- lookup parent from repository -->
</parent>

<properties>
    <project.build.sourceEncoding>UTF-8</project.build.sourceEncoding>
<project.reporting.outputEncoding>UTF-8</project.reporting.outputEncoding>
    <java.version>1.8</java.version>
    <spring-cloud.version>Finchley.M7</spring-cloud.version>
</properties>

<dependencies>
    <dependency>
```

```
        <groupId>org.springframework.boot</groupId>
        <artifactId>spring-boot-starter-web</artifactId>
    </dependency>
    <dependency>
        <groupId>org.springframework.cloud</groupId>
        <artifactId>spring-cloud-starter-netflix-eureka-
client</artifactId>
    </dependency>

    <dependency>
        <groupId>org.springframework.boot</groupId>
        <artifactId>spring-boot-starter-test</artifactId>
        <scope>test</scope>
    </dependency>
</dependencies>

<dependencyManagement>
    <dependencies>
        <dependency>
            <groupId>org.springframework.cloud</groupId>
            <artifactId>spring-cloud-dependencies</artifactId>
            <version>${spring-cloud.version}</version>
            <type>pom</type>
            <scope>import</scope>
        </dependency>
    </dependencies>
</dependencyManagement>
```

As you can see, I have added two dependencies here, one for the Spring web module and another for the Spring cloud Netflix Eureka client. You can choose to create this application as a Gradle project. Let's next look at the configuration of the `build.gradle` file.

The Gradle build configuration

Let's see the following configuration:

```
apply plugin: 'java'
apply plugin: 'eclipse'
apply plugin: 'org.springframework.boot'
apply plugin: 'io.spring.dependency-management'

group = 'com.dineshonjava'
version = '0.0.1-SNAPSHOT'
sourceCompatibility = 1.8

repositories {
```

```
    mavenCentral()
    maven { url "https://repo.spring.io/snapshot" }
    maven { url "https://repo.spring.io/milestone" }
}


ext {
    springCloudVersion = 'Finchley.M7'
}

dependencies {
    compile('org.springframework.boot:spring-boot-starter-web')
    compile('org.springframework.cloud:spring-cloud-starter-netflix-eureka-
client')
    testCompile('org.springframework.boot:spring-boot-starter-test')
}

dependencyManagement {
    imports {
        mavenBom "org.springframework.cloud:spring-cloud-
dependencies:${springCloudVersion}"
    }
}
```

This file has dependencies for the Spring web module and the Spring cloud Netflix Eureka client module. Now let's register this client with Eureka.

Registering a client with Eureka

Registering a client with Eureka means that a client provides it's own meta-information, such as hostname with port, health indicator URL, and homepage. Each instance of a service sends heartbeat messages to the Eureka server; if Eureka doesn't receive the heartbeat over a configurable timetable, the instance is normally removed from the registry.

Let's create the `main` application class annotated with `@SpringBootApplication` for this client application. By default, Spring Discovery Client doesn't enable, so we have to use either `@EnableDiscoveryClient` or `@EnableEurekaClient` to enable it. Here is an example Eureka client:

```
package com.dineshonjava.eurekaclient;

import org.springframework.boot.SpringApplication;
import org.springframework.boot.autoconfigure.SpringBootApplication;
import org.springframework.cloud.netflix.eureka.EnableEurekaClient;
```

```
@SpringBootApplication
@EnableEurekaClient
public class EurekaClientApplication {

    public static void main(String[] args) {
         SpringApplication.run(EurekaClientApplication.class, args);
    }
}
```

Let's create a REST service to be registered with Eureka server.

```
package com.dineshonjava.eurekaclient;

import org.springframework.web.bind.annotation.GetMapping;
import org.springframework.web.bind.annotation.RestController;

@RestController
public class HelloController {
    @GetMapping("/hello")
     public String greeting() {
         return "Hello to the Dineshonjava from EurekaClient!";
     }
}
```

Now let's create an application configuration file for this client application, in the form of an `application.yml` file, as follows:

```
spring:
  application:
    name: spring-cloud-eureka-client

server:
  port: 80

eureka:
  client:
    serviceUrl:
      defaultZone: ${EUREKA_URI:http://localhost:8761/eureka}
    instance:
    preferIpAddress: true
```

This configuration file has a Spring application name to uniquely identify our client in the list of registered applications, it also has server port 80. But we can let Spring Boot choose a random port for us, because later we are accessing this service with its name, and finally, we have to tell our client where to locate the registry.

Let's run this client application and go to `http://localhost:8761` again on the browser.
Now you can see the client registration status on the Eureka Dashboard. Let's look at the
following screenshot:

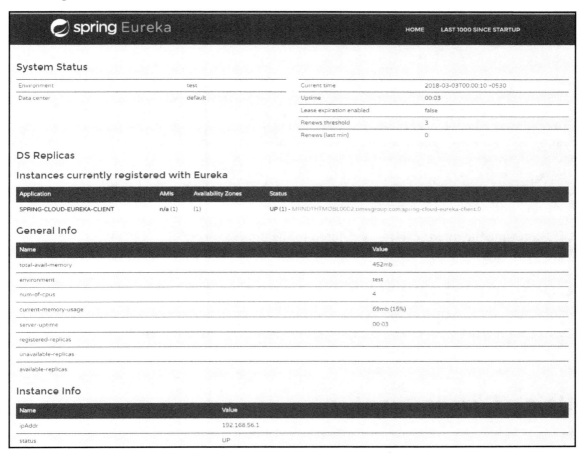

As you can see, now it has one registered instance of a REST service. The registered service
name is `SPRING-CLOUD-EUREKA-CLIENT` as we have given the application name in the
configuration file. You can set up `home-page-url`, `health-check-url`, and `status-page-url-path` as follows:

```
spring:
  application:
    name: spring-cloud-eureka-client

server:
```

```
    port: 80

eureka:
  client:
    service-url:
      default-zone: ${EUREKA_URI:http://localhost:8761/eureka}
  instance:
    prefer-ip-address: true
    status-page-url-path: https://${eureka.instance.hostName}/info
    health-check-url: https://${eureka.instance.hostName}/health
    home-page-url: https://${eureka.instance.hostName}/
```

Eureka internally registers these properties for status and homepage and publishes a non-secure URL for status and homepage. In the preceding configuration file, I have overridden those properties explicitly to secure HTTP protocol.

The `${eureka.instance.hostName}` property will be resolved from a defined hostname under the `eureka.instance` property. And you can set your hostname at runtime using environment variables, for example, `eureka.instance.hostname=${HOST_NAME}`.

Let's consume the microservices registered to the Eureka server.

Consuming the REST service

In this section, we will explore several ways to consume the REST services hosted on the Eureka Server. Let's create a web application that is consuming the REST service using `com.netflix.discovery.EurekaClient`.

Using EurekaClient

Let's create the `HomeController` class and auto-wire `com.netflix.discovery.EurekaClient`:

```
package com.dineshonjava.eurekaclient;

import org.springframework.beans.factory.annotation.Autowired;
import org.springframework.web.bind.annotation.GetMapping;
import org.springframework.web.bind.annotation.Controller;

import com.netflix.appinfo.InstanceInfo;
import com.netflix.discovery.EurekaClient;
import com.netflix.discovery.shared.Application;

@Controller
```

```
public class HomeController {
    @Autowired
    private EurekaClient eurekaClient;
    public String serviceUrl() {
        Application application = eurekaClient.getApplication("spring-cloud-
eureka-client");
        InstanceInfo instanceInfo = application.getInstances().get(0);
        String hostname = instanceInfo.getHostName();
        int port = instanceInfo.getPort();
        // we can find many information related to the instance
        return instanceInfo.getHomePageUrl();
    }
    ...
}
```

As you can see, we have put `EurekaClient` into our controller with which we could receive service information by service name as an `Application` object.

 Don't use EurekaClient in the `@PostConstruct` or `@Scheduled` methods. Because it is initialized in SmartLifecycle (with phase=0), the earliest you can rely on it being available is in another SmartLifecycle with a higher phase.

By default, `EurekaClient` uses Jersey for HTTP communication. But you can avoid using it by excluding Jersey from the Maven dependencies. Spring Cloud will auto-configure the `org.springframework.web.client.RestTemplate` template of the Spring. Spring Cloud provides alternatives to the native Netflix `EurekaClient`. So, if you don't want to use the native Netflix `EurekaClient`, Spring cloud supports Feign and also Spring `RestTemplate`. They use logical Eureka service identifiers instead of physical URLs.

Using DiscoveryClient

Spring Cloud also provides `org.springframework.cloud.client.discovery.DiscoveryClient` for consuming a REST service. `DiscoveryClient` is not related to Netflix and it provides a simple API for discovery clients. Let's see the following example:

```
package com.dineshonjava.eurekaclient;
import java.net.URI;
import java.util.List;
import org.springframework.beans.factory.annotation.Autowired;
import org.springframework.cloud.client.ServiceInstance;
import org.springframework.cloud.client.discovery.DiscoveryClient;
import org.springframework.web.bind.annotation.GetMapping;
```

[117]

```
import org.springframework.web.bind.annotation.Controller;
@Controller
public class HelloController {
@Autowired
private DiscoveryClient discoveryClient;
public URI serviceUrl() {
List<ServiceInstance> list = discoveryClient.getInstances("spring-cloud-
eureka-client");
if (list != null && list.size() > 0 ) {
return list.get(0).getUri();
}
return null;
}
...
}
```

This example has used `DiscoveryClient` to get the URI of the instance. You can use this URI to consume the REST service with Spring's `RestTemplate`.

Use of either `EurekaClient` or `DiscoveryClient` is not suitable because these clients return the information about the services registered with Eureka. Eventually you have to call these services using `RestTemplate` or `HttpClient`. Explicitly, you have to manage the loads to these services. Spring Cloud Netflix Ribbon can be used to manage the load; it is a load balancer in the Spring Cloud-based application.

This chapter will also cover some details about client-side load balancing on the microservice architecture. We have used Service Discovery to communicate with services and find each other. Now I am going to discuss client-side load balancing using Neflix Ribbon.

Client-side load balancing using Netflix Ribbon

Client-side load balancing is used to balance incoming loads to the microservices because each service is typically deployed as multiple instances, so, for fault-tolerance and load-sharing, how do we decide which service instance to use?

Implementing client-side load balancing provides a way to distribute the load across multiple instances. The Discovery server returns the location of these multiple instances. The multiple instances are only for resilience and load-sharing, but the client needs to pick only one instance of the service. So, Spring Cloud Netflix Ribbon comes into the picture and provides several algorithms for client-side load-balancing. Spring also provides a smart `RestTemplate`.

Spring's `RestTemplate` is a smart client to call microservices registered on the Eureka server, and it automatically integrates two Netflix utilities, such as the Eureka Service Discovery and Ribbon client-side load balancer. Eureka returns the URL of all available instances. Ribbon determines the best available service to use. Just inject the load-balanced `RestTemplate` by using the `@LoadBalanced` annotation. And Spring Cloud provides `@LoadBalanced` annotation, it has built-in Service discovery and load balancing. Service Discovery is automatic lookup by using logical service-name of registered microservice.

Let's see following Maven dependency required for Ribbon:

```
<dependencies>
....
<dependency>
<groupId>org.springframework.boot</groupId>
<artifactId>spring-boot-starter-web</artifactId>
</dependency>
<dependency>
<groupId>org.springframework.cloud</groupId>
<artifactId>spring-cloud-starter-netflix-eureka-client</artifactId>
</dependency>
<dependency>
<groupId>org.springframework.cloud</groupId>
<artifactId>spring-cloud-starter-netflix-ribbon</artifactId>
</dependency>
....
</dependencies>
```

As you can see, the `spring-cloud-starter-netflix-ribbon` starter will add the Ribbon libraries to your application. This includes the starters that we have added to create a web application and register this application to the Eureka as a service, such as `spring-boot-starter-web` and `spring-cloud-starter-netflix-eureka-client`.

Ribbon is a client-side load balancer that gives you a lot of control over the behavior of HTTP and TCP clients. And `RestTemplate` can be automatically configured to use Ribbon. To create a load-balanced `RestTemplate`, create an `@Bean RestTemplate` and use the `@LoadBalanced` qualifier:

```
package com.dineshonjava.ribbonclient;
import org.springframework.boot.SpringApplication;
import org.springframework.boot.autoconfigure.SpringBootApplication;
import org.springframework.cloud.client.loadbalancer.LoadBalanced;
import org.springframework.cloud.netflix.eureka.EnableEurekaClient;
import org.springframework.context.annotation.Bean;
import org.springframework.web.client.RestTemplate;
@SpringBootApplication
```

```
@EnableEurekaClient
public class RibbonClientApplication {
public static void main(String[] args) {
SpringApplication.run(RibbonClientApplication.class, args);
}
@Bean
@LoadBalanced
public RestTemplate restTemplate() {
return new RestTemplate();
}
}
```

As you can see, the `main` application class has a bean definition for the `RestTemplate`. If you want to use `RestTemplate` in your application then you have to define a bean method for `RestTempplate` because a `RestTemplate` bean is no longer created via auto-configuration. It must be created by individual applications.

Now let's create a service by using this `RestTemplate` and call the service registered with Eureka:

```
package com.dineshonjava.ribbonclient.service;
import org.springframework.beans.factory.annotation.Autowired;
import org.springframework.cloud.client.loadbalancer.LoadBalanced;
import org.springframework.stereotype.Service;
import org.springframework.web.client.RestTemplate;
@Service
public class HelloServiceClient {
@Autowired
@LoadBalanced
RestTemplate restTemplate;
public String sayHello(){
return restTemplate.getForObject("http://SPRING-CLOUD-EUREKA-CLIENT/hello",
String.class);
}
}
```

As you can see, here we have autowired the load-balanced `RestTemplate` to call the services. The `RestTemplate` is nothing but a high-level implement of the HTTP Client and exposed several methods to call services. But these methods need a URI, and the URI needs to use a virtual host name that is service name, not a host name.

Let's see the application configuration class, that is, `application.yml`:

```
spring:
  application:
    name: spring-cloud-ribbon-client

server:
  port: 8181

eureka:
  client:
    service-url:
      default-zone: ${EUREKA_URI:http://localhost:8761/eureka}
  instance:
    prefer-ip-address: true
```

This configuration file has defined the application name as `spring-cloud-ribbon-client`, the server port as `8181`, and other configurations as the same as we used earlier in this chapter.

Let's run this client application and open the browser with the `http://localhost:8761/` URL:

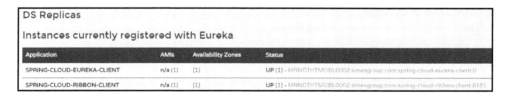

As you can see, on the preceding Eureka Dashboard, there are two services registered as `SPRING-CLOUD-EUREKA-CLIENT`, and `SPRING-CLOUD-RIBBON-CLIENT`.

After running this example, we'll open our browser and go to `http://localhost:8181/say-hello` and it should display something like the following:

As you can see, `RestTemplate` called the `SPRING-CLOUD-EUREKA-CLIENT` service registered with Eureka to fetch the **Hello to the Dineshonjava from Eureka Client!** string.

Spring Cloud also supports another client that internally implements load-balancing functionality. Let's discuss another client that is already aware of the cloud registry. Here there is no need to get the information about a service's instance such as URI. You just give the application name.

Using the registry-aware Spring Cloud Netflix FeignClient client

Let's look at a simple example about Feign Client. In `Chapter 8`, *Simplify HTTP API with Feign Client*, we will discuss more about the Spring Cloud Netflix Feign Client. Feign Client is a `discovery-aware` Spring `RestTemplate` using interfaces to communicate with endpoints. This client is a registry server-aware client. It will be used as the `Discovery-server-aware` Spring `RestTemplate` using an interface with service endpoints to communicate, and these interfaces will be automatically implemented at runtime. The Spring Cloud Netflix Feign Client is using `services-names` instead of the `service-urls`.

Feign already uses Ribbon, so if you are using `@FeignClient` then this section also applies.

Let's see the simple example of this Feign Client. First, to set up Feign Client on your application, you have to add the following dependencies to your `pom.xml`:

```
<dependencies>
    <dependency>
        <groupId>org.springframework.boot</groupId>
        <artifactId>spring-boot-starter-web</artifactId>
    </dependency>
    <dependency>
```

```
        <groupId>org.springframework.cloud</groupId>
        <artifactId>spring-cloud-starter-netflix-eureka-
client</artifactId>
    </dependency>
    <dependency>
        <groupId>org.springframework.cloud</groupId>
        <artifactId>spring-cloud-starter-openfeign</artifactId>
    </dependency>

</dependencies>
```

As you can see, I have added four Maven dependencies to the `pom.xml` file. These dependencies are `spring-cloud-starter-openfeign`, `spring-cloud-starter-netflix-eureka-client`, `spring-boot-starter-web`, and `spring-boot-starter-thymeleaf`. `spring-cloud-starter-openfeign` provides Feign client. Let's see the following Feign client interface:

```
package com.dineshonjava.feignclient.service;

import org.springframework.cloud.openfeign.FeignClient;
import org.springframework.web.bind.annotation.GetMapping;

@FeignClient("spring-cloud-eureka-client")
public interface HelloServiceClient {
    @GetMapping("/hello")
    String sayHello();
}
```

As you can see, this interface has one method in this example with the `@GetMapping` annotation. And you can also see this interface is annotated with the `@FeignClient` annotation with the `spring-cloud-eureka-client` service name. We don't need to implement this interface in our example as Spring will do it at runtime. But remember, the `@FeignClient` annotation will work only when you have enabled the Spring Cloud Netflix Feign Client support for your application by using the `@EnableFeignClients` annotation on the configuration class that is annotated with `@Configuration`:

```
package com.dineshonjava.feignclient;

import org.springframework.boot.SpringApplication;
import org.springframework.boot.autoconfigure.SpringBootApplication;
import org.springframework.cloud.netflix.eureka.EnableEurekaClient;
import org.springframework.cloud.openfeign.EnableFeignClients;

@SpringBootApplication
```

```
@EnableEurekaClient
@EnableFeignClients
public class FeignClientApplication {

    public static void main(String[] args) {
        SpringApplication.run(FeignClientApplication.class, args);
    }
}
```

As you can see, the `main` application class is annotated with three annotations: `@SpringBootApplication`, `@EnableEurekaClient`, and `@EnableFeignClients`. The `@SpringBootApplication` annotation is used for auto-configuration related to Spring Cloud and `@EnableEurekaClient` is used to register this application a service to the Eureka server. Finally, the `@EnableFeignClients` annotation is used to enable the Netflix Feign module to your Spring cloud application.

Let's create an application controller class and auto-wire the Feign client interface into this controller:

```
package com.dineshonjava.feignclient.controller;

import org.springframework.beans.factory.annotation.Autowired;
import org.springframework.stereotype.Controller;
import org.springframework.ui.ModelMap;
import org.springframework.web.bind.annotation.GetMapping;

import com.dineshonjava.feignclient.service.HelloServiceClient;

@Controller
public class HelloWebController {
    @Autowired
    HelloServiceClient helloServiceClient;
    @GetMapping("/say-hello")
    String sayHello(ModelMap model){
        model.put("message", helloServiceClient.sayHello());
        return "hello";
    }
}
```

This web controller has one request handler method, `sayHello()`, and it populates the model object with the message returned by the feign client, that is, `HelloServiceClient`, and fetched data from our REST service. Here, dependency for starters, such as `spring-boot-starter-web` and `spring-boot-starter-thymeleaf`, is used to present a view.

Let's see the following view for this web application example:

```
<!DOCTYPE html>
<html xmlns:th="http://www.thymeleaf.org">
    <head>
        <title>Say Hello Page | Dineshonjava.com</title>
    </head>
    <body>
        <h2 th:text="${message}"/>
    </body>
</html>
```

This is the `thymeleaf` view file, which renders the view and value of the message return from the controller.

So `.yml` configuration file will be same as we have used previously. In this example, I am using the `.yml` format for the configuration file. So, this file will be the same as the one we used for the REST service, the only differences being the application name and server port. You can see this file as follows:

```
spring:
  application:
    name: spring-cloud-feign-client

server:
  port: 8080

eureka:
  client:
    service-url:
      default-zone: ${EUREKA_URI:http://localhost:8761/eureka}
    instance:
    prefer-ip-address: true
```

Let's run this application and see the Eureka Dashboard again:

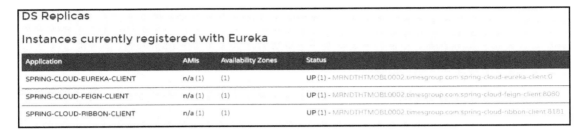

DS Replicas			
Instances currently registered with Eureka			
Application	**AMIs**	**Availability Zones**	**Status**
SPRING-CLOUD-EUREKA-CLIENT	n/a (1)	(1)	UP (1) - MRNDTHTMOBL0002.timesgroup.com:spring-cloud-eureka-client:0
SPRING-CLOUD-FEIGN-CLIENT	n/a (1)	(1)	UP (1) - MRNDTHTMOBL0002.timesgroup.com:spring-cloud-feign-client:8080
SPRING-CLOUD-RIBBON-CLIENT	n/a (1)	(1)	UP (1) - MRNDTHTMOBL0002.timesgroup.com:spring-cloud-ribbon-client:8181

Now you can see that there are three services currently registered with Eureka server—SPRING-CLOUD-EUREKA-CLIENT, SPRING-CLOUD-FEIGN-CLIENT, and SPRING-CLOUD-RIBBON-CLIENT.

After running this example, we'll open our browser, go to http://localhost:8080/say-hello, and it should display something like the following:

Summary

You should now know what a microservice architecture is, as well as its advantages and challenges, and how Spring Cloud solves these microservice challenges by using several Spring Cloud modules, such as Discovery Service and Client-side Load Balancing.

We can now implement a service registry using the Spring Netflix Eureka server and register some Eureka clients with it. We have also implemented several client applications using EurekaClient and Feign client. The Feign client resolves the Discovery Service by using service-name, and it by default provides support for load balancing as well. That means if you are using the Feign client to access the services registered with Eureka, you don't need to add Ribbon explicitly to manage the load across the multiple instances of a service.

With Feign Client and our registry, we can easily locate and consume the REST service, even when the location changes.

In the next chapter, we will explore and implement a RESTful microservices example.

6
Building Spring Boot RESTful Microservice

In this chapter, we will be building a RESTful atomic microservice that performs CRUD operations on in-memory databases (either HSQL or H2) using Spring Cloud and Spring Data. This service will be enabled for service discovery registration to the Eureka Server as we have created in Chapter 5, *Spring Cloud Netflix and Service Discovery*; and configures the service through bootstrap.yml and application.yml.

In the previous chapter, we learned about microservice architecture and its advantages and challenges. We also created the Eureka Server and Eureka Client, and registered this Client with Eureka Server. But in this chapter, we are going to create a simple microservice example using Spring Boot and Cloud.

At the end of this chapter, you will have a better understanding of microservices and how to create a simple microservice that focuses on a targeted situation rather than solving too many problems. This chapter will cover the following points:

- Microservices with Spring Boot
- A simple microservice example:
    - Brief introduction to Spring Data
    - Brief introduction to bootstrap.yml and application.yml
- Developing a simple microservices example
- Creating discovery server:
    - @EnableEurekaServer
- Creating microservice (the Producer):
    - @EnableEurekaClient
    - @EnableDiscoveryClient
    - @RestController

- Creating microservice consumers
- `@SpringBootApplication` and `@SpringCloudApplication`

Let's see these topics in detail.

Microservices with Spring Boot

As we have already discussed, the microservice architecture allows us to divide a large system into a number of collaborating components. As you know, the Spring Framework provides loosely coupled components at the component level; similarly, the microservice with Spring Boot provides loosely coupled processes at the process level.

Here we are dividing a monolithic application into smaller microservices, and deploying each service as a single responsibility within a bounded context.

By using the auto-configuration behavior of Spring Boot, we can easily create several microservices. Spring Boot provides Starters that we can add to the microservice application and deploy with the embedded containers.

Spring Cloud extends Spring Boot into the realm of cloud-native microservices, making the development of distributed microservices quite practical. Spring Boot's real power is in creating microservice-based applications. Spring Boot also supports distributed configurations for cloud-native applications.

Let's see where to use different configuration files for the Spring Boot and Spring Cloud applications.

Brief introduction to bootstrap.yml and application.yml

In the Spring Boot application, the configuration files are either `application.properties` or `application.yml`. The `application.yml` config file will contain application-related configurations, such as server port, JPA configuration, and data source configuration.

In the case of the Spring Cloud application, we need some configurations that would be used in multiple microservices. We require two types of configuration files in the case of the Spring Cloud application. These files are:

- The Bootstrap application configuration file (`bootstrap.yml`)
- The application configuration file (`application.yml`)

By default, Bootstrap properties are added with high precedence, so they cannot be overridden by local configuration. The `bootstrap.yml` (or `bootstrap.properties`) file is loaded before `application.yml` (or `application.properties`). The Bootstrap application configuration file is similar to the `application.yml` file, but it will be loaded at the Bootstrap phase of the application context.

The `bootstrap.yml` file is typically used for the case of the Spring Cloud Config Server application. You can specify `spring.application.name` and `spring.cloud.config.server.git.uri` inside the `bootstrap.yml` file, as we have seen in the Chapter 4, *Getting Started with Spring Cloud and Configuration*, and also add some encryption/decryption information. A parent Spring `ApplicationContext` (known as **Bootstrap Application Context**) loads the Bootstrap Application configuration file, `bootstrap.yml`.

The Spring Cloud application usually loads the configuration data from the Spring Cloud Config Server. So, loading the URL and other connection configurations, such as passwords and encryption/decryption information, first we need that Bootstrap configuration. Thus, we have to use the `bootstrap.yml` file to put in the configurations that are used to load the real configuration data.

Let's see the following example for the `bootstrap.yml` file:

```
spring:
  application:
    name: foo
  cloud:
    config:
      uri: ${SPRING_CONFIG_URI:http://localhost:8888}
```

As you can see in the preceding Bootstrap configuration file, it typically contains two properties, such as the location of the configuration server, `spring.cloud.config.uri`, and the name of the application, `spring.application.name`. So, at the startup time of the Spring Cloud application, it makes an HTTP call to load these attributes from the Config Server.

You can disable the Bootstrap process completely by setting `spring.cloud.bootstrap.enabled=false`.

Let's discuss a simple microservice example in the next section.

A simple microservice example

We will discuss a simple microservice example with Spring Boot and Cloud. In a previous chapter, we saw an example of the Bank application with three microservices—AccountService, CustomerService, and Notification Service.

Without the microservice architecture, let's see the following diagram of the monolith application with these three modules:

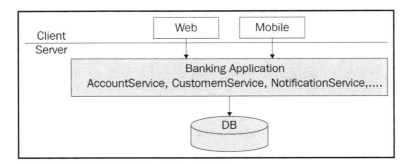

In the preceding diagram, you can see that **Banking Application** has three modules—**AccountService**, **CustomerService**, and **Notification Service**. AccountService manages the account of the customer in the banking system, such open account, get details of an account, update details of an account, and close an account.

Let's divide this monolithic banking application into separate pieces according to the **AccountService**, **CustomerService**, and **NotificationService** modules. These modules process independently of each other. We can deploy each service separately without hampering other services. Its scope is microscopic and focuses only on a unit of task rather than too many tasks. Let's see the following diagram of this banking application based on the microservice architecture:

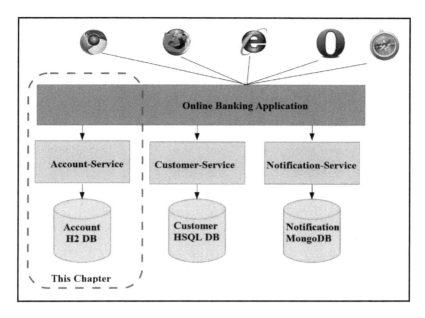

As you can see in the preceding diagram, we created the banking application with a microservices-based architecture. The banking application has been divided into a set of sub-applications, called **microservices**.

I am going to discuss how to implement a large system by building the simplest possible subsystems step-by-step. Therefore, I will only implement a small part of the big system—the user account service. I will discuss only one module of this large banking application. Let's see the following diagram of one of modules of the application:

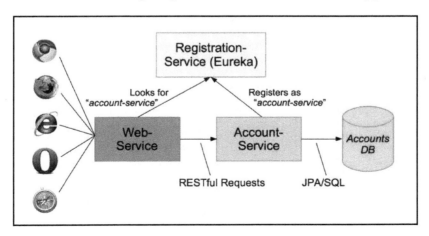

I am going to create an **AccountService** microservice for one of the modules of the Banking application. The web application makes a request to access data from **AccountService** using the RESTful API. We need to add a discovery service, so that other processes can find each other.

Finally, we will create an account resource exposing several RESTful services using the proper URIs and HTTP methods, as follows:

- **Retrieve all accounts**: @GetMapping("/account")
- **Get details of a specific account**: @GetMapping("/account/{accountId}")
- **Delete an account**: @DeleteMapping("/account/{accountId}")
- **Create a new account**: @PostMapping("/account")
- **Update account details**: @PutMapping("/account/{accountId}")

As you can see, the preceding URIs provide all the CRUD operations for the account microservice.

Creating a discovery service

Let's create a discovery service. As we know, a discovery service can solve the following problems of the cloud-native application:

- How do services find each other?
- What happens if we run multiple instances for a service?

Let's see the following diagram with the cloud-native problems:

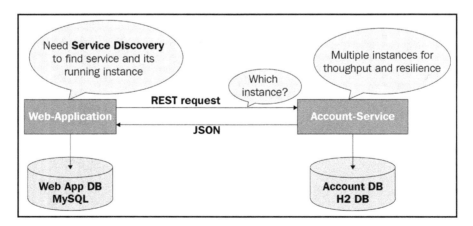

We have already discussed the preceding diagram in detail in Chapter 5, *Spring Cloud Netflix and Service Discovery*.

Let's see the following Maven dependencies required for the discovery service:

```xml
<parent>
    <groupId>org.springframework.boot</groupId>
    <artifactId>spring-boot-starter-parent</artifactId>
    <version>2.0.2.RELEASE</version>
    <relativePath/> <!-- lookup parent from repository -->
</parent>

<properties>
    ...
    <spring-cloud.version>Finchley.M8</spring-cloud.version>
</properties>

<dependencies>
    <dependency>
        <groupId>org.springframework.cloud</groupId>
        <artifactId>spring-cloud-starter-netflix-eureka-
server</artifactId>
    </dependency>
</dependencies>

<dependencyManagement>
    <dependencies>
        <dependency>
            <groupId>org.springframework.cloud</groupId>
            <artifactId>spring-cloud-dependencies</artifactId>
            <version>${spring-cloud.version}</version>
            <type>pom</type>
            <scope>import</scope>
        </dependency>
    </dependencies>
</dependencyManagement>
```

The preceding Maven configuration is included in Spring Cloud with the Finchley.M8 version and accordingly, in this version, it manages all transitive dependencies required for Spring Cloud.

So now `spring-cloud-starter-eureka-server` dependency is present in the Maven build configuration (`pom.xml`), and because of this dependency, the application will be started as a Eureka Server. As you can see, the `spring-cloud-starter-eureka-server` dependency starter is part of the Spring Cloud project and it uses the latest Spring Cloud release train (currently `Finchley.M8`) to manage your Maven dependency versions for other cloud-related dependencies.

After adding the Starter dependency for the Eureka Server, we now need to add a Eureka Service registry. It is a very simple and regular Spring Boot application with one additional annotation apart from `@SpringBootApplication`. This annotation is added to enable the service registry. So, you can use Spring Cloud's `@EnableEurekaServer` annotation to create and enable a Eureka registry server. The application can talk to this registry server and register itself.

Let's see the following code to create the discovery registry service and enable it to register the microservices:

```
package com.dineshonjava.eurekaserver;

import org.springframework.boot.SpringApplication;
import org.springframework.boot.autoconfigure.SpringBootApplication;
import org.springframework.cloud.netflix.eureka.server.EnableEurekaServer;

@SpringBootApplication
@EnableEurekaServer
public class EurekaServerApplication {

    public static void main(String[] args) {
        SpringApplication.run(EurekaServerApplication.class, args);
    }
}
```

As you can see, the preceding code is a very simple Spring Boot application class. Spring Boot's opinionated design makes it easy to create a Eureka Server just by annotating the entry point class with `@EnableEurekaServer`. This class is only required to implement the registry service.

You can see I have used two annotations:

- `@SpringBootApplication`
- `@EnableEurekaServer`

As you know, the `@SpringBootApplication` annotation enables your application to load the auto-configurations related to the Spring Cloud, and the `@EnableEurekaServer` annotation enables and starts this application as a Eureka Server.

Let's see the required basic configuration for this server application in the `application.properties` or `application.yml` file:

```
server:
  port: 8761

eureka:
  instance:
    hostname: localhost
  client:
    registerWithEureka: false
    fetchRegistry: false
    serviceUrl:
      defaultZone:
http://${eureka.instance.hostname}:${server.port}/eureka/
```

As per the preceding configuration, when this Eureka Server application starts, it will listen for registrations on server port `8761`. All our microservices, at the time of start, will register themselves with this Eureka Server by making a call to this Eureka Server application running at server port `8761`. Other services or web applications can query this Eureka Server to find other registered services. You can access the Eureka dashboard by using the `http://localhost:8761` URI, because Eureka also provides a simple status dashboard:

The dashboard shows that the Eureka Server is running smoothly, but currently there are no instances registered with Eureka.

Now that we have created and started up a service registry, let's move on to create a client that registers itself with the Eureka registry server and also uses either Spring Cloud `DiscoveryClient` or `EurekaClient` to expose its own registry with the host and port.

Creating a microservice (the Producer)

We will discuss and create a microservice, `account-service`, as we have seen in the preceding diagram. This microservice registers itself with the registry service or discovery service with its logical service name as `account-service`.

First, we need to add the required Maven dependencies. Again, use the `spring-cloud` release train to manage versions:

```
<properties>
    ...
    <spring-cloud.version>Finchley.M8</spring-cloud.version>
</properties>

<dependencies>
    <dependency>
        <groupId>org.springframework.boot</groupId>
        <artifactId>spring-boot-starter-data-jpa</artifactId>
    </dependency>
    <dependency>
        <groupId>org.springframework.boot</groupId>
        <artifactId>spring-boot-starter-web</artifactId>
    </dependency>
    <dependency>
        <groupId>org.springframework.cloud</groupId>
        <artifactId>spring-cloud-starter-netflix-eureka-
client</artifactId>
    </dependency>
    <dependency>
        <groupId>com.h2database</groupId>
        <artifactId>h2</artifactId>
        <scope>runtime</scope>
    </dependency>
</dependencies>

<dependencyManagement>
    <dependencies>
        <dependency>
```

```
            <groupId>org.springframework.cloud</groupId>
            <artifactId>spring-cloud-dependencies</artifactId>
            <version>${spring-cloud.version}</version>
            <type>pom</type>
            <scope>import</scope>
        </dependency>
    </dependencies>
</dependencyManagement>
```

The preceding Maven configuration has the `spring-cloud-starter-netflix-eureka-client` dependency for `@EnableEurkaClient` instead of the `@EnableDiscoveryClient` annotation. But you can also use the `@EnableDiscoveryClient` annotation to register this service with the registry server. And this configuration also has the `spring-boot-starter-data-jpa` dependency for creating the Spring Data JPA repository, `spring-boot-starter-web` for creating `@RestController`, and the `h2` in-memory database to save the data associated with the account application.

Let's see the following `main` class of the Spring Boot application for `accountservice`:

```
package com.dineshonjava.accountservice;

import org.springframework.boot.SpringApplication;
import org.springframework.boot.autoconfigure.SpringBootApplication;
import org.springframework.cloud.netflix.eureka.EnableEurekaClient;

@SpringBootApplication
@EnableEurekaClient
public class AccountServiceApplication {

    public static void main(String[] args) {
            SpringApplication.run(AccountServiceApplication.class, args);
    }
}
```

The preceding `main` application class is annotated with `@SpringBootApplication` and `@EnableEurekaClient`. `@SpringBootApplication` is used for the Spring Boot auto-configuration, as we have already discussed. The next annotation, `@EnableEurekaClient`, is used to activate the Netflix `EurekaClient` implementation.

We can also enable discovery with the `@EnableDiscoveryClient` annotation on a `@Configuration` class or the `@SpringBootApplication` entry point class. `@EnableDiscoveryClient` activates the Netflix Eureka `DiscoveryClient` implementation.

There are multiple implementations of `Discovery Service`, such as Eureka, Consul, and Zookeeper. In this example, we have used `@EnableEurekaClient` explicitly but it will be available only when the `spring-cloud-starter-netflix-eureka-client` dependency is available on your application classpath, and it only works for Eureka. You could also use `@EnableDiscoveryClient`; it lives in `spring-cloud-commons` and picks the implementation on the classpath. And there is no difference between either using the `@EnableEurekaClient` or the `@EnableDiscoveryClient` annotation. They are effectively the same.

Let's create a configuration file, `application.properties` (or `application.yml`), with a couple of configuration settings:

```
spring:
  application:
    name: account-service

server:
  port: 6060

eureka:
  client:
    service-url:
      default-zone: ${EUREKA_URI:http://localhost:8761/eureka}
    instance:
    prefer-ip-address: true
```

This file tells us the application name is `account-service`, and the server port will be `6060`. And this tells the application where the Eureka Server is to register itself with the `account-service` logical service name.

Now let's start `account-service` and you can see that it will be registered with Eureka discovery service:

The `ACCOUNT-SERVICE` microservice is registered with Eureka discovery service, as you can see under **Instances** currently registered with Eureka in the Dashboard.

The `@EnableEurekaClient` annotation makes this application `account-service` into both a Eureka *instance* by registering itself, as you can see in the preceding dashboard, and also a *client*, so that it can access or query other registered services. We can control the behavior of this instance, and also we can see the health of this instance by configuring some settings with the `eureka.instance.*` configuration keys.

Let's see other classes of this service. We have created a REST Controller by using the `@RestController` annotation. You can refer to my book, *Spring 5 Design Patterns*—it explains the Spring MVC module in details. Here I am just going to use the `@RestController` annotation without explaining much about the Spring MVC module, to create the REST controller to handle RESTful API calls:

```
package com.dineshonjava.accountservice.controller;
import java.util.List;
import org.springframework.beans.factory.annotation.Autowired;
import org.springframework.web.bind.annotation.DeleteMapping;
```

```
import org.springframework.web.bind.annotation.GetMapping;
import org.springframework.web.bind.annotation.PathVariable;
import org.springframework.web.bind.annotation.PostMapping;
import org.springframework.web.bind.annotation.PutMapping;
import org.springframework.web.bind.annotation.RequestBody;
import org.springframework.web.bind.annotation.RestController;

import com.dineshonjava.accountservice.domain.Account;
import com.dineshonjava.accountservice.repository.AccountRepository;

@RestController
public class AccountController {
    @Autowired
    AccountRepository accountRepository;
    @PostMapping(value = "/account")
    public Account save (@RequestBody Account account){
        return accountRepository.save(account);
    }
    @GetMapping(value = "/account")
    public Iterable<Account> all (){
        return accountRepository.findAll();
    }
    @GetMapping(value = "/account/{accountId}")
    public Account findByAccountId (@PathVariable Integer accountId){
        return accountRepository.findAccountByAccountId(accountId);
    }
    @PutMapping(value = "/account")
    public Account update (@RequestBody Account account){
        return accountRepository.save(account);
    }
    @DeleteMapping(value = "/account")
    public void delete (@RequestBody Account account){
        accountRepository.delete(account);
    }
    ...
}
```

This REST controller has several request handler methods to perform the CRUD operations. The `save()` request handler method creates a new account, we can read all accounts using the `all()` handler method, the `update()` handler method updates the existing account of a given account ID. And also we can delete an account using the `delete()` handler method.

The `AccountController` REST controller has an `AccountRepository` property. This repository is an interface extending with the `CrudRepository` interface of the Spring Data JPA. We will cover Spring Data in the next section. This repository uses the `H2` database to store all information about the account. You can find complete a example on GitHub about this account service application.

Let's see whether the following URIs have been exposed by this REST controller of the account microservice:

- **Create a new account**: `@PostMapping("/account")`
- **Read all accounts**: `@GetMapping("/account")`
- **Get details of a specific account**: `@GetMapping("/account/{accountId}")`
- **Update account details**: `@PutMapping("/account/{accountId}")`
- **Delete an account**: `@DeleteMapping("/account")`

The preceding endpoints have been used by the web application to access the account microservice.

Let's create microservice consumers.

Creating microservice consumers

To consume this RESTful microservice, let's create a consumer web application. This web application will consume RESTful service endpoints. Spring provides several ways to consume microservices, but in this web application, we will use the `RestTemplate` class. This `RestTemplate` class allows you to send HTTP requests to a RESTful server and fetch data in a number of formats, such as JSON and XML.

The format of data depends on the presence of marshalling classes on the classpath of the web application. The web application will support the JSON format if Jackson JARS are present in the classpath. Similarly, it will support the XML format if JAXB JARS are present in the classpath.

In this web application, the `WEB-APPLICATION` component depends on the backend microservice (`ACCOUNT-SERVICE`). This application will talk to the account microservice by using a logical service name rather than hardcoding the location of the microservice, and this web application asks Eureka to resolve the host and port of this microservice.

Let's see the following `main` application class of this web application:

```
package com.dineshonjava.webapplication;

import org.springframework.boot.SpringApplication;
import org.springframework.boot.autoconfigure.SpringBootApplication;
import org.springframework.cloud.client.loadbalancer.LoadBalanced;
import org.springframework.cloud.netflix.eureka.EnableEurekaClient;
import org.springframework.context.annotation.Bean;
import org.springframework.web.client.RestTemplate;

@SpringBootApplication
@EnableEurekaClient
public class WebApplication {

    public static void main(String[] args) {
        SpringApplication.run(WebApplication.class, args);
    }
    @LoadBalanced
    @Bean
    RestTemplate restTemplate() {
        return new RestTemplate();
    }
}
```

This class has the `@EnableEurekaClient` annotation to register itself with the registry service. And, one more thing; I have configured a bean that is `RestTemplate` using the `@LoadBalanced` annotation. That means our web application has load-balanced `RestTemplate`.

Load-balanced RestTemplate

The `RestTemplate` bean will be intercepted and auto-configured by Spring Cloud (due to the `@LoadBalanced` annotation) to use a custom `HttpRequestClient` that uses Netflix Ribbon to do the microservice lookup. Ribbon is also a load balancer, so if you have multiple instances of a service available, it picks one for you. (Neither Eureka nor Consul on their own performs load balancing, so we use Ribbon to do it instead.)

 From the Brixton Release Train (Spring Cloud 1.1.0.RELEASE), the `RestTemplate` is no longer created automatically. Previously it was created for you, which caused confusion and potential conflicts.

The `loadBalancer` takes the logical service name (as registered with the discovery server) and converts it to the actual hostname of the chosen microservice. A `RestTemplate` instance is thread-safe and can be used to access any number of services in different parts of your application.

Let's see the configuration file of this web application:

```
spring:
  application:
    name: web-application

server:
  port: 6464

eureka:
  client:
    service-url:
      default-zone: ${EUREKA_URI:http://localhost:8761/eureka}
    instance:
      prefer-ip-address: true
```

After configuration file creation, let's run this `main` application class and see the following Eureka dashboard:

As you can see, **WEB-APPLICATION** is registered with the Eureka discovery service. Let's see the `WebAccountService` class, which accesses the account microservice by using names rather than server addresses:

```java
package com.dineshonjava.webapplication.service;

import java.util.List;

import org.springframework.beans.factory.annotation.Autowired;
import org.springframework.cloud.client.loadbalancer.LoadBalanced;
import org.springframework.stereotype.Service;
import org.springframework.web.client.RestTemplate;

import com.dineshonjava.webapplication.domain.Account;
import com.dineshonjava.webapplication.exception.AccountNotFoundException;

@Service
public class WebAccountsService {
    @Autowired
    protected RestTemplate restTemplate;
    // ACCOUNTS-SERVICE is the name of the microservice we're calling
    protected String serviceUrl = "http://ACCOUNT-SERVICE";
    public Account getByNumber(String accountNumber) {
        Account account = restTemplate.getForObject(serviceUrl
                + "/account/{accountId}", Account.class, accountNumber);
        if (account == null)
            throw new AccountNotFoundException(accountNumber);
        else
            return account;
    }
    public List<Account> getAllAccounts(){
        return restTemplate.getForObject(serviceUrl+ "/account",
List.class);
    }
    ...
    ...
}
```

The `service` class accesses the backend microservice for this web application. The `@LoadBalanced` annotated `RestTemplate` will resolve application names (`ACCOUNT-SERVICE`) to a real server name and port by querying Eureka. The `@LoadBalanced` annotation tells Spring Boot to customize `RestTemplate` with `ClientHttpRequestFactory` that does a Eureka lookup before making the HTTP call. To make this work, you'll need to add a new config setting to `application.properties`:

```
ribbon.http.client.enabled=true
```

You can find complete web application from GitHub (`https://github.com/PacktPublishing/Mastering-Spring-Boot-2.0`).

Let's discuss the Spring Data project of the Spring Framework in the next section.

Brief introduction to Spring Data

Spring Data is a mutation of Spring Source Projects, designed with the purpose of unifying and easing the access to different kinds of data storage, such as relational databases and NoSQL data stores. Spring Data aims to provide a consistent and reliable platform to access data while keeping the special traits of the data stores intact. The model of Spring Data is based on Spring-based programming.

Using Spring Data provides easy-to-utilize data storing technologies, such as:

- Relational databases
- Non-relational databases
- Map-reduced frameworks
- Cloud-based data services

Developers of Spring Data interact and work together with the many companies and developers of these technologies to bring you Spring Data. Spring Data projects are like umbrella projects with many sub-projects specific to the technology you require.

There are many features of Spring Data, and some are:

- A powerful repository
- Customized object-mapping abstractions
- Query derivations from the names of the repository
- Domain-based classes that provide basic properties are implemented

- Transparent auditing, such as created and last changed, are supported
- Customized repository codes can be integrated into the projects
- Easy Spring integration can be done through customized XML namespaces or JavaConfig
- Advanced integration can be done with Spring MVC models

To manage the different independent projects under the Spring Data projects, a Bill of Materials is published with the set of dependencies for all the projects. The released trains are classified by names instead of versions. Spring Data's central goal is to provide a well-known and reliable, Spring based coding model for hiding verbosity.

It makes it simple to utilize information get to innovations, all kinds of databases, outline structures, and cloud-based services. This is an umbrella venture that contains numerous sub-projects that are particular to a given database. The activities are produced by cooperating with a significant number of organizations and engineers that are behind these energizing advances.

Apache Ignite repository

Spring Data Framework gives a brought-together and broadly utilized API that permits abstracting fundamental information stockpiling from the application layer. Spring Data causes you to abstain from locking to a particular database merchant, making it simple to change, starting with one database then onto the next with negligible endeavors.

Apache Ignite actualizes the Spring Data `CrudRepository` interface that backs the fundamental CRUD activities and gives access to the Apache Ignite SQL Grid by means of the bound-together Spring Data API.

Spring Data MongoDB

Spring Data for MongoDB is part of the umbrella Spring Data venture that plans to give a natural and steady Spring-based programming model to new datastores while holding store-particular highlights and abilities.

The Spring Data MongoDB venture gives coordination the MongoDB report database. Key practical territories of Spring Data MongoDB are a POJO-driven model for connecting with a MongoDB DBCollection and effortlessly composing repository-style information to layer.

Spring MongoDB data highlights

Here are some highlights of the Spring MongoDB data:

- Spring setup bolster utilizing Java-based `@Configuration` classes or an XML namespace for a Mongo driver occasion and imitation sets
- The `mongo` template assistant class builds efficiency performing normal Mongo activities
- Incorporates coordinated protest mapping among records and POJOs
- Special case interpretation into Spring's versatile Data Access Exception chain of importance
- Highlight Rich Object Mapping coordinated with Spring's Conversion Service
- Explanation-based mapping metadata, yet extensible to help other metadata positions
- Steadiness and mapping life cycle occasions
- Low-level mapping utilizing MongoReader/MongoWriter reflections
- Java-based Query, Criteria, and Update DSLs
- Programmed usage of Repository interfaces, including support for custom discoverer strategies
- QueryDSL coordination to help compose safe inquiries
- Cross-store persistence, support for JPA Entities with fields straightforwardly endured/recovered utilizing MongoDB
- Log4j log appender
- GeoSpatial
- Guide Reduce
- JMX organization and checking
- CDI bolster
- GridFS

Spring Data JPA

Spring Data JPA, some portion of the bigger Spring Data group, makes it simple to effortlessly execute JPA-based repositories. This module manages an upgraded bolster for JPA-based information to get layers. It makes it simpler to fabricate Spring-fueled applications that utilize information gets to advancements.

Summary

We created a microservice called `ACCOUNT-SERVICE` and registered this service with the Eureka discovery service. We also created a consumer of the microservice as a web application, and it registered itself with the Eureka discovery service to consume the `accountservice` by using its logical service name rather than using a hardcoded hostname and server port.

Netflix's Eureka works as service discovery and client. Spring Cloud provides support to Netflix's Eureka to provide solutions to the cloud-native problems.

Netflix's Ribbon provides client-side load balancing with the Spring's `RestTemplate`. Spring Cloud promotes service registration and `client-side load-balancing` features to create a more resilient system.

We have also discussed some parts of the Spring Data project. How Spring creates a repository using interfaces. In this chapter, we have created a repository and built a CRUD operation using the H2 database.

In the next chapter, we will explore and implement asynchronous reactive systems.

Creating API Gateway with Netflix Zuul Proxy

In the previous chapter, we created microservices and registered with the Eureka registry server. This chapter will explore the need for the API Gateway pattern for microservices communication, either from UI components or from inter-service calls. We will implement API Gateway using the Netflix Zuul API. We will see how to set up Zuul Proxy in your application.

Spring Cloud provides support for Netflix Zuul to implement the API Gateway proxy for routing and filtering the actual microservice requests. This chapter will explore the following points and you will get a better understanding of API Gateway and Zuul proxy.

This chapter will cover the following topics:

- The need for an API Gateway pattern
- API Gateway pattern components
- Implementing the API Gateway using Netflix Zuul proxy
- Including Zuul using Maven dependency
- Enabling the Zuul service proxy
- Configuring Zuul properties
- Adding Zuul filters

The need for an API Gateway pattern

In the microservices architecture, lots of API services work together for the distributed application. There could be more than 100 API services and UI components talking to each other for a business goal. So, these UI components must know about all microservices endpoints with a port to call these API services if you are not using API Gateway.

An API Gateway mechanism is required when you want to implement the common aspects for your distributed application, such as CORS, authentication, security, and monitoring, in terms of this design. If you are not using API Gateway, then you have to implement these aspects into all API services, so the same code will be repeated over all microservices. To avoid this problem, we have to use a common service or entry point where all common aspect code is written and the client will call that common service.

Let's see the following diagram of a distributed application without an API Gateway service:

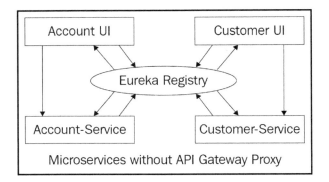

As you can see, each UI component must be aware of each service endpoint using the Eureka Server. The UI component of the **Customer-Service** must have information about the endpoint of the `Customer` microservice that is registered with the Eureka Server. Similarly, the UI component of the account must be aware of the endpoints of the `Account` microservice. It is sometimes very complex to maintain and remember the endpoints of each API service, and our microservices implementations don't want to expose these endpoints to the outside world for security reasons. We want to keep these API services private. In this case, instead of letting UI components know about all the actual endpoints of the API services, we can provide API Gateway, which will delegate all API calls to the individual microservices working behind the scenes.

API Gateway is a unified proxy interface delegating the calls to several microservices-based on the URL pattern. In this chapter, we will implement this API Gateway proxy using Spring Cloud's Zuul Proxy. This API Gateway interface allows us to expose a set of public services to the outside client without any security breaches. Let's see the following diagram with an API Gateway interface to call API services:

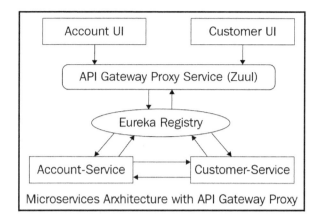

As you can see in the preceding diagram, the UI component calls the API services through API Gateway. Now, each UI component doesn't need to know the actual endpoint of the individual microservice. We have exposed a single service, that is, the API Gateway service with a host and port for all UI components. This API Gateway service is also known as *Edge Service* because this service sits on top of all the other microservices in a distributed application. All clients will call this Edge Service as a proxy for all internal microservices.

Let's see the pros and cons of using the API Gateway proxy service in the next section. There are many reasons to use the API Gateway service on microservices-based applications, we have discussed some of them. There are listed pros and cons of the API Gateway pattern in the next sections.

Pros of the API Gateway pattern

These are the advantages of using an API Gateway proxy in your distributed application:

- API Gateway provides an easier way for clients to call API services
- You can apply client-specific policies, such as authentication and rate-limiting, at a single place rather than across multiple services
- You can also expose selected APIs to the clients with exposing internal microservices endpoints
- Microservices endpoints can be changed without forcing the clients to refactor consuming logic
- You can implement any routing rules or any filter implementation
- API Gateway is like an Edge microservice and is independently scalable

You have seen some pros of using the API Gateway proxy service in your microservices architecture, and now let's look at some cons of using this API Gateway pattern.

Cons of the API Gateway pattern

These are the disadvantages of using an API Gateway proxy in your distributed application:

- API Gateway is the single entry point to apply all common aspects, it could be risky sometimes because of the single point of failure if proper measures are not taken to make it highly available
- Managing API information of various microservices might be difficult in the API Gateway service

We have discussed some pros and cons of using the API Gateway pattern in your microservices-based application. Let's see the API Gateway pattern components in the next section.

API Gateway pattern components

The API Gateway pattern is based on calling API services using a proxy. The API Gateway proxy service has mainly four types of filters. These filters intercept the HTTP requests coming from the client applications. You can also add your own custom filters for a specific URL pattern. Let's see the following diagram that displays API Gateway's components:

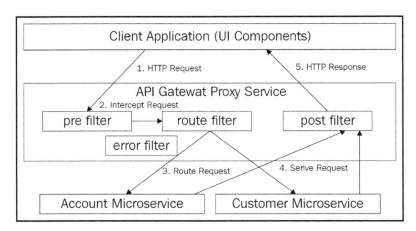

API Gateway has mainly four filters as follows:

- **Pre filter**: These filters will be invoked before the HTTP request is routed

- **Post filter**: These filters will be invoked after the HTTP request has been routed

- **Route filter**: These filters will be used to route the HTTP request

- **Error filter**: These filters will be invoked when an error occurs while handling the HTTP request

As per the preceding diagram, the **Client Applications** send the **HTTP request** to the API Gateway service, the **pre filter** intercepts the HTTP request coming from the client applications and forwards it to the **route filter** to route these requests to the internal individual microservices, such as **Account Microservice** and **Customer Microservice**. The microservices send a response to the **post filter**, and finally, the post filter forwards the **HTTP Response** to the **Client Applications**.

We have discussed the API Gateway pattern in the microservices architecture. Let's implement this pattern using Spring Cloud's Netflix Zuul API in your microservice application.

Implementing API Gateway using Netflix Zuul Proxy

Let's implement routing for your microservice application. We have discussed the importance of routing for API services. In this chapter, we have created two microservices— `Account` and `Customer`. Also, we have a Eureka registry application. For example, `/api/accounts` is mapped to the `Account` service and `/api/customers` is mapped to the `Customer` service.

In this example, we have used Netflix's Zuul API to implement the API Gateway proxy to route API calls. Spring has strong bonding with Netflix Zuul and provides a Spring Cloud Netflix Zuul module. Zuul is a JVM-based router and also used as server-side loadbalancer by Netflix.

Here, we will call both the `Account` and `Customer` services by using the Zuul proxy, which can be used to create API Gateway. Also, we have to create another microservice application for API Gateway Edge service.

Let's create a Spring Boot project using the web interface of Spring Initializr (`http://start.spring.io/`). The application name will be `Api-Zuul-Service` and select **Zuul and Eureka Discovery** module. This Edge Service will be a Eureka client itself.

Let's include Spring Cloud's Netflix Zuul library in your microservice application.

Including Zuul using Maven dependency

First, we need to add a dependency to the Zuul support from Spring Cloud to our UI application's `pom.xml` file:

```
<dependencies>
...
<dependency>
<groupId>org.springframework.cloud</groupId>
<artifactId>spring-cloud-starter-netflix-eureka-client</artifactId>
</dependency>
<dependency>
<groupId>org.springframework.cloud</groupId>
<artifactId>spring-cloud-starter-netflix-zuul</artifactId>
</dependency>
<dependency>
<groupId>org.springframework.boot</groupId>
<artifactId>spring-boot-starter-test</artifactId>
<scope>test</scope>
</dependency>
...
</dependencies>
```

As you can see in the Maven configuration file, we have added the Zuul library with `spring-cloud-starter-netflix-zuul` artifactId and `org.springframework.cloud` groupId. And also we have added the `spring-cloud-starter-netflix-eureka-client` dependency to register this `api-gateway-service` with the Eureka registry server.

As of now, we have added the Zuul Maven dependency to our Spring Boot application but, by default, Zuul will not be enabled, so we have to enable the Zuul proxy service. Let's see in the next section.

Enabling the Zuul service proxy

Now add the `@EnableZuulProxy` annotation on top of the
`ApiZuulServiceApplication` Spring Boot application class. This annotation will enable
the Zuul service proxy in our application and will also enable all the features of an API
Gateway layer. Along with the `@EnableZuulproxy` annotation, we have also added
another `@EnableDiscoveryClient` annotation on top of
the `ApiZuulServiceApplication` class. Let's see the following `main` application class of
the `api-gateway-service` application:

```
package com.dineshonjava.apizuulservice;
import org.springframework.boot.SpringApplication;
import org.springframework.boot.autoconfigure.SpringBootApplication;
import org.springframework.cloud.client.discovery.EnableDiscoveryClient;
import org.springframework.cloud.netflix.zuul.EnableZuulProxy;
@EnableZuulProxy
@EnableDiscoveryClient
@SpringBootApplication
public class ApiZuulServiceApplication {
public static void main(String[] args) {
SpringApplication.run(ApiZuulServiceApplication.class, args);
}
}
```

As you can see, the `ApiZuulServiceApplication` class is annotated with the
`@EnableZuulProxy` annotation to enable the Zuul proxy service in our microservice
application. Now, we will see how to configure Zuul properties in our
`application.properties` or `application.yml` file. In this chapter, I have used
the `application.yml` configuration file to configure Zuul properties, but we can also use
the `bootstrap.properties` file to configure come configurations that are required at the
startup time of the application.

Configuring Zuul properties

Let's configure Zuul properties in our application using the `application.yml`
configuration file. These are the configurations we have created for our application
configuration file:

```
spring:
application:
name: API-GATEWAY
server:
port: 8080
```

```
eureka:
client:
service-url:
default-zone: ${EUREKA_URI:http://localhost:8761/eureka}
instance:
prefer-ip-address: true
zuul:
ignoredServices: '*'
prefix: /api
routes:
account-service:
path: /accounts/**
serviceId: ACCOUNT-SERVICE
customer-service:
path: /customers/**
serviceId: CUSTOMER-SERVICE
host:socket-timeout-millis: 30000
```

In the preceding application configuration file, first, we have configured the application name as API-GATEWAY and the server port with 8080 for the Edge Service application. And we have defined configurations related to the Eureka client for registering this Edge Service application with the Eureka Server.

 If you want to use routing based on service IDs, you need to provide Eureka on the classpath and have to register this service with the Eureka registry server. You can also use Zuul without the Eureka Server, but you have to provide the exact URL of the service where it will be redirected: zuul.routes.account-service.url=http://localhost:6060.

Finally, we have configured Zuul properties in the application configuration file. First, we have to skip all the default services from the Zuul proxy by using the following configuration:

```
zuul:
ignoredServices: '*'
account-service:
path: /accounts/**
```

In the preceding example, all services are ignored except account-service.

We can also use a common prefix for URLs, such as /api, for which we want Zuul to proxy by setting zuul.prefix property:

```
zuul:
prefix: /api
```

We can also customize the path mappings of services as follows:

```
zuul:
routes:
account-service:
path: /accounts/**
serviceId: ACCOUNT-SERVICE
```

Here, `zuul.routes.account-service.path` will route all traffic to request the service with the `ACCOUNT-SERVICE` service ID. Now, the `http://localhost:8080/api/accounts/account` URL will be forwarded to the `ACCOUNT-SERVICE` microservice. Let's configure another microservice `Customer` similar to `Account` microservice in the example.

Finally, we have configured the Zuul `host` socket timeout with the following configuration:

```
zuul:
host:
socket-timeout-millis: 30000
```

In the preceding configuration, we have configured it to instruct Spring Boot to wait for the response for `30000` ms.

Now, our microservice application for the API Gateway service is ready to run and test. Let's start Eureka Server, `AccountService`, `CustomerService`, and `APIZuulService` application.

Let's open the Eureka dashboard with the `http://localhost:8761/` URL, as follows:

Instances currently registered with Eureka

Application	AMIs	Availability Zones	Status
ACCOUNT-SERVICE	n/a (1)	(1)	UP (1) - MRNDTHTMOBL0002.timesgroup.com:account-service:6060
API-GATEWAY	n/a (1)	(1)	UP (1) - MRNDTHTMOBL0002.timesgroup.com:API-GATEWAY:8080
CUSTOMER-SERVICE	n/a (1)	(1)	UP (1) - MRNDTHTMOBL0002.timesgroup.com:customer-service:6161

In the preceding screenshot, you can see our three microservices are running and registered with Eureka.

Let's hit the following URL of `Customer` service for customer UI application. `http://localhost:8080/api/customers/customer/1001`, you will see this URL will be routed to the `Customer` service internally with the `http://localhost:6161/customer/1001` URL.

Let's see the following screenshot for the public API call for `Customer` service using API Gateway `http://localhost:8080/api/customers/customer/1001`:

As you can see, we have called the `Customer` microservice using the API Gateway Zuul proxy. Internally, this Zuul proxy calls the `Customer` service with the `http://localhost:6161/customer/1001` URL. Similarly, the Account UI component can call the `Account` microservice using the API Gateway Zuul proxy service using the `http://localhost:8080/api/accounts/account/100` URL:

As you can see, we have called the `Account` microservice using the API Gateway Zuul proxy. Internally, it will call the actual service with the `http://localhost:6060/account/100` URL.

Adding Zuul filters

We can also add custom filters in the Zuul microservice for implementing some cross-cutting concerns, such as security and rate-limiting. In the *API Gateway components* section, we discussed four filters—`pre`, `post`, `route`, and `error`. We can create these filters by extending the `com.netflix.zuul.ZuulFilter` class. We have to override `filterType`, `filterOrder`, and `shouldFilter`, and run methods. Let's see the following `PreFilter` custom filter:

```
package com.dineshonjava.apizuulservice.filters;
import java.util.UUID;
import javax.servlet.http.HttpServletRequest;
import com.netflix.zuul.ZuulFilter;
import com.netflix.zuul.context.RequestContext;
import com.netflix.zuul.exception.ZuulException;
public class PreFilter extends ZuulFilter{
@Override
public Object run() throws ZuulException {
RequestContext ctx = RequestContext.getCurrentContext();
HttpServletRequest request = ctx.getRequest();
if (request.getAttribute("AUTH_HEADER") == null) {
//generate or get AUTH_TOKEN, ex from Spring Session repository
String sessionId = UUID.randomUUID().toString();
ctx.addZuulRequestHeader("AUTH_HEADER", sessionId);
}
return null;
}
@Override
public boolean shouldFilter() {
return true;
}
@Override
public int filterOrder() {
return 0;
}
@Override
public String filterType() {
return "pre";
}
}
```

In the preceding class, we have created `PreFilter` by extending the `ZuulFilter` abstract class of Netflix's Zuul API. Similarly, we can create `RouteFilter`, `PostFilter`, and `ErrorFilter`. You can find the complete code on the GitHub repository at `https://github.com/PacktPublishing/Mastering-Spring-Boot-2.0`. In the preceding filter class, we modified the `run()` method by adding `AUTH_HEADER` as a request header using `RequestContext.addZuulRequestHeader()`. This header will be forwarded to the internal microservices.

After creating Zuul filters, we have to register these filters with the Zuul proxy service by creating the bean definitions.

Registering Zuul filters

Let's create the bean definition of these filters, as follows:

```
@EnableZuulProxy
@EnableDiscoveryClient
@SpringBootApplication
public class ApiZuulServiceApplication {
public static void main(String[] args) {
SpringApplication.run(ApiZuulServiceApplication.class, args);
}
@Bean
public PreFilter preFilter() {
return new PreFilter();
}
@Bean
public PostFilter postFilter() {
return new PostFilter();
}
@Bean
public ErrorFilter errorFilter() {
return new ErrorFilter();
}
@Bean
public RouteFilter routeFilter() {
return new RouteFilter();
}
}
}
```

Let's run the preceding class again and access any public API Gateway service for `Customer` or `Account` and check the console of the eclipse:

```
Console ☒  Progress  Problems
account-zuul-service - ApiZuulServiceApplication [Spring Boot App] C:\Program Files\Java\jre1.8.0_161\bin\javaw.exe (17-May-2018, 2:51:04 AM)
Inside pre filter : GET Request URL : http://192.168.225.208:8080/api/customers/customer/1001
Inside Route Filter
Inside Post Filter
```

As you can see in the console log, as we have refreshed the `http://192.168.225.208:8080/api/customers/customer/1001` API call, all filters are executed and print log on the console, respectively.

Summary

We learned about the API Gateway pattern for the microservices architecture and also discussed the need for API Gateway for microservices-based applications. API Gateway has several benefits of being used in cloud-based distributed applications. In this chapter, we discussed how to implement the API Gateway proxy service using Spring Cloud's Netflix Zuul API.

We implemented a microservice, Edge Service, to provide a Zuul-based proxy service on top of the internal multiple microservices. The Edge Service can be used for common functionality implementations or cross-cutting concerns.

We also created multiple Zuul filters and registered with the Zuul proxy service.

In the next chapter, we will explore the Feign client in microservices-based applications.

Simplify HTTP API with Feign Client

8

In the previous chapters, we developed microservices and client applications for these microservices using load-balancing `RestTemplate`, `EurekaClient`, and `DiscoveryClient`. This way of client implementation requires a lot of boilerplate code for enabling microservices to communicate with each other. In light of these discussions, we will learn about Feign, which is nothing but a declarative HTTP client developed by Netflix.

In this chapter, we will explore what Feign is and how it works. We will also have a detailed discussion on how Feign can be extended or customized for business needs with a reference implementation for a custom encoder, decoder, Hystrix, and exception handling with unit testing.

We will learn how Feign simplifies the HTTP API clients. We don't need to use a lot of boilerplate code to make the HTTP API clients application to access the microservices. You just simply put in an annotated interface, while the actual implementation will be created at the runtime.

By the end of this chapter, you will have a better understanding of the declarative REST client, Feign client, and how to access the microservices using only annotated interfaces without implementing these interfaces by yourself.

This chapter will cover the following points:

- Feign basics
- Feign inheritance support
- Multiple interfaces
- Advanced usage
- Feign and Hystrix
- Logging
- Exception handling
- Custom encoders and decoders
- Unit testing Feign clients

Let's look at these topics in detail.

Declarative REST client – Feign basics

According to the Feign documentation:

> *"Feign is a Java to HTTP client binder inspired by Retrofit, JAXRS-2.0, and WebSocket. Feign's first goal was reducing the complexity of binding Denominator uniformly to HTTP APIs regardless of ReSTfulness."*

Netflix has developed a declarative web service client called *Feign*. It is very easy to create compared to other web service clients, such as Spring's `RestTemplate`, `DiscoveryClient`, and `EurekaClient`. To create a Feign REST client, create an interface and annotate this interface with an annotation provided by the Netflix Feign library. You don't need to implement this interface in your cloud application to use the microservice. The Feign client provides support to use Feign annotations and JAX-RS annotations. And you can also use the Spring MVC annotations and the same `HttpMessageConverters` as we used in the Spring web module, the Feign client supports all annotations of the Spring MVC module for a REST application. It also provides support for pluggable encoders and decoders. Feign, by default, provides the functionality of Ribbon and Eureka to provide a load-balanced HTTP client.

In the previous chapters, we created microservices and its consumers. In the examples, `account-consumer` (that is, a web application or another microservice `CUSTOMER-SERVICE`) consumed the REST services exposed by the `account-service` producer using `RestTemplate`. Let's look at the following diagram, which illustrates the consumption of microservices without using Feign:

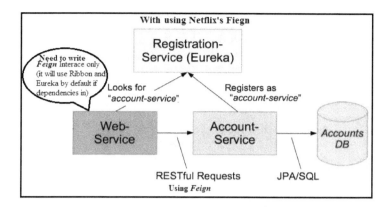

As you can see, microservices communicating with each other without the Feign client required a lot of boilerplate code related to Eureka, Ribbon, and load-balancing. The required code also increases the complexity in the client application when the number of microservices increases. Let's see the following requirements for which we have to write a lot of code:

- To make a resilient system we have to create a load-balancing client using Ribbon
- To know the `Service` instance and then the Base URL of a microservice using Eureka
- To make use of `RestTemplate` for consuming service

The following code shows how to consume an `account` microservice:

```
package com.dineshonjava.webapplication.service;

import java.util.List;

import org.springframework.beans.factory.annotation.Autowired;
import org.springframework.cloud.client.loadbalancer.LoadBalanced;
import org.springframework.stereotype.Service;
import org.springframework.web.client.RestTemplate;

import com.dineshonjava.webapplication.domain.Account;
import com.dineshonjava.webapplication.exception.AccountNotFoundException;

@Service
public class WebAccountsService {
    @Autowired
     @LoadBalanced
     protected RestTemplate restTemplate;
    protected String serviceUrl = "http://ACCOUNT-SERVICE";
```

```
public Account getByNumber(String accountNumber) {
    Account account = restTemplate.getForObject(serviceUrl
            + "/account/{accountId}", Account.class,
            accountNumber);
    if (account == null)
        throw new AccountNotFoundException(accountNumber);
    else
        return account;
}
...
...
}
```

Now, let's use the Feign declarative REST client and see how it resolves the complexity of communicating with microservices. Let's see the following diagram using the Feign client:

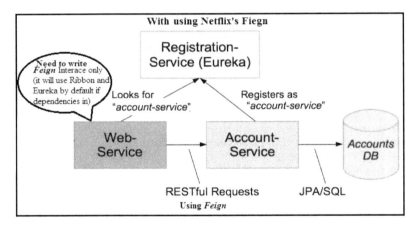

We don't need to write the code for Eureka, Ribbon, and load-balancing, it's automatically added if these libraries or dependencies are available on the classpath of your client application. You don't even need to write a class for the client code, just create an interface with the @FeignClient annotation with a logical service name as the annotation argument. This is a much easier and cleaner way of using Netflix Feign. If the Netflix Ribbon dependency is also in the classpath, then Feign takes care of load-balancing by default.

Let's see how to include Feign in the client application.

Including Feign in the cloud application

First we will include the Netflix Feign dependency in the `pom.xml` file:

```
<parent>
    <groupId>org.springframework.boot</groupId>
    <artifactId>spring-boot-starter-parent</artifactId>
    <version>2.0.2.RELEASE</version>
    <relativePath/> <!-- lookup parent from repository -->
</parent>

<properties>
    ...
    <spring-cloud.version>Finchley.M8</spring-cloud.version>
</properties>

<dependencies>
    ...
    <dependency>
            <groupId>org.springframework.boot</groupId>
            <artifactId>spring-boot-starter-web</artifactId>
    </dependency>
    <dependency>
            <groupId>org.springframework.cloud</groupId>
            <artifactId>spring-cloud-starter-netflix-eureka-
             client</artifactId>
    </dependency>
    <dependency>
            <groupId>org.springframework.cloud</groupId>
            <artifactId>spring-cloud-starter-openfeign</artifactId>
    </dependency>
    ...
</dependencies>
```

To include Feign in your client application project based on the Spring Cloud, use the Starter with the `org.springframework.cloud` group and the `spring-cloud-starter-openfeign` artifact ID.

Now, let's define a Feign client by creating an interface with the @FeignClient annotation. This interface is working as a client to access microservices registered on the discovery server. *But how do we access these services?* We have to specify the name value as account-service on the @FeignClient annotation (it is the logical service name of the account microservice using Eureka for discovery). Let's see the following code for this interface:

```
package com.dineshonjava.customerservice.service;

import java.util.List;

import org.springframework.cloud.openfeign.FeignClient;
import org.springframework.web.bind.annotation.GetMapping;
import org.springframework.web.bind.annotation.PathVariable;

import com.dineshonjava.customerservice.domain.Account;

@FeignClient("account-service")
public interface AccountService {
    @GetMapping(value = "/account/customer/{customer}")
    List<Account> findByCutomer (@PathVariable("customer") Integer
    customer);
            @PutMapping(value = "/account/{accountId}", consumes =
    "application/json")
              Account update(@PathVariable("storeId") Integer
     accountId, Account account);
    @DeleteMapping(value = "/account/{accountId}")
    void delete(@PathVariable("accountId") Integer accountId);
    @PostMapping(value = "/account/customer/", consumes =
    "application/json")
            Account update(@RequestBody Account account);
}
```

We have used the @FeignClient("account-service") annotation with the account-service logical service name. And we have defined the method call to be made to consume this account REST microservice exposed by the account-service module with the /account/customer/{customer} endpoint.

To make sure this @FeignClient annotation is working, we have to enable the Feign client cloud behavior in your application. Finally, we annotate the Spring Boot main class with @EnableFeignClients. Let's see the following main class of the application:

```
package com.dineshonjava.customerservice;

import org.springframework.boot.SpringApplication;
import org.springframework.boot.autoconfigure.SpringBootApplication;
import org.springframework.cloud.openfeign.EnableFeignClients;
```

```
@SpringBootApplication
@EnableFeignClients
public class CustomerServiceApplication {

    public static void main(String[] args) {
        SpringApplication.run(CustomerServiceApplication.class, args);
    }
}
```

Next create another microservice, CUSTOMER-SERVICE, and it will access the account microservice to fetch all accounts associated with a customer in the banking application. Let's see the following class that will use the accountService by using Feign:

```
package com.dineshonjava.customerservice.controller;

import org.springframework.beans.factory.annotation.Autowired;
import org.springframework.web.bind.annotation.DeleteMapping;
import org.springframework.web.bind.annotation.GetMapping;
import org.springframework.web.bind.annotation.PathVariable;
import org.springframework.web.bind.annotation.PostMapping;
import org.springframework.web.bind.annotation.PutMapping;
import org.springframework.web.bind.annotation.RequestBody;
import org.springframework.web.bind.annotation.RestController;

import com.dineshonjava.customerservice.domain.Customer;
import com.dineshonjava.customerservice.repository.CustomerRepository;
import com.dineshonjava.customerservice.service.AccountService;

@RestController
public class CustomerController {
    @Autowired
    CustomerRepository customerRepository;
    @Autowired
    AccountService accountService;
    @PostMapping(value = "/customer")
    public Customer save (@RequestBody Customer customer){
        return customerRepository.save(customer);
    }
    @GetMapping(value = "/customer")
    public Iterable<Customer> all (){
        return customerRepository.findAll();
    }
    @GetMapping(value = "/customer/{customerId}")
    public Customer findByAccountId (@PathVariable Integer customerId){
        Customer customer =
    customerRepository.findByCustomerId(customerId);
        customer.setAccount(accountService.findByCutomer(customerId));
```

```
            return customer;
      }
      @PutMapping(value = "/customer")
      public Customer update (@RequestBody Customer customer){
            return customerRepository.save(customer);
      }
      @DeleteMapping(value = "/customer")
      public void delete (@RequestBody Customer customer){
            customerRepository.delete(customer);
            accountService.delete(customer);
      }
}
```

An interface `AccountService` annotated with `@FeignClient` has autowired with this controller class of the customer microservice. The complete code of these microservices (`AccountService`,`Customer Service`, and, web application service) is available on GitHub:
`https://github.com/PacktPublishing/Mastering-Spring-Boot-2.0`.

 Feign clients can be used to consume text-based HTTP APIs only, which means that they cannot handle binary data, for example, file uploads or downloads.

Let's run these microservices along with the Eureka Server, following the console output with the registered services with Eureka:

```
Initializing Spring FrameworkServlet 'dispatcherServlet'
FrameworkServlet 'dispatcherServlet': initialization started
FrameworkServlet 'dispatcherServlet': initialization completed in 34 ms
Registered instance CUSTOMER-SERVICE/MRNDTHTMOBL0002.timesgroup.com:customer-service:6161 with status UP (replication=false)
Registered instance ACCOUNT-SERVICE/MRNDTHTMOBL0002.timesgroup.com:account-service:6060 with status UP (replication=false)
```

Now access the following URL endpoint of the customer microservice:

`http://192.168.225.208:6161/customer/1001`

This will fetch information about the customer whose customer ID is `1001` and also fetch the account associated with this customer from the account microservice. Let's see the following output:

In this example, there are two accounts associated with the `1001` customer ID. In the next section, let's look at how to override the default configurations of the Feign client.

Overriding Feign defaults

The default configuration is used by each Spring Cloud Feign using `FeignClientsConfiguration`. Spring Cloud creates a new configuration context on-demand for each named client using the `FeignClientsConfiguration` file. This configuration file has almost all the required attributes of `FeignClient`, such as `feign.Decoder`, `feign.Encoder`, and `feign.Contract`. But Spring Cloud allows you to override these configuration attributes by adding an additional configuration file on top of `FeignClientsConfiguration`.

Spring Cloud Netflix provides the following beans as default configurations for Feign:

- **Decoder feignDecoder**: `ResponseEntityDecoder` class provides `feignDecode` bean
- **Encoder feignEncoder**: `SpringEncoder` class provides `feignEncoder` bean
- **Logger feignLogger**: `Slf4jLogger` class provides `feignLogger` bean
- **Contract feignContract**: `SpringMvcContract` class provides `feignContract` bean
- **Feign.Builder feignBuilder**: `HystrixFeign.Builder` class provides `feignBuilder` bean
- **Client feignClient**: If Ribbon is enabled it is a `LoadBalancerFeignClient`, otherwise the default Feign client is used

We can override all these listed default configurations for Feign either using the custom configuration file or the configuration properties file (YMAL or properties).

Let's see the following example of the configuration file:

```
@FeignClient(name = "account-service", configuration =
AccountConfiguration.class)
public interface AccountService {
    //..
}
```

Now, this `AccountService` client will be used for both the `FeignClientsConfiguration` and `AccountConfiguration` configurations, but the same attributes will be overridden by the attributes in the `AccountConfiguration` file.

 In the Feign client configuration, we don't need to annotate the `AccountConfiguration` class with `@Configuration`. If you have annotated it with the `@Configuration` annotation, then take care to exclude it from any `@ComponentScan` because this configuration will become the default source for `feign.Decoder`, `feign.Encoder`, `feign.Contract`, and so on. So, you have to avoid putting it with the common configuration files and put this file in a separate, non-overlapping package from any `@ComponentScan` or `@SpringBootApplication`, or you can also explicitly exclude this configuration file from the component scanning by using `@ComponentScan`.

The `@FeignClient` annotation also supports placeholders in the name and URL attributes of this annotation. Let's see the following example:

```
@FeignClient(name = "${feign.name}", url = "${feign.url}", configuration =
AccountConfiguration.class)
public interface AccountService {
    //..
}
```

Let's see the following configuration file that will be used with the `@FeignClient` annotation:

```
@Configuration
public class AccountConfiguration {
    @Bean
    public Contract feignContract() {
        return new feign.Contract.Default();
    }

    @Bean
    public BasicAuthRequestInterceptor basicAuthRequestInterceptor() {
        return new BasicAuthRequestInterceptor("user", "password");
    }
}
```

This configuration file replaces `SpringMvcContract` with `feign.Contract.Default` and adds a `RequestInterceptor` bean.

Spring Cloud also allows you to override the default configuration of the `@FiegnClient` annotation using configuration properties, let's see the following `.yml` file:

```
feign:
  client:
    config:
      feignName:
        connectTimeout: 5000
        readTimeout: 5000
        loggerLevel: full
        errorDecoder: com.dineshonjava.decode.CustomErrorDecoder
        retryer: com.dineshonjava.CustomRetryer
        requestInterceptors:
          - com.dineshonjava.interceptor.AccountRequestInterceptor
          - com.dineshonjava.interceptor.CustomRequestInterceptor
        decode404: false
        encoder: com.dineshonjava.CustomEncoder
        decoder: com.dineshonjava.CustomDecoder
        contract: com.dineshonjava.CustomContract
```

Spring Cloud also allows you to configure default configuration in the `@EnableFeignClients` attribute, `defaultConfiguration`. The given configuration in the `@EnableFeignClients` annotation will apply to all Feign clients. Let's see the following:

```
package com.dineshonjava.customerservice;

import org.springframework.boot.SpringApplication;
import org.springframework.boot.autoconfigure.SpringBootApplication;
import org.springframework.cloud.openfeign.EnableFeignClients;

@SpringBootApplication
@EnableFeignClients(defaultConfiguration=BasicFeignConfig.class)
public class CustomerServiceApplication {

    public static void main(String[] args) {
            SpringApplication.run(CustomerServiceApplication.class, args);
    }
}
```

Suppose we have both the `@Configuration` bean and configuration properties in our project, then configuration properties will be used. The configuration properties file overrides the `@Configuration` values. But you can change the priority to `@Configuration` by setting `feign.client.default-to-properties` to `false`.

Spring Cloud also allows you to create the Feign client manually, let's see it in the next section.

Creating Feign clients

You can create your own Feign client by using `Feign.builder()` to configure our interface-based client. Let's see the following class, which creates two Feign clients using the same interface:

```
@Import(FeignClientsConfiguration.class)
@RestController
class CustomerController {
    private AccountService customerAccuntService;
    private AccountService adminAccuntService;

  @Autowired
public CustomerController(
    Decoder decoder, Encoder encoder, Client client, Contract contract) {
    this.customerAccuntService = Feign.builder().client(client)
```

```
        .encoder(encoder)
        .decoder(decoder)
                .contract(contract)
        .requestInterceptor(new BasicAuthRequestInterceptor("customer",
        "customer"))
        .target(AccountService.class, "http://ACCOUNT-SERVICE");

    this.adminAccountService = Feign.builder().client(client)
            .encoder(encoder)
            .decoder(decoder)
            .contract(contract)
            .requestInterceptor(new BasicAuthRequestInterceptor("admin",
        "admin"))
        .target(AccountService.class, "http://ACCOUNT-SERVICE");
        }
    }
```

We have created two Feign clients of
the `AccountService` type, `cutomerAccountService` and `adminAccountService`, using
the Feign Builder API.

Feign inheritance support

We can also inherit interfaces to avoid boilerplate code for the same type of services. Feign
allows grouping common operations into convenient base interfaces. Let's see the following
example:

```
@FeignClient(name="account-service")
public interface AccountService {
    @GetMapping(value = "/account/customer/{customer}")
    List<Account> findByCutomer (@PathVariable("customer") Integer
    customer);
    ...
}
```

We can inherit this interface in the creation of another `FeignClient` service:

```
@FeignClient("users")
public interface AdminAccountService extends AccountService {
    ...
}
```

Multiple interfaces

Spring Cloud Netflix allows you to create multiple Feign client interfaces. These are defined as `Target<T>`, which allow for dynamic discovery and decoration of requests prior to execution:

```
AccountService accountService = Feign.builder().target(new
CloudIdentityTarget<AccountService>(user, apiKey));
```

Advanced usage of the Feign client

Feign supports inheritance and multiple inheritance; it helps to remove boilerplate code for a service to follow the same conventions. You can create a base API interface and inherit it for a specific API interface.

Let's see the example:

```
interface BaseAPI<T> {
  @GetMapping("/health")
  T get();

  @GetMapping("/all")
  List<T> all();
}
```

Let's define a specific API interface by inheriting the base interface methods:

```
interface CustomAPI extends BaseAPI<T> {
  @GetMapping("/custom")
  T custom();
}
```

Sometimes the resource representations are also consistent. So, you can declare to accept type parameters on the base API interface and you can inherit this base API interface to the specific interfaces. Let's see the example:

```
@Headers("Accept: application/json")
interface BaseApi<T> {

  @GetMapping("/api/{key}")
  T get(@PathVariable("key") String key);

  @GetMapping("/api")
  List<T> list();
```

```
    @Headers("Content-Type: application/json")
    @PutMapping("/api/{key}")
    void put(@PathVariable("key") String key, T value);
}

interface AccountApi extends BaseApi<Account> { }

interface CustomerApi extends BaseApi<Customer> { }
```

You can use the Feign to develop APIs interfaces, per our requirements, by using inheritances and defining base API interfaces for common conventions and common configurations related to the resource representation either for headers or responses.

Feign logging

As you know, logging is very important for every project. The Feign client only responds to a DEBUG level and, by default, the file name of the log is the full class name of the interface used to create the Feign client. A logger is created for each Feign client. The log level can be changed by setting the `logging.level.project.user.UserClient` property in the configuration property.

Let's see the following `application.yml` configuration file:

```
logging:
    level:
      project:
          user:
             UserClient: debug
```

You have the following choices of log level for your client application:

- **NONE**: No logging (DEFAULT)
- **BASIC**: This level of log responds to the request method and URL and the response status code and execution time
- **HEADERS**: This level of log responds to the basic information along with the request and response headers
- **FULL**: This level of log responds to the headers, body, and metadata for both requests and responses

Define the log level by using the Java configuration file for the Feign client, let's see the following example, set `Logger.Level` to `FULL`:

```
@Configuration
public class AccountConfiguration {
    @Bean
    Logger.Level feignLoggerLevel() {
        return Logger.Level.FULL;
    }
}
```

Exception handling

By default, Spring Cloud Netflix Feign throws `FeignException` for any type errors in any situation, but it is not always suitable and you don't want this same exception for every situation in your project. Netflix Feign allows you to set your own application-specific exception instead. You can do it easily by providing your own implementation of `feign.codec.ErrorDecoder` to `Feign.builder.errorDecoder()`.

Let's see an example of such an `ErrorDecoder` implementation:

```
public class AccountErrorDecoder implements ErrorDecoder {

    @Override
    public Exception decode(String methodKey, Response response) {
        if (response.status() >= 400 && response.status() <= 499) {
            return new AccountClientException(
                    response.status(),
                    response.reason()
            );
        }
        if (response.status() >= 500 && response.status() <= 599) {
            return new AccountServerException(
                    response.status(),
                    response.reason()
            );
        }
        return errorStatus(methodKey, response);
    }
}
```

Now you can use the preceding created exception by providing your `Feign.builder()`. Let's see the following example:

```
return Feign.builder()
             .errorDecoder(new AccountErrorDecoder())
             .target(AccountService.class, url);
```

`AccountErrorDecoder` sets a custom error decoder to the Feign Builder API. This code is simply adding a custom error decoder to the Feign client. We can create custom decoders and encoders for the Feign Builder API.

Custom encoders and decoders

The Feign Builder API allows us to create custom encoders for a request, and decoders for a response, to the Feign client.

Custom encoder

Let's create a custom encoder for a request body.

The request body data has been sent to the server by a POST method using either the String or byte[] parameter. You can add a Content-Type header:

```
interface AccountService {
    @PostMapping("/account/")
    @Headers("Content-Type: application/json")
    Account create(@RequestBody Account account);
}
```

Let's configure your own custom encoder; now it will be the `type-safe request` body. Let's see the following example using the `feign-gson` extension:

```
class Account {
    Integer accountId;
    Double balance;
    Integer customerId;
    String accountType;
    String branchCode;
    String bank;

public Account(Integer accountId, Double balance, Integer customerId,
String accountType, String branchCode,
            String bank) {
```

```
            super();
            this.accountId = accountId;
            this.balance = balance;
            this.customerId = customerId;
            this.accountType = accountType;
            this.branchCode = branchCode;
            this.bank = bank;
        }
        ...
    }

    interface AccountService {
        @PostMapping("/account/")
        @Headers("Content-Type: application/json")
        Account create(@RequestBody Account account);
    }
    ...
    AccountService client = Feign.builder()
                            .encoder(new GsonEncoder())
                            .target(AccountService.class,
                        "http://ACCOUNT_SERVICE");

    client.create(new Account(1001, 2304.32, 100, 'SAVING', 'HDFC0011',
    'HDFC'));
```

Custom decoder

`Feign.builder()` allows you to create a custom decoder and also allows you to add this decoder to the configuration of the Feign client to decode a response. You have to configure a non-default decoder if your interface returns some custom type or a type besides `Response`, `String`, `byte[]`, or `void`. Let's see following example of using the `feign-gson` extension:

```
    AccountService client = Feign.builder()
                        .decoder(new GsonDecoder())
                        .target(AccountService.class, "http://ACCOUNT-
                        SERVICE");
```

As you can see in the preceding code, `GsonDecoder` has been added as a response decoder to this Feign client. We can also create a custom decoder class for this Feign client.

Netflix Feign also supports Hystrix for the circuit-breaker pattern. Let's see this in the next section.

Feign and Hystrix

To create a resilient system, we have to implement reactive patterns, such as circuit-breaker patterns. The Feign client supports the circuit-breaker pattern by using Hystrix. We will discuss Hystrix and how we can write fallback methods in Chapter 10, *Building Resilient Systems Using Hystrix and Turbine*. Feign clients have direct support for fallbacks. If Hystrix is on the classpath and feign.hystrix.enabled=true, Feign will wrap all methods with a circuit-breaker. Returning com.netflix.hystrix.HystrixCommand is also available.

To implement the Feign client with Hystrix, just implement the interface with the fallback code, which will then be used when the actual call to the endpoint delivers an error.

Let's see the following example:

```
@FeignClient(name = "account-service", fallback =
HystrixClientFallback.class)
interface HystrixClient {
    @GetMapping("/account/{accountId}")
    Account get(@PathVariable Integer accountId);
}

class HystrixClientFallback implements HystrixClient {
    @Override
    public Account get() {
        return new new Account();
    }
}
```

As you can see in the preceding code, we have created the HystrixClient interface annotated with @FeignClient with its two attributes, name and fallback. The fallback attribute sets up with the HystrixClientFallback class, which has a fallback method. This fallback method will be executed when the circuit is open or there is an error. The fallback attribute of the given @FeignClient enables fallbacks to the class name that implements the fallback methods.

The HystrixClientFallback class has implemented the HystrixClient interface, overridden its get() method, and returned an account object with a default constructor.

You can also access the failure cause that made the fallback trigger, you can use the fallbackFactory attribute inside @FeignClient:

```
@FeignClient(name = "account-service", fallbackFactory =
HystrixClientFallbackFactory.class)
protected interface HystrixClient {
```

```
@GetMapping("/account/{accountId}")
 Account get(@PathVariable Integer accountId);
}

@Component
static class HystrixClientFallbackFactory implements
FallbackFactory<HystrixClient> {
    @Override
    public HystrixClient create(Throwable cause) {
        return new HystrixClient() {
            @Override
             public Account get() {
                 return new new Account("fallback; reason was: " +
                 cause.getMessage());
             }
        };
    }
}
}
```

We have learned how to set up circuit-breaker pattern by using Hystrix in the Feign client. This makes our system more resilient. We will discuss Hystrix more in Chapter 10, *Building Resilient Systems Using Hystrix and Turbine.*

 Prior to the Spring Cloud Dalston release, if Hystrix was on the classpath, Feign would have wrapped all the methods in a circuit-breaker by default. This default behavior was changed in Spring Cloud Dalston in favor of an opt-in approach.

Finally, let's see how to write a unit test using the Feign client in the cloud application.

Unit testing Feign clients

Let's create a unit test class; this test class can have several test methods but in this example, we have created three @Test methods, to test our client. The test will use static imports from the org.hamcrest.CoreMatchers.* and org.junit.Assert.* packages:

```
@Test
public void findAllAccountTest() throws Exception {
   List<Account> accounts = accountService.findAll();
   assertTrue(accounts.size() > 4);
}
@Test
public void findOneAccountTest() throws Exception {
    Account account = accountService.findByAccountId(1001);
```

```
        assertThat(account.getCustmer().getCustomerName(),
        containsString("Arnav"));
    }
    @Test
    public void createAccountTest() throws Exception {
        Account account = new Account(1001, 2304.32, 100, 'SAVING',
        'HDFC0011', 'HDFC')
        accountService.create(account);
        account = accountService.findByAccountId(1001);
        assertThat(account.getBank(), containsString("HDFC"));
    }
```

We have written unit test cases to test the `accountService` Feign client. In the first test method, we fetched all accounts in a list—the size of the list must be greater than five. In the second test method, we fetched one account with the `1001` account ID—the associated customer name must be `Arnav`. In the third test method, we created an account using the `accountService` Feign client.

Summary

In this chapter, we introduced and explained Feign, a declarative HTTP client developed by Netflix. We have learned how Feign simplifies HTTP API clients. We don't need to use a lot of boilerplate code to make the HTTP API clients application to access the microservices. You just simply use an annotated interface while the actual implementation will be created at the runtime.

The reader can learn to use Feign client and Hystrix support with the Feign client. This chapter has also implemented a custom encoder/decoder with exception handling for the Feign requests and responses. We have created some unit test cases to test the Feign client. The reader can also learn to use and customize the configurable options, such as logging and request compression.

In the next chapter, we will explore and implement event-driven systems.

Building Event-Driven and Asynchronous Reactive Systems

9

This chapter will provide a detailed overview of event-driven architecture to build event-driven microservices as cloud-native applications. We will look at some of the important concepts and themes behind handling data consistency in distributed systems, we will be building a reference application using Spring Cloud and Reactor in the following chapter.

In the previous chapters, we have created microservice applications and we have seen how to implement routing for distributed applications using the Netflix Zuul API, and we implemented a REST client using the declarative Feign client.

By the end of this chapter, you will have a better understanding of the event-driven microservices architecture and how to build an event-driven and asynchronous reactive system using Spring Cloud Stream. This chapter will explore the need and solution for asynchronous service communication, using reactive programming, with a reference application using ReactiveX and Reactive Spring.

This chapter will cover the following topics:

- Event-driven architecture patterns
- Introduction to reactive programming
- Spring Reactive
- ReactiveX
- Introduction to Command Query Responsibility Segregation
- Introduction to Event Sourcing
- Introduction to Eventual consistency
- Building an event-driven Reactive Asynchronous System

Event-driven architecture patterns

An event-driven architecture is a software architecture pattern that supports the production, deduction, consumption, and reaction to events. This is a commonly distributed architecture that is asynchronous and is used to develop highly scalable systems.

The main purpose of event-driven architecture patterns is to intercept the events and process them asynchronously. There are two types of topologies contained by event-driven architectures.

Mediator topology

Mediator topology contains a single event queue and a mediator that arranges for the events in the queue to be directed to their respective processors. The events are then passed through a filter or a preprocessor of events from an event channel.

The event queue can be implemented in the form of a simple message queue or an interface that passes messages in a large distributed system. The second form of implementation also requires the involvement of complex messaging protocols, such as Rabbit MQ, and Kafka.

Broker topology

Broker topology does not contain any event queue. In fact, the processors themselves are responsible for extracting the events and processing them. After one event is done processing, the processors have to indicate to another event, and then extract and process it. As per the name of the topology, the processor here acts as a broker to the chain of events, processing one event and then publishing another to process, and so the cycle goes on.

Some of the event-driven web frameworks include:

- Spring Reactor (JAVA)
- ReactiveX
- Netty (JAVA)
- Vert.X (JVM Languages)
- React PHP (PHP)

Since the event-driven architecture is asynchronous, the pattern lacks atomicity because no execution sequence is available for the events. The event processors are implemented to be highly distributed and asynchronous, hence the results are expected to be provided at any time in the future, most probably depending on the sequence of the callback.

Testability of this pattern is a bit difficult because of the asynchronous nature of the event-driven architecture. However, the performance of the event-driven architecture patterns is great because of the asynchronous and non-blocking nature of its executions. This allows the processes to be parallel and there is no queuing overhead involved.

Even though the scalability score of event-driven architecture is high, the effort of development is doubled. While the asynchronous nature of the pattern allows the architecture to be highly scalable, it also makes the testing of the pattern and its components difficult. The decoupled nature of the architecture also allows the processors to process the events parallel to each other, parallelism increasing the scalability even further.

One of the resulting benefits of the event-driven architecture pattern is that it allows the application to maintain data consistency over multiple servers and services without the help of any distributed transactions. However, this functionality also makes the complete model more complex, making it harder to understand and more difficult to be developed. The application will also automatically update the database and publish events.

Introduction to reactive programming

Reactive programming is customizing with non-concurrent information streams. That means it is coded with asynchronous data.

Streams are shoddy and omnipresent. Anything can be a stream—factors, client inputs, properties, reserves, information structures, and so forth. For instance, envision your Twitter channel as an information stream in a similar manner to snap occasions. You can tune in to that stream and respond as needs be.

Over that, you are given an astounding tool stash of capacities to consolidate, make, and channel any of those streams. That is the place the *practical* enchantment kicks in. A stream can be utilized as a contribution to another. Indeed, even different streams can be utilized as contributions to another stream. You can consolidate two streams. You can channel a stream to get another that has just those occasions you are keen on. You can delineate esteems starting with one stream then on to the next new one.

Let's see the following uses of reactive programming:

- **External service calls**: Many of the backend services these days implement the RESTful model and operate over HTTP. This makes their underlying protocols synchronous and blocking. External service calls help you avoid waiting for every IO completion.

- **Concurrent message consumers**: Message processing in the reactive programming framework includes measuring micro-benchmarks and is fast and efficient. The results of messages routing are at the staggering rate of tens of millions per second.

Let's see the following technologies and frameworks based on the reactive programming model in the next section.

Spring Reactive

Spring Reactive is a framework for Reactive web applications with reactive programming based. At the very least, reactive programming allows you to create applications with non-blocking services.

Most Java-based applications are built on the Servlet API, which was created with support for synchronous and blocking semantics. However, with increasing support for non-blocking I/O and asynchronous events, Spring MVC found it feasible to add an HTTP request that handles the existing applications.

But it is also true that introducing non-blocking I/O in an existing environment of frameworks and applications is not as easy or effective. For this reason, Spring Reactive was introduced to deal with asynchronous and non-blocking I/O. In the traditional Spring MVC, there is now a `TestController` section for Reactive web applications. This directs the applications to a new reactive engine with integration tests.

For Spring Reactive to work efficiently and effectively, the Reactive Stream spec is the most important aspect. The spec allows the connection among async component providers such as HTTP servers, web frameworks, and database drivers.

The Reactive Stream spec is small and consists of only four interfaces and some rules. To compose the asynchronous logic, however, the Reactive Stream spec needs an infrastructure, as it is exposed as an API. Spring Reactive uses a small library, known as Reactor Core, that is focused and serves as a foundation for other functions, libraries, and frameworks that wish to build on Reactive Streams.

Their quality lies in their ability to serve more demand simultaneously, and to deal with activities with inactivity, for example, asking for information from a remote server, all the more productively. Not at all like customary preparing, which hinders the present string while at the same time holding up an outcome, a Reactive API that holds up costs nothing, asks for just the measure of information it can process, and carries new abilities, since it manages the stream of information, not just singular components one by one.

Spring Reactive programming models allow for writing non-blocking services and applications. It shifts your imperative programming approach to the async, non blocking and functional styled code at time of interacting external resources.

I needed to think about three illustrations—a situation where the already present Java 8 `CompletableFuture` is reverted as a type; where RxJava's `Observable` is reverted as a type; and a third with Spring Reactor Core's Flux compose.

ReactiveX

ReactiveX is a library for asynchronous and event-driven programs. It supports sequences of data and events by extending the observer pattern. It has operators that allow declaring sequences while being free of worries regarding things such as low-level threading, thread safety, synchronization, and non-blocking IOs. ReactiveX is functional, reactive, and operates on discrete values that have changed over time.

The ReactiveX Observable model was designed to help you deal with asynchronous events as easily as arrays. It removes the complexity of the callback, making your code more readable and less vulnerable to bugs. Some of the advantages of the ReactiveX Observable model are:

- **Composable**: The ReactiveX Observable model makes creating a flow of asynchronous events very easy and helps compose their flows and the sequence of the event. Although other techniques, such as Java Future, are very straightforward for the use of asynchronous events, they add unnecessary non-trivial complexity.

- **Flexible**: This model supports many different types of values instead of just scalar values. This allows the model some flexibility and elegance that helps in other use cases.

- **Less opinionated**: The observable model can be implemented using thread loops, event loops, non-blocking I/O, or whatever implementation meets your requirements. It is not biased toward particular sources of concurrency and asynchronicity.

- **No callbacks**: Callbacks create a lot of problems in the code when used with the nested execution of asynchronous events.

- **Polyglot implementation**: ReactiveX is implementing a number of different languages in the `Observable` model.

Let's see another pattern for making a system reactive and event-driven asynchronous.

Introduction to Command Query Responsibility Segregation

This pattern is based on the idea of **command-query separation** (**CQS**). So, according to CQS, we have to divide our command and query separately to make the system more reactive and robust. This command means the query to write something into the database to change the state of the domain, and the query means ready only query that doesn't change the state of the domain. These queries are based on the ready on access either from another database or somewhere in the cache. Let's look at the following:

- Commands, changing state of the system
- Queries, getting some information from the system

The CQRS naturally fits with some other architectural patterns, such as event-based programming models. It's common to see CQRS systems split into separate services communicating with event collaboration. This allows these services to easily take advantage of Event Sourcing.

This architectural pattern improves the performance of a distributed application where the application is required to process complex domain-driven programming. So, it separates this domain-driven module from the other part where we are querying data for representation and reading only. We can use either messaging or event-driven software architecture asynchronously with non-blocking calls to write into the database. Let's see the following application architecture and see how the CQRS pattern is used in the system architecture:

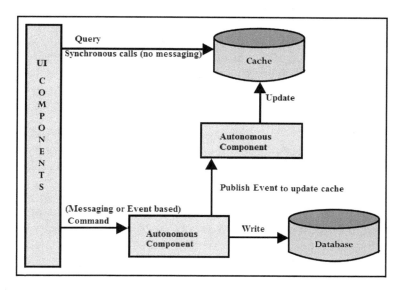

As you can see, the system has divided into two different parts, such as read only query (the components used for reading) and command query (the components used for writing). The commands are responsible for performing an action or changing states of the system. The **Autonomous Component** is a piece of business logic that can update the Domain model and inform the client about whether this change has been accepted or not. The **Autonomous Component** also notifies everyone whenever any changes are detected. In the preceding diagram, the first AC component publishes a domain event to update the database and also notifies another AC component to update cache using in the application.

The second part is querying data for representation for the client, it is getting information from the system without changing its state. This part uses only the View model rather than the Domain model. This CQRS pattern is all about the separation of concerns between the Domain and View models, and these models can operate asynchronously to improve the performance of the application. Let's see another pattern that is commonly used with the CQRS pattern—the Event Sourcing pattern.

Introduction to the Event Sourcing pattern

According to the Event Sourcing pattern, to capture all changes to the system states as a sequence of events is known as event sourcing.

We can say that all information and data in the system is persisted in the form of events, and an event is nothing but a piece of information to tell the system about something that has occurred, such as domain creation, update, and deletion. The generated events are immutable by nature, you cannot modify or delete them. So, it is totally based on the occurrences in the system, if something has occurred in the system, the events will be triggered.

The main concept behind the Event Sourcing pattern is capturing every change of the state of an application during processing into an event object. These event objects are stored in the sequence to be triggered in the same scope as the application-processing scope.

Suppose we have a distributed application with two microservices, Account and Customer for example, and we want to trigger a notification to the customers for any new customer added or any modification to the data of customers. And also we want to trigger a mobile notification when any change happens to the accounts associated with customers. Let's see the following diagram:

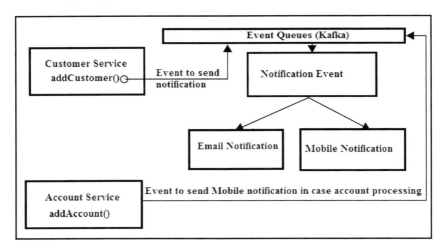

In this example, as you can see in the preceding diagram, we have introduced the Event Sourcing pattern, and added a step to this process. Now the service creates an event object to record the change and processes it to update the customer and account.

We have seen an Event Sourcing-based system with Command Query Responsibility Segregation, which has two parts, command and querying. The command query is all about writing databases, and querying is all about reading data for the frontend. But having separate models raises questions about the data consistency for those models which are used in the frontend. Let's see how to maintain data consistency in the distributed event-driven system using Eventual consistency.

Introduction to Eventual consistency

Eventual consistency is a consistency model for the event-based distributed application to achieve high availability. If there are no changes for domain into a system, then it will return the last updated value for that domain. Eventual consistency is also known as optimistic replication and strongly used in distributed systems.

In the diagram of the CQRS pattern, we have used the cache for returning data for queries sent by the client, so, the cache will be updated if there are no changes for domain into a system. In fact, almost every cache is based on Eventual consistency.

Typically in event-sourced systems with Command Query Responsibility Segregation that need to display data to a client, we have three components that must cooperate:

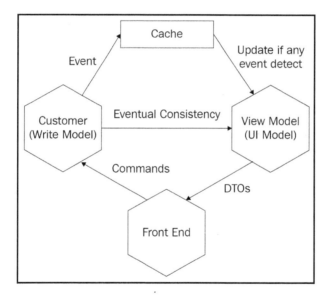

As you can see, the **Write Model** accepts **Commands** and generates **Event** to its database and **Cache** to be updated. The read model accepts events and returns data objects to the frontend client.

We have discussed some patterns for the event-driven distributed system, such as event-driven architecture, Command Query Responsibility Segregation, Event Sourcing, and the Eventual consistency model. Now we will implement an event-driven asynchronous system using a messaging queue, such as Kafka and Spring Cloud Stream, in the next section.

Building an event-driven Reactive Asynchronous System

Let's build a sample project that demonstrates how to create a real-time streaming application using event-driven architecture, Spring Cloud Stream, Spring Boot, Apache Kafka, and Spring Netflix Eureka. Let's see the application architecture:

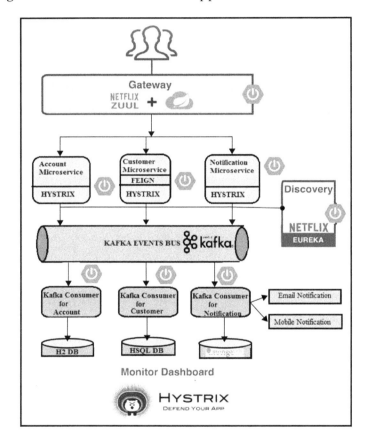

We have used Netflix Hystrix to implement the circuit breaker pattern, we will discuss it in `Chapter 10`, *Building Resilient Systems Using Hystrix and Turbine*. We also configured the API Gateway proxy using Netflix Zuul, as we have already discussed in `Chapter 7`, *Creating API Gateway with Netflix Zuul Proxy*.

In previous chapters, we have discussed using microservices architectures to decouple large and complex systems into simple independent micoservices. In this chapter, we are discussing the Event-driven microservices architecture, it is a methodology used to produce, handle events, and implement applications where events transmit among decoupled software components and services.

We are going to create an application with microservices, such as `Account`, `Customer`, and `Notification`. Whenever we create a customer record or create an account for a customer, a notification service sends an email and a mobile notification.

We have three decoupled services—`Account`, `Customer`, and `Notification`. All of them are independently deployable applications. And also we have the edge service for API Gateway using Netflix Zuul. The `Account` service can be used to create, read, update, delete customer accounts. The `Account` service sends a message to the Kafka topic when a new account is created.

Similarly, the `Customer` service is used to create, read, update, delete a customer in the database. The `Customer` service sends a message to the Kafka topic when a new customer is created. And the `Notification` service sends email and SMS notifications. The `Notification` service listens on topics from incoming customer and account messages and then processes these messages by sending notifications to the given email and mobile.

The `Account` and `Customer` microservices have their own H2 database, and `Notification` service uses MongoDB. In this application, we will use the Spring Cloud Stream module to provide abstract messaging mechanisms in the application; it is a framework for building event-driven microservice applications.

Introducing Spring Cloud Streaming

Spring Cloud Stream is a framework to build message-driven microservice applications. It abstracts away the message producer and consumer code from message-broker-specific implementations. Spring Cloud Stream provides input and output channels to service communications to the outside world. Spring Cloud Stream is created on top of Spring Boot, it can create a standalone and production-grade applications.Spring Integration provides the message broker's connectivity to the Spring Cloud Stream. Message brokers, such as Kafka and RabbitMQ, can be added easily by just injecting a binding dependency to the code of your application.

Let's see the Maven dependency for Spring Cloud Stream:

```
<dependency>
<groupId>org.springframework.cloud</groupId>
<artifactId>spring-cloud-stream-reactive</artifactId>
</dependency>
```

In the preceding Maven dependency, we have added the Spring Cloud Stream dependency reactive model. Let's see how to enable the application to connect with the message broker:

```
@EnableBinding(NotificationStreams.class)
public class StreamsConfig {
}
```

In the preceding code, the `@EnableBinding` annotation is used to enable connectivity between the application and message broker. This annotation takes one or more interfaces as parameters, in our case, we have passed the `NotificationStreams` interface as a parameter, let's see this interface:

```
public interface NotificationStreams {
String INPUT = "notification-in";
String OUTPUT = "notification-out";
@Input(INPUT)
SubscribableChannel subscribe();
@Output(OUTPUT)
MessageChannel notifyTo();
}
```

As you can see, the interface declares input and/or output channels. This is our custom interface in this example but you can also use interfaces such as Source, Sink, and Processor, provided by the Spring Cloud Stream:

- **Source**: This interface can be used for an application that has a single outbound channel
- **Sink**: This interface can be used for an application that has a single inbound channel
- **Processor**: This interface can be used for an application that has both an inbound and an outbound channel

And also in the preceding code, the `@Input` annotation is used to identify an input channel by using this identifier it receives message which enter to the application. Similarly, the `@Output` annotation is used to identify an output channel, by using this identifier, published messages leave the application.

The `@Input` and `@Output` annotations take the name parameter as a channel name, if name is not provided, then by default name of the annotated method will be used. In this application, we have used Kafka as a message broker. Let's learn more about Kafka.

Adding Kafka to your application

Apache Kafka is a publish-subscribe-based high-performance and horizontally-scalable messaging platform. It is fast, scalable, and distributed by design. LinkedIn develops it. Spring Cloud Stream supports binder implementations for Kafka and RabbitMQ. First, we have to install Kafka in your machine. Let's see how to install it.

Installing and running Kafka

Let's download Kafka from `https://kafka.apache.org/downloads` and untar it using the following commands:

```
> tar -xzf kafka_2.12-1.1.0.tgz
> cd kafka_2.12-1.1.0
```

Let's start ZooKeeper and Kafka on Windows:

```
> bin\windows\zookeeper-server-start.bat configzookeeper.properties
> bin\windows\kafka-server-start.bat configserver.properties
```

You can start ZooKeeper and Kafka on Linux by using the following commands:

```
> bin/zookeeper-server-start.sh config/zookeeper.properties
> bin/kafka-server-start.sh config/server.properties
```

After starting Kafka on your machine, let's add the Kafka Maven dependency in your application:

```
<dependency>
<groupId>org.springframework.cloud</groupId>
<artifactId>spring-cloud-stream-binder-kafka</artifactId>
</dependency>
<dependency>
<groupId>org.springframework.cloud</groupId>
<artifactId>spring-cloud-stream-binder-kafka-streams</artifactId>
</dependency>
```

As you can see, we have added Spring Cloud Stream and Kafka binder. After adding these dependencies, let's configure the configuration properties for Kafka.

Configuration properties for Kafka

Let's see the following `application.yml` configuration file for a microservice:

```
spring:
  application:
    name: customer-service
  cloud:
    stream:
      kafka:
        binder:
          brokers:
          - localhost:9092
      bindings:
        notification-in:
          destination: notification
          contentType: application/json
        notification-out:
          destination: notification
          contentType: application/json
```

As you can see, this file configures the address of the Kafka server to connect to, and the Kafka topic we use for both the inbound and outbound streams in our code. The `contentType` properties tell Spring Cloud Stream to send or receive our message objects as strings in the streams.

Service used to write to Kafka

Let's see the following service class that is responsible for writing to Kafka in our application:

```
@Servicepublic class NotificationService {

  private final NotificationStreams notificationStreams;

  public NotificationService(NotificationStreams notificationStreams) {
    super();
    this.notificationStreams = notificationStreams;
  }

  public void sendNotification(final Notification notification) {
```

```
MessageChannel messageChannel = notificationStreams.notifyTo();
messageChannel.send(MessageBuilder.withPayload(notification)
    .setHeader(MessageHeaders.CONTENT_TYPE, MimeTypeUtils.APPLICATION_JSON)
    .build());
  }
}
```

In the preceding service class, the `sentNotification()` method uses an injected `NotificationStreams` object to send message represented by the `Notification` object in our application. Let's see the following `Controller` class that will trigger sending the message to Kafka.

Rest API controller

Let's see a Rest Controller class that we'll use to create a REST API endpoint. This controller will trigger sending a message to Kafka using the `NotificationService` Spring Bean:

```
@RestController
public class CustomerController {
...
@Autowired
CustomerRepository customerRepository;
@Autowired
AccountService accountService;
@Autowired
NotificationService notificationService;
@PostMapping(value = "/customer")
public Customer save (@RequestBody Customer customer){
Notification notification = new Notification("Customer is created",
"admin@dineshonjava.com", "9852XXX122");
notificationService.sendNotification(notification);
return customerRepository.save(customer);
}
...
...
}
```

As you can see in the preceding Controller class of `Customer` service, this class has a dependency with `NotificationService`. The `save()` method is responsible for creating a customer in the corresponding database, and also it creates a notification message using the `Notification` object and sends it to Kafka using the `sendNotification()` method of `NotificationService`. Let's see another side how Kafka listen to this message using topic name notification.

Listening to a Kafka topic

Let's create a listener `NotificationListener` class that will be used to listen to messages on the Kafka notification topic and send email and SMS notifications to the customer:

```
@Component
public class NotificationListener {
@StreamListener(NotificationStreams.INPUT)
public void sendMailNotification(@Payload Notification notification) {
System.out.println("Sent notification to email: "+notification.getEmail()+"
Message: "+notification.getMessage());
}
@StreamListener(NotificationStreams.INPUT)
public void sendSMSNotification(@Payload Notification notification) {
System.out.println("Notified with SMS to mobile:
"+notification.getMobile()+" Message: "+notification.getMessage());
}
}
```

The `NotificationListener` class has two methods—`sendMailNotification()` and `sendSMSNotification()`. These methods will be invoked by Spring Cloud Stream with every new `Notification` message object on the Kafka notification topic. These methods are annotated with `@StreamListener`. This annotation makes the method listener cause it to receive events for stream processing.

This chapter doesn't have the complete code for this event-driven application, you can find the complete code in the GitHub repository at `https://github.com/PacktPublishing/Mastering-Spring-Boot-2.0`.

Let's run this application and test how this event-driven works. First, we have to ensure we run Kafka and Zookeeper as we discussed in the previous section. The Kafka server will be run at `http://localhost:9092`.

Now let's run `EurekaServer`, `ApiZuulService`, `AccountService`, `CustomerService`, and `NotificationService`. Let's open Eureka dashboard on the browser:

Instances currently registered with Eureka			
Application	**AMIs**	**Availability Zones**	**Status**
ACCOUNT-SERVICE	n/a (1)	(1)	UP (1) - MRNDTHTMOBL0002.timesgroup.com:account-service:6060
API-GATEWAY	n/a (1)	(1)	UP (1) - MRNDTHTMOBL0002.timesgroup.com:API-GATEWAY:8080
CUSTOMER-SERVICE	n/a (1)	(1)	UP (1) - MRNDTHTMOBL0002.timesgroup.com:customer-service:6161
NOTIFICATION-SERVICE	n/a (1)	(1)	UP (1) - MRNDTHTMOBL0002.timesgroup.com:notification-service:6262

As you can see, all services are running now, let's create a `Customer` object to trigger the event to Kafka. Here I am using Postman as a REST client, we will discuss in Postman in `Chapter 11`, *Testing Spring Boot Application*. Let's see the following diagram, where we have created a new customer using the `http://localhost:8080/api/customers/customer` API endpoint through Zuul API Gateway:

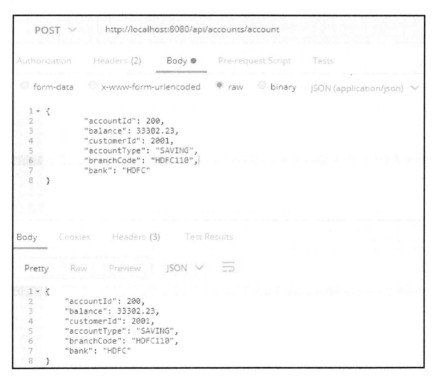

As you can see, we have entered a new customer record in the database. As we have discussed, whenever a new customer is created, it will trigger a message to Kafka to send email and SMS notifications using the `Notification` microservice. Let's see the following console output of the `Notification` microservice:

We have created a new customer using `Customer` service and it will trigger a notification to be sent to the customer using the Kafka broker. It is a message-driven asynchronous call.

Similarly, whenever we create an account record for a new customer, Kafka will listen for another new notification message for the account creation:

Let's verify the console of the `Notification` microservice:

```
Console 🔲  Progress  Problems  Search
Chapter-09-notification-service - NotificationServiceApplication [Spring Boot App] C:\Program Files\Java\jre1.8.0_161\bin\javaw.exe
Sent notification to email: admin@dineshonjava.com Message: Customer is created
Notified with SMS to mobile: 9852XXX122 Message: Customer is created
```

As you can see, we have created an account record for the customer, it has triggered a message to Kafka to send email and SMS notifications to the customer, let's check the customer record for the customer we just created by visiting `http://localhost:8080/api/customers/customer/2001`:

```
localhost:8080/api/custo  X

← → C  ⓘ localhost:8080/api/customers/customer/2001

{
    customerId: 2001,
    customerName: "Rushika Rajput",
    mobile: "94312XX223",
    email: "rushikaxxx@mail.com",
    city: "Noida",
  - account: [
      - {
            accountId: 200,
            balance: 33302.23,
            customerId: 2001,
            accountType: "SAVING",
            branchCode: "HDFC110",
            bank: "HDFC"
        }
    ]
}
```

As you can see, the customer has complete information including an associated account object. So, in this chapter, we created an event-driven microservice using the Spring Cloud Stream, Kafka Event Bus, Spring Netflix Zuul, and Spring Discovery service. You can find the complete code for this chapter in the GitHub repository `https://github.com/PacktPublishing/Mastering-Spring-Boot-2.0`.

Summary

We have explored some design patterns, such as event-driven architecture patterns, Command Query Responsibility Segregation, Event Sourcing, and Eventual consistency. Spring Cloud Stream provides another way to create a distributed application based on the event-driven and message-driven architecture.

We created a system based on the event-driven architecture with multiple microservices. We used Kafka as a message broker and Spring Cloud Stream to provide support for the Kafka and RabbitMQ binder. But, in this chapter, we implemented this event-driven system using Kafka.

In the next chapter, we will explore and implement a Resilient System using Hystrix and Turbine.

10
Building Resilient Systems Using Hystrix and Turbine

In this chapter, we will explore the circuit-breaker pattern with a reference implementation using the Netflix Hystrix library, looking at configuring the Turbine dashboard to aggregate Hystrix streams from multiple services. We will also cover some important aspects of the Turbine dashboard to aggregate the data streams from multiple services.

In microsystem architecture, we have seen that a monolithic application is divided into several pieces of software, and each is deployed as an individual service. This system is known as a *distributed system*. It has a lot of benefits, as we discussed in `Chapter 4`, *Getting Started with Spring Cloud and Configuration*. Due to the distributed nature of cloud-native applications, they have more potential failure modes than monolith applications. As the number of services will be increased in distributed systems, it will also increase the chance of cascading failures.

As each incoming request must now potentially touch tens or even hundreds of different microservices, some failure in one or more of those dependencies is virtually guaranteed. Let's see the famous quote regarding fault tolerance:

> *"Without taking steps to ensure fault tolerance, 30 dependencies each with 99.99% uptime would result in 2+ hours downtime/month (99.99%30= 99.7% uptime = 2+ hours in a month)."*

> *– Ben Christensen, Netflix engineer*

In this chapter, we will discuss a pattern to prevent the cascading failures of these microservices and avoid negative availability services in the distributed systems.

By the end of this chapter, you will have a better understanding of fault tolerance, and the circuit-breaker pattern, how to use the Netflix Hystrix library to prevent cascading failures in a distributed system, and how to enable Hystrix and Turbine dashboard to monitor the failures.

This chapter will cover the following points:

- Circuit-breaker pattern
- Using the Hystrix library with a reference implementation
- Customizing the default configuration
- Hystrix Metrics Stream
- Hystrix Dashboard
- Turbine dashboard
- REST consumer with Hystrix and Feign

Let's look at these topics in detail.

Circuit-breaker pattern

In distributed software systems, it is very common to make several remote calls to the services running in the different machines with different environments across a network. As you know, remote calls can fail due to the overload from clients without a response until a timeout limit is reached. So, it is a very serious problem for distributed systems. In monoliths, it is not very common to call remote services outside of the application, monoliths mostly require in-memory calls. There is a big difference between in-memory calls and remote calls, remote calls can fail.

The circuit-breaker can help prevent these failures in a distributed software system. The idea behind the circuit-breaker is very simple, you just create a circuit-breaker object for a remote function call that monitors for cascading failures in the distributed software systems. Every circuit-breaker has a threshold of failures, once it is reached, the circuit-breaker opens in the system. All further calls to the circuit-breaker return with an error, an empty object, or hardcoded values without the protected call being made at all.

The circuit-breaker prevents failures from constantly recurring in a system. Design patterns provide solutions for the recurring issues, tasks, and bugs a developer comes across during software programming. One of the lesser-known examples of these design patterns is the circuit-breaker design pattern. The circuit-breaker pattern plans to open the *circuit* in the wake of hitting a configurable edge of mistaken method calls. A characteristic fit is the utilization of an interceptor to gauge the execution and screen the exceptions; subsequent to achieving the limit, the interceptor returns without calling the objective.

Let's see the following diagram of a distributed software system:

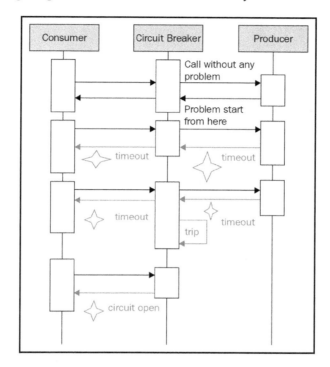

In this diagram, a **Consumer** calls the remote services of the **Producer** through the **Circuit Breaker**. This **Circuit Breaker** monitors the failures. If any problem occurs in the system related to network failures, the system hangs due to overload that is situation of the **timeout, Circuit Breaker** monitor all such type failure and prevents cascading failure once it reached threshold of failures. The **Circuit Breaker** opens and serves the request without calling the remote service produced by the **Producer** in the distributed software system.

While timeouts constrain framework asset utilization, the circuit-breaker pattern is more useful. An electrical switch recognizes failures and keeps the mobile app from endeavoring to play out an activity that is destined to fall flat. As opposed to the HttpClient Retry design, this design pattern tends to eradicate recurring bugs.

You can utilize the circuit-breaker design pattern to spare client-side assets from any calls that are bound to fail, and additionally to spare assets of the server side. In case the server is in a wrong state, for example an overload state, which is not a smart thought to include additional heap on the server as a rule.

The circuit-breaker design pattern enlivens and screens a secured work call. Contingent upon the present state, the call will either be rejected or executed. As a rule, a circuit-breaker actualizes three kinds of states:

- Closed
- Open
- Half-open

Let's see the following diagram about the circuit-breaker states:

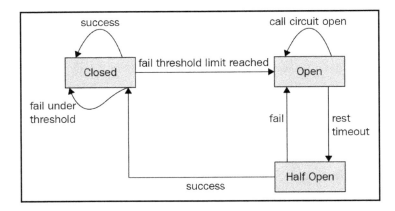

The circuit-breaker will be **Closed** for all **success** remote calls or **fail under threshold** for certain threshold. Once the failures cross the limit of the threshold, the circuit-breaker opens. And after, the circuit will **reset timeout** and move to a **half Open** state, once it successful it will be closed.

Inside the closed state, transactions and their metrics will now be saved and the call is executed. These measurements are important to execute. It's more about the system's health. In the case the health of the system is affected, the circuit-breaker passes away from any confining open state. Within this state, the majority of the calls are dismissed instantly with no calls that are. The motivation behind the open state is to give the server side time to recoup and redress the issue.

At the point when the circuit-breaker goes to an open state, a timeout clock is begun. In the event that this clock lapses, the electrical switch changes into a half-open state. Inside the half-open state, most of the calls are executed once in a while to check whether the issue has been settled. Assuming everything is alright, at that point the state changes back to closed.

The circuit-breaker channel actualizes a *before* execution and an *after* execution strategy. Inside the *before* execution technique, the system verifies whether the demand execution is permitted. A devoted circuit-breaker example is utilized for each objective host, keeping in mind the end goal to dodge reactions. In the case that this call is permitted, the HTTP exchange shall be maintained to keep up the measurements. This exchange metric question will be closed inside the *after* execution technique by appointing the outcome to the exchange. A 5xx status reaction will be translated as an error.

The circuit-breaker example can, likewise, be executed on the server side. The extent of the server-side channel is the objective task rather than the objective host. If the objective task being prepared is incorrect, calls will be instantly dismissed with the error status. Utilizing a server-side channel guarantees that a wrong activity won't be permitted to devour an excessive number of assets.

In the next section, let's look at how Spring Cloud supports this circuit-breaker pattern by using Netflix Hystrix as a fault tolerance in the distributed microservices.

Using the Hystrix library with a reference implementation

Spring Cloud supports Netflix utilities, and Netflix has produced a library based on the circuit-breaker pattern implementation called *Hystrix*. In a microservice architecture, we can use the Hystrix library to prevent cascading failures, because it is very common in the microservice architecture to have several individual services hosted on different machines across a network. The microservice-based system has multiple layers of service calls.

In a microservice architecture, the failure of a lower-level service can be caused due to the cascading failure of the whole distributed system. So, Netflix Hystrix provides a way to prevent the failure of a whole system by using fallback calls and the developer can provide a fallback. Each circuit-breaker has its own threshold for failure. In Hystrix, if a particular service is called more than `circuitBreaker.requestVolumeThreshold` (default: 20 requests) and failure attempt percentage is more than `circuitBreaker.errorThresholdPercentage` (default: >50%) in a trip defined by `metrics.rollingStats.timeInMilliseconds` (default: 10 seconds), then Hystrix opens and a call is not made to that particular service.

Let's see how the Hystrix fallback prevents cascading failures:

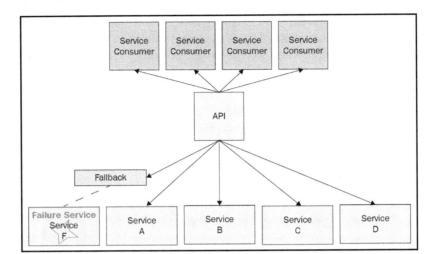

Hystrix **Fallback** prevents cascading failures in the distributed system, which has several services, such as **Service A**, **Service B**, **Service C**, **Service D**, and **Service E**. **Service Consumer** calls these remote services using the **API** gateway, but any specific service failure can be the cause of the whole system failure. Having an open circuit stops this whole failure of the system and allows the failing services time to heal. This fallback is provided by the developer and it can be another Hystrix protected call, empty object, or some static data. The developer can also define a chain of **Fallback** to make a call for a business task that turns another fallback into static data or an empty business object. It is totally dependent on the business need.

Let's see how to include and configure the Hystrix in our application.

Configuring Hystrix in your application

We will cover Spring Cloud Netflix Hystix with an example we discussed in the previous chapters. We will use the same example and implement the circuit-breaker pattern, which creates a strategy against cascading failure at lower levels of services in a distributed system. We will configure Hystrix in our application of `customer` and `Account` microservices, as we discussed in the previous chapters:

- `Account` microservice: This microservice will give some basic functionality to the `Account` entity. We will call this `Account` service from `customer` service to understand circuit-breaker. It will run on port `6060` in localhost.
- `Customer` microservice: This is also a REST-based microservice where we will implement the circuit-breaker using Hystrix. The `Account` microservice will be invoked from this `Customer` microservice and we will see the fallback path once the `Account` service is unavailable. It will run on port `6161` in localhost.

Hystrix is monitoring methods that call the remote services for failing calls. If there is such a failure, it will open the circuit and forward the call to a fallback method. The Hystrix library will tolerate failures up to a threshold. As the threshold is reached, it opens the circuit-breaker to forward all subsequent calls to the fallback method, to prevent failure of the whole system at once and it gives a time to failure service for recovering from its failing state to a healthy state.

Maven dependency

Add the Starter with the `org.springframework.cloud` group and the `spring-cloud-starter-netflix-hystrix` artifact ID to include Hystrix in your application. Let's see the following Maven dependency in the `pom.xml` file:

```
<dependency>
    <groupId>org.springframework.cloud</groupId>
    <artifactId>spring-cloud-starter-netflix-hystrix</artifactId>
</dependency>
```

Add this Maven dependency to your project to include the Hystrix library.

Enabling circuit-breaker

Add the `@EnableCircuitBreaker` annotation to the `main` configuration application to enable the circuit-breaker in your project. Let's see the following code:

```
package com.dineshonjava.customerservice;

import org.springframework.boot.SpringApplication;
import org.springframework.boot.autoconfigure.SpringBootApplication;
import org.springframework.cloud.client.circuitbreaker.EnableCircuitBreaker;
import org.springframework.cloud.client.loadbalancer.LoadBalanced;
import org.springframework.cloud.netflix.eureka.EnableEurekaClient;
```

```
import org.springframework.context.annotation.Bean;
import org.springframework.web.client.RestTemplate;

@SpringBootApplication
@EnableEurekaClient
@EnableCircuitBreaker
public class CustomerServiceApplication {

    public static void main(String[] args) {
        SpringApplication.run(CustomerServiceApplication.class, args);
    }
    ...
         ...
}
```

I have used the `@EnableCircuitBreaker` annotation to enable the circuit-breaker pattern in the application. Let's see how to add Hystrix functionalities in the service layer of the application.

Adding the Hystrix annotation in services

Netflix Hystrix provides an annotation, `@HystrixCommand`, which we can use at the service layer to add the functionality of the circuit-breaker pattern. Let's see the following code:

```
package com.dineshonjava.customerservice.service;

import java.util.ArrayList;
import java.util.List;

import org.springframework.beans.factory.annotation.Autowired;
import org.springframework.cloud.client.loadbalancer.LoadBalanced;
import org.springframework.stereotype.Service;
import org.springframework.web.client.RestTemplate;

import com.dineshonjava.customerservice.domain.Account;
import com.netflix.hystrix.contrib.javanica.annotation.HystrixCommand;

@Service
public class AccountServiceImpl implements AccountService {
    @Autowired
    @LoadBalanced
    RestTemplate restTemplate;
    @HystrixCommand(fallbackMethod = "defaultAccount")
    public List<Account> findByCutomer(Integer customer) {
        //do stuff that might fail
```

```
            return restTemplate.getForObject("http://ACCOUNT-
            SERVICE/account/customer/{customer}", List.class, customer);
    }
        public List<Account> defaultAccount() {
                /* something useful */;
        return new ArrayList<>();
            }
    }
```

We have used an annotation, @HystrixCommand(fallbackMethod =
"defaultAccount"), on top of the findByCutomer(Integer customer) method. And
the fallbackMethod attribute denotes the defaultAccount() method for a fallback
condition. The fallback method can have any access modifier. As you know, Netflix has
produced a very powerful library for fault tolerance. Hystrix allows you to wrap the code
in HystrixCommand objects after wrapping that code in a circuit-breaker.

Spring Cloud creates a proxy for those Spring Beans that are annotated with the
@HystrixCommand annotation, and that proxy is connected to the Hystrix circuit-breaker.
And that circuit-breaker monitors when to open and close the circuit, and also takes
decisions in the case of a failure to perform an action. You can also use the
commandProperties attribute with a list of @HystrixProperty annotations to configure
@HystrixCommand.

It's important to remember that the Hystrix command and fallback should be placed in the
same class and have the same method signature (optional parameter for failed execution
exception).

As we have declared a method, defaultAccount, it will be used to process fallback logic
in case of any errors. If you need to run the defaultAccount fallback method as separate
Hystrix command, then you need to annotate it with the HystrixCommand annotation:

```
@HystrixCommand(fallbackMethod = "defaultAccount")
public Account getAccountById(String id) {
    return accountService.getAccountById(id);
}

@HystrixCommand
private Account defaultAccount(String id) {
  return new Account();
}
```

As you can see, we have marked a fallback method with `@HystrixCommand`, now this `defaultAccount` fallback method also has another fallback method:

```
@HystrixCommand(fallbackMethod = "defaultAccount")
    public Account getAccountById(String id) {
        return accountService.getAccountById(id);
    }

    @HystrixCommand(fallbackMethod = "defaultUserSecond")
     private Account defaultAccount(String id) {
        return new Account();
    }
    @HystrixCommand
    private Account defaultAccountSecond(String id) {
        return new Account("1002", "2000");
    }
```

We have declared second a `defaultAccountSecond` fallback method as a fallback method of the first `defaultAccount` fallback method.

The Hystrix library also allows you to pass the extra parameter in order to get an exception thrown by a command. Let's see the following example:

```
@HystrixCommand(fallbackMethod = "fallback1")
public Account getAccountById(String id) {
    throw new RuntimeException("getAccountById command raised error");
}

@HystrixCommand(fallbackMethod = "fallback2")
Account fallback1(String id, Throwable e) {
    throw new RuntimeException("fallback1 raised error");
}

@HystrixCommand(fallbackMethod = "fallback3")
Account fallback2(String id) {
    throw new RuntimeException("fallback2 raised error");
}

@HystrixCommand(fallbackMethod = "staticFallback")
Account fallback3(String id, Throwable e) {
    throw new RuntimeException("fallback3 raised error");
}

Account emptyObjectFallback(String id, Throwable e) {
    return new Account();
}
```

This code has several fallback methods, with an extra parameter of the `Throwable` type and each fallback has its own fallback method with an extra `Throwable` parameter to propagate an exception at the command to the `fallback` method.

Error propagation

The `@HystrixCommand` annotation has the ability to specify exceptions types that should be ignored:

```
@HystrixCommand(ignoreExceptions = {BadRequestException.class})
public Account findAccountById(String id) {
    return accountService.findAccountById(id);
}
```

If `accountService.findAccountById(id)` throws an exception of the `BadRequestException` type, then this exception will be wrapped in `HystrixBadRequestException` and be-thrown without triggering the fallback logic.

Let's create a REST controller for the `customer` service.

Implementing a REST controller in customer service

Let's implement a `CustomerController` REST controller to the `Customer` microservice and expose endpoints for the CRUD operations. The `/customer/{customerId}` endpoint will simply return the customer details of a given customer ID along with its associated `account` details. For the `account` details, it will call another microservice that is already developed and deployed with its host and port number, exposing some endpoints such as `/account/customer/{customer}`. Let's see the following REST controller class:

```
package com.dineshonjava.customerservice.controller;

import java.util.ArrayList;
import java.util.List;

import org.springframework.beans.factory.annotation.Autowired;
import org.springframework.web.bind.annotation.DeleteMapping;
import org.springframework.web.bind.annotation.GetMapping;
import org.springframework.web.bind.annotation.PathVariable;
import org.springframework.web.bind.annotation.PostMapping;
import org.springframework.web.bind.annotation.PutMapping;
```

```
import org.springframework.web.bind.annotation.RequestBody;
import org.springframework.web.bind.annotation.RestController;

import com.dineshonjava.customerservice.domain.Customer;
import com.dineshonjava.customerservice.repository.CustomerRepository;
import com.dineshonjava.customerservice.service.AccountService;

@RestController
public class CustomerController {
    @Autowired
    CustomerRepository customerRepository;
    @Autowired
    AccountService accountService;
    @PostMapping(value = "/customer")
    public Customer save (@RequestBody Customer customer){
        return customerRepository.save(customer);
    }
    @GetMapping(value = "/customer")
    public Iterable<Customer> all (){
        List<Customer> customers = new ArrayList<>();
        for(Customer customer : customerRepository.findAll()){
customer.setAccount(accountService.findByCutomer(customer.getCustomerId()))
;
        }
        return customers;
    }
    @GetMapping(value = "/customer/{customerId}")
    public Customer findByAccountId (@PathVariable Integer customerId){
        Customer customer =
customerRepository.findByCustomerId(customerId);
        customer.setAccount(accountService.findByCutomer(customerId));
        return customer;
    }
    @PutMapping(value = "/customer")
    public Customer update (@RequestBody Customer customer){
        return customerRepository.save(customer);
    }
    @DeleteMapping(value = "/customer")
    public void delete (@RequestBody Customer customer){
        customerRepository.delete(customer);
    }
}
```

As you can see, there are two properties that have been injected, `AccountService` and `CustomerRepository`. `CustomerRepository` is used to access the customer data and `AccountService` is a delegating service for the `Account` microservice. Let's see how to create an `AccountService.java` delegate layer to call the `Account` service:

```java
package com.dineshonjava.customerservice.service;

import java.util.ArrayList;
import java.util.List;

import org.springframework.beans.factory.annotation.Autowired;
import org.springframework.cloud.client.loadbalancer.LoadBalanced;
import org.springframework.stereotype.Service;
import org.springframework.web.client.RestTemplate;

import com.dineshonjava.customerservice.domain.Account;
import com.netflix.hystrix.contrib.javanica.annotation.HystrixCommand;

@Service
public class AccountServiceImpl implements AccountService {
    @Autowired
    @LoadBalanced
    RestTemplate restTemplate;
    @HystrixCommand(fallbackMethod = "defaultAccount")
    public List<Account> findByCutomer(Integer customer) {
        return
restTemplate.getForObject("http://ACCOUNT-SERVICE/account/customer/{custome
r}", List.class, customer);
    }
    private List<Account> defaultAccount(Integer customer) {
            List<Account> defaultList = new ArrayList<>();
        defaultList.add(new Account(0000, 1.000, 0000, "UNKNOWN
ACCOUNT TYPE", "UNK", "FALLBACK BANK"));
            return defaultList;
        }
}
```

In the code for `AccountService`, we have performed the following steps to enable the Hystrix circuit-breaker:

1. `Account` microservice is invoked by the Spring Framework provided by `RestTemplate`.

2. Use the `@HystrixCommand(fallbackMethod = "defaultAccount")` annotation to add the Hystrix command to enable a fallback method, and we will have to add another `defaultAccount` method with the same signature as the command method has `findByCutomer(Integer customer)`, which will be invoked when the actual `Account` service will be down.

3. Add the `defaultAccount(Integer customer)` fallback method, which will return a default value.

This Hystrix-enabled `Customer` microservice will use the `Account` microservice registered with the Eureka registry server. The account REST service will be the same as the one we created in the previous chapters. You can find the complete example on GitHub (`https://github.com/PacktPublishing/Mastering-Spring-Boot-2.0`).

Let's build and test the `customer` service.

Building and testing customer service

Let's create builds for the Eureka server, `customer`, and `Account` service using the `mvn clean install` command and after that run all these services using the Java command. You can find `customer` service in port `6161`. And `Account` service is available at port `6060`. But we are using the Spring Cloud Eureka registry server, so you don't need to use the actual hostname and port to call `Account` service in the `customer` service, just use the logical service name (`http://ACCOUNT-SERVICE`).

Now fetch the `customer` service by opening the browser and type
`http://localhost:6161/customer/1001`. It should show the following output in the
browser:

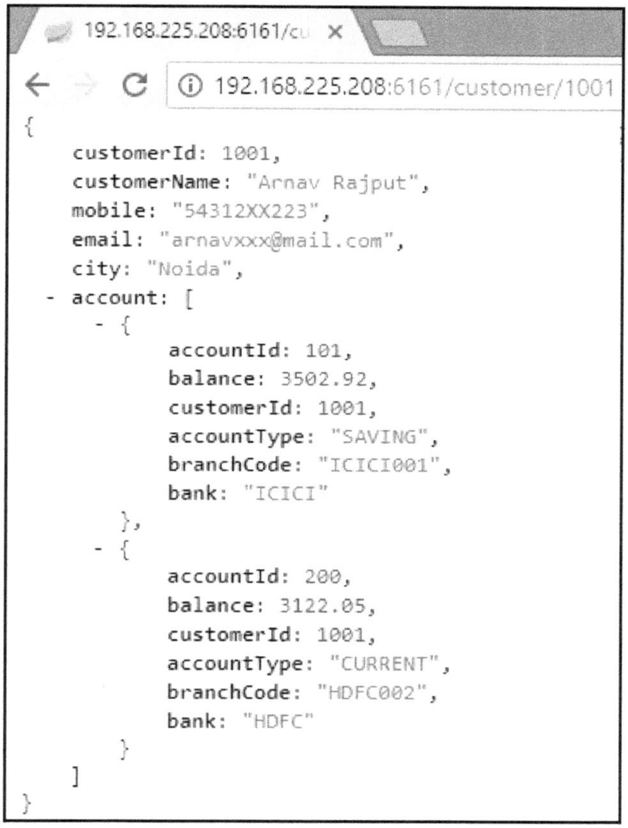

As you can see in the preceding screenshot, the customer with the `1001` customer ID has
been rendered with two accounts by calling the `Account` service internally by the
`customer` service. So if both services are running fine, the `customer` service is displaying
the data returned by the `Account` service. That means the circuit-breaker is in the CLOSED
state right now. Now let's move to test the Hystrix circuit-breaker by shutting down the
`Account` service. After shutdown, the `Account` service and refreshed same URI endpoint
as we have opened is at `http://localhost:6161/customer/1001`.

Let's see the following screenshot after refreshing the browser with the given URI:

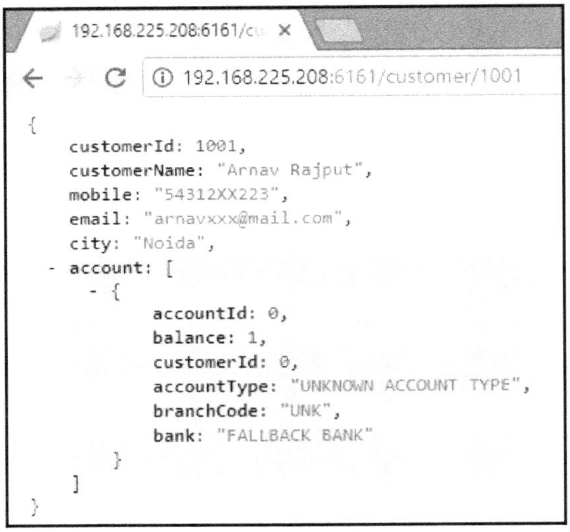

This time it will return the fallback method response. Here, Hystrix comes into the picture, it monitors the `Account` service in frequent intervals and as it is down, the Hystrix component has opened the circuit and enabled the fallback path.

Let's start the `Account` service again; after a few times, go back to the `customer` service, and refresh the browser again so you can see the response in normal flow.

Now we will explore how the Hystrix library allows us to customize the default configuration.

Customizing the default configuration

The Hystrix library allows you to customize the default configuration by using some properties for command and fallback. The command properties can be set using `commandProperties` of the `@HystrixCommand` annotation:

```
@HystrixCommand(commandProperties = {
    @HystrixProperty(name =
"execution.isolation.thread.timeoutInMilliseconds", value = "300")
})
public Account findAccountById(String id) {
    return accountService.findAccountById(id);
}
```

We have customized the default timeout to 300 milliseconds. Similar to `commandProperties`, we can customize the thread pool properties by using the `threadPoolProperties` of `@HystrixCommand`:

```
@HystrixCommand(commandProperties = {
        @HystrixProperty(name =
"execution.isolation.thread.timeoutInMilliseconds", value = "300")
    },
    threadPoolProperties = {
        @HystrixProperty(name = "coreSize", value = "30"),
        @HystrixProperty(name = "maxQueueSize", value = "101"),
        @HystrixProperty(name = "keepAliveTimeMinutes", value = "2"),
        @HystrixProperty(name = "queueSizeRejectionThreshold", value =
        "15"),
        @HystrixProperty(name = "metrics.rollingStats.numBuckets",
        value = "12"),
        @HystrixProperty(name =
        "metrics.rollingStats.timeInMilliseconds", value = "1200")
    })
public Account findAccountById(String id) {
    return accountService.findAccountById(id);
}
```

We have set `threadPoolProperties`, such as `coreSize`, `maxQueueSize`, `keepAliveTimeMinutes`, and `queueSizeRejectionThreshold`. Sometimes we are required to set some common properties to all Hystrix commands. The Hystrix library also allows us to set default properties at the class level so that these can be applicable for all Hystrix commands.

Netflix's Hystrix provides the `@DefaultProperties` annotation. It is a class-level annotation that allows us to set default command properties, such as `groupKey`, `threadPoolKey`, `commandProperties`, `threadPoolProperties`, `ignoreExceptions`, and `raiseHystrixExceptions`.

By default, specified properties will be used for each command within an annotated class by using the `@DefaultProperties` annotation unless a command specifies those properties explicitly using the corresponding `@HystrixCommand` parameters. Let's see the following:

```
@DefaultProperties(groupKey = "DefaultGroupKey")
class AccountService {
    @HystrixCommand // hystrix command group key is 'DefaultGroupKey'
    public Object commandInheritsDefaultProperties() {
        return null;
    }
```

```
@HystrixCommand(groupKey = "SpecificGroupKey") // command overrides
default group key
public Object commandOverridesGroupKey() {
    return null;
}
}
```

Let's enable the Hystrix Metrics Stream in the next section.

Hystrix Metrics Stream

You can also enable the Hystrix Metrics Stream by adding a dependency on `spring-boot-starter-actuator`. Hystrix will expose the metrics stream by using `/hystrix.stream` as a management endpoint:

```
<dependency>
    <groupId>org.springframework.boot</groupId>
    <artifactId>spring-boot-starter-actuator</artifactId>
</dependency>
```

Also add the following configurations to the application property file (`application.propeties`):

```
management.endpoint.health.enabled=true
management.endpoints.jmx.exposure.include=*
management.endpoints.web.exposure.include=*
management.endpoints.web.base-path=/actuator
management.endpoints.web.cors.allowed-origins=true
management.endpoint.health.show-details=always
```

These configurations are required to expose the Hystrix Metrics Stream in Spring Boot 2.0.

Let's access the `/hystrix.stream` endpoint on the browser to see the Hystrix Metrics Stream. The `http://localhost:6161/actuator/hystrix.stream` URI represents a continuous stream that Hystrix generates. This stream is generated by Hystrix to monitor health and all the service calls that are being monitored. Let's see the sample output in the screenshot:

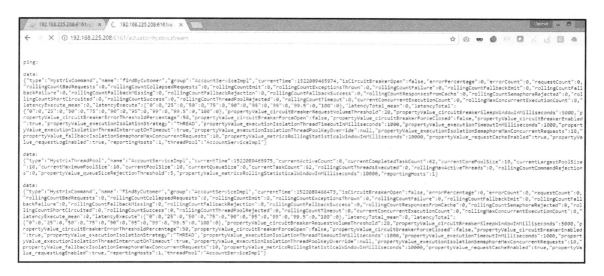

You can see in the preceding screenshot which JSON data represents the status for the health checkup of the services and the monitoring data stream for the service calls. It is very difficult to monitor because it looks like a very complex JSON format. Hystrix provides a Hystrix Dashboard for the Hystrix Metrics Stream and it will render the same data in GUI format in a very simple way. In the next section, we will explore Hystrix Dashboard.

Implementing Hystrix Dashboard in our project

Hystrix Dashboard provides benefits to monitoring the set of metrics on a dashboard. It displays the health of each circuit-breaker in a very simple way. Let's include Hystrix Dashboard in your project by using the Starter with the `org.springframework.cloud` and group and the `spring-cloud-starter-netflix-hystrix-dashboard` artifact ID:

```
<dependency>
    <groupId>org.springframework.cloud</groupId>
    <artifactId>spring-cloud-starter-netflix-hystrix-dashboard</artifactId>
</dependency>
```

We have to add in the `pom.xml` file. But it is not enough to add Hystrix Dashboard in your project, we have to add one more annotation, `@EnableHystrixDashboard`, to your Spring Boot `main` class:

```
@SpringBootApplication
@EnableEurekaClient
@EnableCircuitBreaker
@EnableHystrixDashboard
public class CustomerServiceApplication {

    public static void main(String[] args) {
            SpringApplication.run(CustomerServiceApplication.class, args);
    }
    ...
}
```

Now run the `main` class as a Spring Boot application to run Hystrix Dashboard in your project. You can visit `/hystrix` endpoint to see the dashboard for an individual-instance `/hystrix.stream` endpoint in a Hystrix client application. Let's access the `http://localhost:6161/hystrix` URI and see the following output on the browser:

The preceding diagram is a visual dashboard in its initial state. Now let's add the `http://localhost:6161/actuator/hystrix.stream` URI in the dashboard and click on the **Monitor Stream** button to get a meaningful dynamic visual representation of the circuit being monitored by the Hystrix component. Let's see the following visual dashboard after providing the stream input in the homepage:

Hystrix provides information about the individual instance using the `/hystrix.stream` endpoints, but in a distributed system, we must have more than one instance. So, getting a collaborated view about all instances in a distributed system is not possible with Hystrix Dashboard. Spring Cloud Netflix provides a solution to aggregate all the information about all the instances, which is Turbine. Let's discuss it in the next section.

Turbine dashboard

Turbine is a tool for aggregating events produced on Hystrix. Suppose that we have a distributed system with more than 10 microservices and each one with Hystrix. So, it is very difficult to monitor all the circuits. Spring Cloud Netflix offers Turbine to provide aggregation for the circuit-breakers. Turbine is a system that aggregates all the `/hystrix.stream` endpoints of all microservices of a distributed system into a combined `/turbine.stream` for use in Hystrix Dashboard.

To include Turbine in your project, add the following Turbine Maven dependency to your pom.xml file:

```
<dependency>
    <groupId>org.springframework.cloud</groupId>
    <artifactId>spring-cloud-starter-netflix-turbine</artifactId>
</dependency>
```

We have added a Maven dependency for Turbine. The spring-cloud-starter-netflix-turbine Starter provides the @EnableTurbine annotation. Annotate your main application class with this annotation to enable Turbine functionality in your project.

Let's see the main application class for this Turbine application:

```
package com.dineshonjava.turbine;

import org.springframework.boot.SpringApplication;
import org.springframework.boot.autoconfigure.SpringBootApplication;
import org.springframework.cloud.netflix.eureka.EnableEurekaClient;
import
org.springframework.cloud.netflix.hystrix.dashboard.EnableHystrixDashboard;
import org.springframework.cloud.netflix.turbine.EnableTurbine;

@SpringBootApplication
@EnableTurbine
@EnableEurekaClient
@EnableHystrixDashboard
public class TurbineApplication {

    public static void main(String[] args) {
        SpringApplication.run(TurbineApplication.class, args);
    }
}
```

The main application class has been annotated with the @EnableTurbine annotation to enable Turbine functionality in your project. Other annotations are the same ones we used in earlier examples in the chapter.

Let's see the following configuration files for this Turbine application (application.yml) file:

```
spring:
  application:
    name: turbine

server:
```

```
    port: 6262

eureka:
  client:
    service-url:
      default-zone: ${EUREKA_URI:http://localhost:8761/eureka}
  instance:
    prefer-ip-address: true
turbine:
  aggregator:
    cluster-config:
    - CUSTOMER-SERVICE
  app-config: CUSTOMER-SERVICE
```

This configuration file has a configuration for application name, server port, and Eureka registry information, and it has Turbine configurations of the aggregator cluster config and `appConfig`, which means we have to add those services with `@HystrixCommand`. Here I have added only one service, (`CUSTOMER-SERVICE`), to the Turbine aggregator for the Turbine dashboard.

Let's run this Turbine application and look the following Eureka Server Dashboard:

DS Replicas

Instances currently registered with Eureka

Application	AMIs	Availability Zones	Status
ACCOUNT-SERVICE	n/a (1)	(1)	UP (1) - MRNDTHTMOBL0002.timesgroup.com:account-service:6060
CUSTOMER-SERVICE	n/a (1)	(1)	UP (1) - MRNDTHTMOBL0002.timesgroup.com:customer-service:6161
TURBINE	n/a (1)	(1)	UP (1) - MRNDTHTMOBL0002.timesgroup.com:turbine:6262

As you can in the preceding screenshot, there are three running instances registered with the Eureka registry server.

Let's open Turbine, following the same steps we completed for Hystrix Dashboard. But here we have to inform the cluster via Turbine as follows:
`http://localhost:6262/turbine.stream?cluster=CUSTOMER-SERVICE`

Now open same screen that we opened with Hystrix with
`http://localhost:6262/hystrix` and use the `/turbine.stream` endpoint
(`http://localhost:6262/turbine.stream?cluster=CUSTOMER-SERVICE`) instead of
the `/hystrix.stream` endpoint to access the Turbine dashboard. It will open the same
screen as Hystrix, but if you have more services, they will appear in an aggregated way.
Let's see the following screenshot:

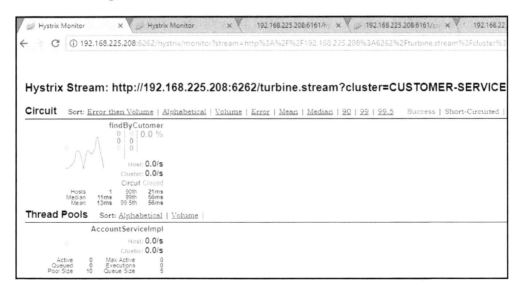

As you can see, it is very similar to the Hystrix Dashboard, but here it is the Turbine dashboard that aggregates all the /hystrix.stream endpoints to a single /turbine.stream endpoint.

Let's discuss the Turbine stream and what t is used for.

Turbine stream

The environments, such as PaaS, the classic Turbine model that pulls metrics from all the distributed Hystrix commands that doesn't work. In such cases, you can push your Hystrix command push metrics to Turbine by using Spring Cloud messaging. These are following dependencies required for your client application:

```
<dependency>
    <groupId>org.springframework.cloud</groupId>
    <artifactId>spring-cloud-starter-netflix-turbine-stream</artifactId>
</dependency>

<dependency>
    <groupId>org.springframework.cloud</groupId>
    <artifactId>spring-cloud-starter-stream-rabbit</artifactId>
</dependency>
```

I have added the spring-cloud-starter-netflix-turbine-stream and the spring-cloud-starter-stream-rabbit Starters. But you can add any messaging broker Starter of Spring cloud, using spring-cloud-starter-stream-*, of your choice. And also, you have to annotate the Spring Boot application class with the @EnableTurbineStream annotation.

REST consumer with Hystrix and Feign

We've used Spring Framework's RestTemplate to consume microservices. Now, we are going to use Spring's Netflix Feign as a declarative REST client, instead of Spring RestTemplate, to consume microservices. We have already discussed the Spring Netflix Feign client to access REST API in Chapter 8, *Simplify HTTP API with Feign Client*. In this section, we will use the Feign client with the circuit-breaker pattern.

If Hystrix is on the classpath and `feign.hystrix.enabled=true`, Feign will wrap all methods with a circuit-breaker.

Prior to the Spring Cloud Dalston release, if Hystrix was on the classpath, Feign would have wrapped all methods in a circuit-breaker by default. This default behavior was changed in Spring Cloud Dalston in favor of an opt-in approach.

To add the Feign client in your project, add the following Maven dependency:

```
<dependency>
    <groupId>org.springframework.cloud</groupId>
    <artifactId>spring-cloud-starter-openfeign</artifactId>
</dependency>
```

Now, let's enable fallbacks for a given `@FeignClient` by setting the class name to the fallback attribute of this annotation that implements the fallback. And also you have to declare your implementation as a Spring Bean. Let's see the following `AccountService` as a Feign client interface:

```
@FeignClient(name="account-service", fallback=AccountServiceFallback.class)
public interface AccountService {
    @GetMapping(value = "/account/customer/{customer}")
    List<Account> findByCutomer (@PathVariable("customer") Integer
customer);
}

class AccountServiceFallback implements AccountService {
    @Override
    private List<Account> findByCutomer(Integer customer) {
        List<Account> defaultList = new ArrayList<>();
        defaultList.add(new Account(0000, 1.000, 0000, "UNKNOWN
         ACCOUNT TYPE", "UNK", "FALLBACK BANK"));
        return defaultList;
    }
}
```

The name property of the `@FeignClient` is mandatory. It is used to look up the application either by service discovery via a Eureka Client or via URL, if this property is given.

Summary

We have covered creating a Spring Cloud Hystrix circuit-breaker and the circuit-breaker Pattern for fault tolerance in the distributed application. We created an application using Spring Netflix Hystrix to test both the circuit's open path and the circuit's closed path. We have implemented the client application to consume REST services by using Spring's `RestTemplate` and also used Spring Cloud's Netflix Feign.

We saw how to customize the default configuration of the Hystrix command and fallback. We also explored error propagation in the Hystrix command.

We created two REST consumer applications, one using `RestTempate` and another using the Feign client. And finally, we created a Hystrix Dashboard to monitor the metrics of your project. The Turbine dashboard helps to aggregate all the `/hystrix.stream` endpoints of all the microservices in the distributed system to a combine the `/turbine.stream` endpoints.

We learned why circuit-breaker implementation is necessary for building distributed systems and how to use the Hystrix library and customize it for business needs. You have also learned to configure the Hystrix Dashboard with data streams from individual services and configure the Turbine dashboard to aggregate the data streams from multiple services.

In the next chapter, we will explore Spring Boot support for testing.

Testing Spring Boot Application

11

Test cases are important for your application, as they not only verify the code but also make sure it does everything you expect it to do. In this chapter, we will explore how to write tests to make sure that things don't break as your application continues to evolve. You could either write tests before or after the code has been written.

Spring doesn't provide an API to write unit tests for an application. Spring promotes loose coupling and interface-driven design. So, it makes it easy to write unit tests for any Spring application. On the other hand, integration tests require some help from Spring Framework, because Spring does bean wiring between the application components in your production application. So, Spring is responsible for configuring and creating the application components in your production application.

Spring provides us with a separate module for testing—Spring test. The Spring test module provides the `SpringJUnit4ClassRunner` class to help load a Spring application context in JUnit-based application tests. But Spring Boot, by default, enables auto-configuring support and provides another class, `SpringRunner`. Spring Boot also offers a handful of useful testing utilities.

We'll start by looking at how to test with a fully Spring Boot-enabled application context. You will learn to unit test Spring Boot services and also learn to mock Spring Boot services. You'll also learn about the different tools available to test service contracts with basic usage. In this chapter, we will create a REST application by exposing some REST URIs and then we will test these using the Postman and SoapUI tools. By the end of this chapter, you will have a better understanding of how Spring Boot supports testing.

This chapter will cover the following points:

- Test-driven development
- JUnit test for Spring Boot

- Using Mockito for mocking services
- Postman for testing RESTful service contracts
- SoapUI for testing RESTful service contracts

Let's look at these topics in detail.

Test-driven development

Test-driven development (**TDD**) is about writing automated tests that verify whether the code actually works. TDD focuses on development with well-defined requirements in the form of tests. Every development process includes testing either in an automated or manual way. Automated tests result in an overall faster development cycle. Efficient TDD is faster than development without tests. Comprehensive test coverage provides confidence in the application development and this confidence enables refactoring for the application. Refactoring is essential to the agile development of an application. Let's see the following diagram:

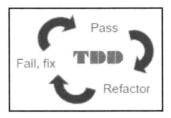

Refactoring promotes agile development; it is easy to discover failures and it fixes them.

Testing makes you think about your design. If your code is hard to test, then the design should be reconsidered. A test case helps you focus on what matters. It helps you not to write code that you don't need and it finds problems early during development. Let's see the different types testing in software.

Unit testing

Unit testing tests one unit of functionality and it keeps dependencies minimal and isolated from the environment, including Spring. We can use simplified alternatives for dependencies such as stubs and/or mocks.

In unit testing, there must not be any external dependencies, because external dependencies aren't available since we are testing a unit. So, remove links with dependencies. The test shouldn't fail because of external dependencies. You can remove external dependencies of your implementation for testing purposes by using stubs and mocks. *Stubs* create a simple test implementation and a *mock* dependency class generated at startup-time using a mocking framework.

Let's see the following diagram related to the unit testing example:

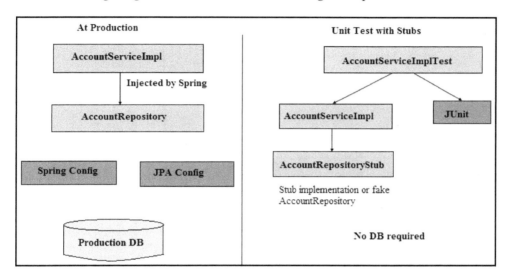

Here, you can see both modes of your application, the production mode and unit test mode. In the production mode, the Spring Framework injects dependencies by using the Spring configuration, but in the unit testing mode, Spring doesn't have any role, and dependencies have been resolved by creating stub implementations. The stub implementations are fake objection creation with dummy data.

In this example, I want to create a unit test for the `AccountServiceImpl` class and test two methods, `findAccountByAccountId()` and `findAllByCustomerId()`. The `findAccountByAccountId()` method will return the account object associated account ID and `findAllByCustomerId()` will return the list of accounts for a customer.

Let's create the `AccountServiceImpl` class and test this class with unit testing:

```
public class AccountServiceImpl implements AccountService {
    @Autowired
    AccountRepository accountRepository;

    public AccountServiceImpl(AccountRepository accountRepository) {
        this.accountRepository = accountRepository;
    }
    @Override
    public Account findAccountByAccountId(Integer accountId) {
        return accountRepository.findAccountByAccountId(accountId);
    }
    @Override
    public List<Account> findAllByCustomerId(Integer customerId) {
        return accountRepository.findAllByCustomerId(customerId);
    }
    . . .
}
```

The preceding service class had a dependency with the `AccountRepoistory` implementation. Let's implement a stub implementation of `AccountRepository` for unit testing the `AccountServiceImpl` class:

```
public class StubAccountRepository implements AccountRepository {
    . . .
    @Override
    public Account findAccountByAccountId(Integer accountId) {
        return new Account(100, 121.31, 1000, "SAVING", "HDFC121",
    "HDFC");
    }
    @Override
    public List<Account> findAllByCustomerId(Integer customerId) {
        List<Account> accounts = new ArrayList<>();
        accounts.add(new Account(100, 121.31, 1000, "SAVING",
      "HDFC121", "HDFC"));
        accounts.add(new Account(200, 221.31, 1000, "CURRENT",
      "ICIC121", "ICICI"));
        return accounts;
    }
    . . .
}
```

The StubAccountRepository class is a stub implementation of AccountRepository, by implementing methods with dummy data without calling the actual database. Let's see the following diagram that explains the two implementations of AccountRepository:

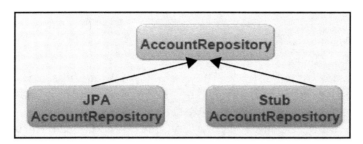

According to the preceding diagram, our application has two implementations of AccountRepository. JPAAccountRepository is used at the production mode, using database integration, but another class, StubAccountRepository, is used for unit testing without integrating database dependency. Let's see the following class to create a unit test using this stub repository:

AccountServiceImplTest is a unit test using a stub repository. Refer to the following code:

```
package com.dineshonjava.accountservice;

import static org.junit.Assert.assertFalse;
import static org.junit.Assert.assertTrue;

import org.junit.Before;
import org.junit.Test;

import com.dineshonjava.accountservice.repository.StubAccountRepository;
import com.dineshonjava.accountservice.service.AccountService;
import com.dineshonjava.accountservice.service.AccountServiceImpl;

public class AccountServiceImplTest {
    AccountService accountService;
    @Before
    public void setUp() {
        accountService = new AccountServiceImpl( new
        StubAccountRepository() );
    }
    @Test
    public void findAccountByAccountId() {
assertTrue(accountService.findAccountByAccountId(100).getBalance().intValue
```

```
() == 121);
    }
    @Test
    public void findAllByCustomerId() {
        assertFalse(accountService.findAllByCustomerId(1000).size() ==
        3);
    }
}
```

The preceding class has three methods. The `setup()` method initializes
`AccountRepository`; it is annotated with the `@Before` annotation. That means `setup()`
will be called before the test methods execute. The other two methods,
`findAccountByAccountId()` and `findAllByCustomerId())`, in the testing class are test
methods and are also annotated with the `@Test` annotation, which indicates that these are
test methods. We have testing logic inside these testing methods and we are using
assertions to write the test logic.

Advantages

Let's see the following advantages of using the stub implementation in unit tests:

- Easy to implement and understand
- Reusable

Disadvantages

Let's see the following disadvantages of using the stub implementation in unit tests:

- A change to an interface requires a change to a stub
- Your stub must implement all methods, even those not used by a specific
  scenario
- If a stub is reused, refactoring can break other tests

Other mock libraries

Apart from the stub implementation, there are many mocking frameworks available; you can use them to create unit tests. There are several mocking libraries available, such as Mockito, jMock, and EasyMock. You need to complete the following steps in order to perform tests with a Mock library:

1. Use a mocking library to generate a mock object that implements the dependent interface on the fly
2. Record the mock with expectations of how it will be used for a scenario
3. Exercise the scenario
4. Verify the mock expectations were met

The preceding mock considerations have the following benefits:

- No additional class to maintain
- You only need to set up what is necessary for the scenario you're testing

The only disadvantage is that these libraries are a little hard to understand at first.

Integration testing

Integration testing is also known as **system testing**; it tests the interactions of multiple units working together. All *units* should work well individually as we've already performed unit testing to confirm that, and integration testing involves testing application classes in the context of their surrounding infrastructure without running the entire project. Use the Apache DBCP connection pool instead of a container-provider pool obtained through JNDI, and use ActiveMQ to avoid expensive commercial JMS licenses.

Let's see the following diagram about integration testing:

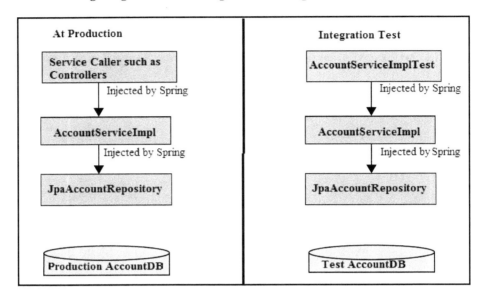

As you can see in the preceding diagram, `AccountServiceImpl` is using the actual `AccountRepository` implementation instead of its stub implementation as we have used in the unit tests. But `JpaAccountRepository` will fetch data from the testing DB instead of the production DB. Spring supports integration testing using the `Spring-test.jar` library, and Spring can use the same application configuration for the testing environment to inject dependencies between the application components.

Spring provides a separate module (`spring-test.jar`) for integration testing and consists of several JUnit test-support classes. Spring has a central support class, which is `SpringJUnit4ClassRunner`. It caches a shared `ApplicationContext` across test methods.

Let's see the following class with integration testing:

```
@RunWith(SpringJUnit4ClassRunner.class)
@ContextConfiguration(classes=SystemTestConfig.class)
public final class AccountServiceImplTest {
    @Autowired
    AccountService accountService;

    @Test
    public void findAccountByAccountId() {
assertTrue(accountService.findAccountByAccountId(100).getBalance().intValue
```

```
() == 121);
    }
    @Test
    public void findAllByCustomerId() {
        assertFalse(accountService.findAllByCustomerId(1000).size() ==
        3);
    }
}
```

The preceding test class, `AccountServiceImplTest`, is annotated with the `@RunWith` annotation by passing the `SpringJUnit4ClassRunner` class; it indicates this test will run with Spring support. The `@ContextConfiguration` annotation is used to include the testing configuration and the `SystemTestConfig` class points to the system test configuration file. You may notice that we didn't use the `@Before` annotation here because the `AccountService` dependency will be injected by Spring, so we don't need to use the `@Before` annotation.

In addition to loading the application context, `SpringJUnit4ClassRunner` also makes it possible to inject beans from the application context into the test itself via autowiring. Because this test is targeting an `AccountService` bean, it is autowired into the test. Finally, the `findAccountByAccountId()` method makes calls to the address service and verifies the results. As we've looked at integration testing, let's look at the benefits of testing with Spring.

Benefits of testing with Spring

Using Spring in integration testing offers the following benefits:

- No need to deploy to an external container to test application functionality, runs everything quickly inside your IDE
- Supports continuous integration testing and allows the reuse of your configuration between test and production environments, and application configuration logic is typically reused

Activating profiles for a test class

The Spring test module provides the `@ActiveProfiles` annotation inside the `test` class. This annotation activates the profile in the test environment. Beans associated with that profile are instantiated and also those beans which are not associated with any profile instantiated. For example, there are two profiles activated—`prod` and `dev`:

```
@RunWith(SpringJUnit4ClassRunner.class)
@ContextConfiguration(classes=TestConfig.class)
@ActiveProfiles( { "prod", "dev" } )
public class AccountServiceImplTest {
    ...
}
```

JUnit tests for the Spring Boot application

Spring Boot provides two modules for test support—`sprint-boot-test` and `spring-boot-test-autoconfigure`. `spring-boot-test` contains core items, and `spring-boot-test-autoconfigure` supports auto-configuration for tests. These modules have a number of utilities and annotations to help when testing your application. It is very simple to add these modules in the Spring Boot application by adding the `spring-boot-starter-test` starter dependency in your Maven file. This starter imports both Spring Boot test modules as well as JUnit, AssertJ, Hamcrest, and a number of other useful libraries. Let's see the following Maven dependency to include test support in the Spring Boot application:

```
<dependency>
    <groupId>org.springframework.boot</groupId>
    <artifactId>spring-boot-starter-test</artifactId>
    <scope>test</scope>
</dependency>
```

The preceding Maven dependency will add the following libraries to your Spring Boot application:

- **JUnit**: This is related to unit testing Java applications
- **Spring test and Spring Boot test**: They add utilities and integration-test support for Spring Boot applications
- **AssertJ**: It is an assertion library
- **Hamcrest**: This library is related to constraints or predicates

- **Mockito**: It is a Java mocking framework
- **JSONassert**: This library is used to assert in JSON support
- **JsonPath**: XPath for JSON

These libraries are useful for writing tests. Spring Boot provides an annotation, @SpringBootTest. This annotation can be used as an alternative to the @ContextConfiguration annotation of the Spring test module. This annotation is used to create ApplicationContext in your tests using SpringApplication. Let's see the following class:

```
package com.dineshonjava.accountservice;

import static org.junit.Assert.assertFalse;
import static org.junit.Assert.assertTrue;

import org.junit.Test;
import org.junit.runner.RunWith;
import org.springframework.beans.factory.annotation.Autowired;
import org.springframework.boot.test.context.SpringBootTest;
import org.springframework.test.context.junit4.SpringRunner;

import com.dineshonjava.accountservice.service.AccountService;

@RunWith(SpringRunner.class)
@SpringBootTest
public class AccountServiceApplicationTests {
    @Autowired
    AccountService accountService;
    @Test
    public void findAccountByAccountId() {
assertTrue(accountService.findAccountByAccountId(100).getBalance().intValue
() == 3502);
    }
    @Test
    public void findAllByCustomerId() {
        assertFalse(accountService.findAllByCustomerId(1000).size() ==
        3);
    }

}
```

The class is annotated with the `@SpringBootTest` annotation, no need to add the `@ContextConfiguration` annotation.

Using Mockito for mocking services

Let's see following quote about the role of mocking:

> *"Mockito is a mocking framework that tastes really good. It lets you write beautiful tests with a clean & simple API. Mockito doesn't give you hangover because the tests are very readable and they produce clean verification errors."*

> – *Mockito. Mockito Framework Site. N.p., n.d. Web. 28 Apr. 2017.*

When running tests, it is sometimes necessary to mock certain components within your application context. For example, you may have a facade over some remote service that is unavailable during development. Mocking can also be useful when you want to simulate failures that might be hard to trigger in a real environment. Let's see the following test class where I have used Mocking:

```
package com.dineshonjava.accountservice;

import static org.hamcrest.CoreMatchers.is;
import static org.hamcrest.CoreMatchers.notNullValue;
import static org.junit.Assert.assertFalse;
import static org.junit.Assert.assertThat;
import static org.junit.Assert.assertTrue;
import static org.mockito.Mockito.*;

import org.junit.Test;
import org.junit.runner.RunWith;
import org.springframework.boot.test.context.SpringBootTest;
import org.springframework.boot.test.mock.mockito.MockBean;
import org.springframework.test.context.junit4.SpringRunner;

import com.dineshonjava.accountservice.domain.Account;
import com.dineshonjava.accountservice.service.AccountService;

@RunWith(SpringRunner.class)
@SpringBootTest
public class AccountControllerTest {
    @MockBean
    AccountService accountService;
    @Test
```

```
    public void findAllByCustomerId() {
        assertFalse(accountService.findAllByCustomerId(1000).size() ==
        3);
    }
    @Test
    public void testAddAccount_returnsNewAccount(){
        when(accountService.save(any(Account.class))).thenReturn(new
        Account(200, 200.20, 1000, "SAVING", "SBIWO111", "SBIW"));
        assertThat(accountService.save(new Account(200, 200.20, 1000,
        "SAVING", "SBIWO111", "SBIW")), is(notNullValue()));
    }
    @Test
    public void findAccountByAccountId() {
assertTrue(accountService.findAccountByAccountId(200).getBalance().intValue
() == 200);
    }

}
```

Spring Boot includes a @MockBean annotation that can be used to define a Mockito mock for a bean inside your ApplicationContext. You can use the annotation to add new beans or replace a single existing bean definition. The annotation can be used directly on test classes, on fields within your test, or on @Configuration classes and fields. When used on a field, the instance of the created mock is also injected. Mock beans are automatically reset after each test method.

Postman for testing RESTful service contracts

Postman is a REST client that started off as a Chrome browser plugin but recently came out with native versions for both Mac and Windows. Postman supports every HTTP method you can think of including some you might not even know about. Let's install Postman in your machine and open it after installation is completed. It is very easy to use, just open Postman and log in with your Google account. Now Postman is ready to test your REST API.

Let's see the following screenshot about Postman testing a REST API:

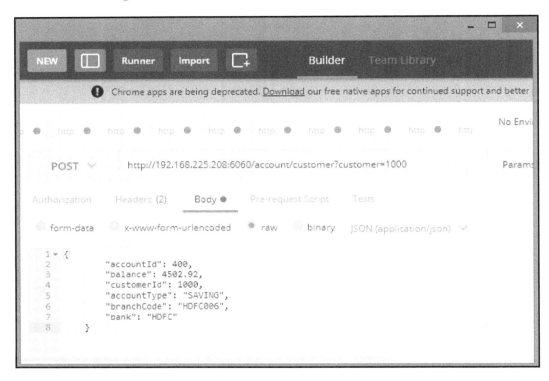

The preceding screenshot is about Postman. Here I have tested a RESTful web service to create an account for a customer with the `1000` customer ID:

```
http://192.168.225.208:6060/account/customer?customer=1000
```

The header contains the following information:

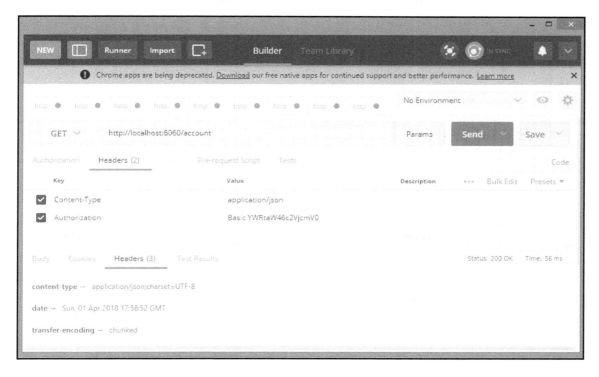

As you can see, it is displaying information about the request and response headers. In the request header, **Content-Type** is **application/json**. In the response header, the content type is also **application/json** and is displaying the date and encoding information of the response of the API.

Postman also allows you to write test cases for an API; let's see the following screenshot:

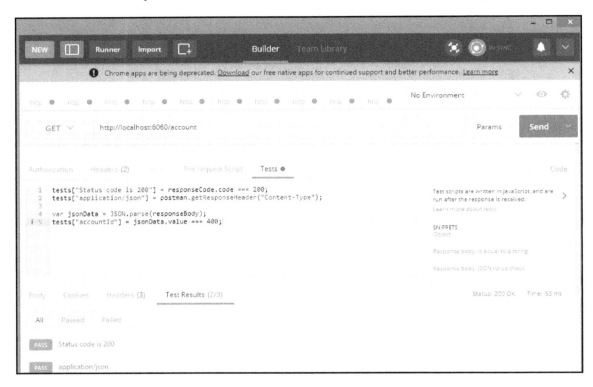

I have created some test cases using the Postman tool; click on the **Tests** tab and, in the right menu, there is a JavaScript snippet. We have created three tests here. The first test case checks the response code, the second test case checks the content type of the response, and the third test checks the return JSON data value.

Summary

Testing is an essential part of any development. Unit testing tests a class in isolation and external dependencies should be minimized. You can consider creating stubs or mocks to unit test. You don't need Spring to unit test. Integration testing tests the interaction of multiple units working together. Spring provides good integration testing support and profiles for different test and deployment configurations.

There are many tools available to test services such as Postman and SoapUI. In this chapter, we saw how to use Postman to test RESTful services. Postman provides support for all HTTP methods with every content type.

In the next chapter, we will explore the Docker container and will create Docker images.

12
Containerizing Microservice

This chapter will provide an introduction to containers, dockerizing the services built in the previous chapter, writing the `Dockerfile` and orchestrating the containers using `docker-compose`, and providing orchestration examples in Kubernetes.

In the previous chapter, we learned about microservice architecture and its advantages and challenges. One of the major challenges in the microservice-distributed application is the deployment of several microservices across multiple machines (VMs). How will they share common resources of VMs? In production, deploying and managing a system composed of many independent services is an operational complexity.

In microservice architecture, you create and deploy services independently, and you have to re-test your services after deployment on the same VMs. A microservice wouldn't impact on the other microservices, but you could never really guarantee that because the service is independent of the other services, it is using common resources of VMs.

In the favor of microservice architecture, containerized deployment is the topping on the pizza. The microservice is already autonomous by its functional service, but the containerization makes microservices more autonomous by self-containing the underlying infrastructure. So, containerization is making the microservices cloud-neutral.

In this chapter, we will introduce the containerized deployment of microservices and concepts of virtual machine images. Readers will get an understanding of building Docker images for microservices, which are developed with Spring Boot and Spring Cloud. We will also explore how to deploy Docker images in production-like environments, and how to manage and maintain these Docker images.

By the end of this chapter, you will have a better understanding of containerization and how to containerize a microservice developed with Spring Boot and Spring Cloud.

This chapter will cover the following points:

- Introducing containers in the microservice architecture
- Getting started with Docker
- Dockerizing any Spring Boot application
- Writing `Dockerfile`
- Using `docker-compose`
- Writing the `docker-compose` file
- Orchestration using `docker-compose`
- Introducing Kubernetes
- Orchestration using Kubernetes

Let's look at these topics in detail.

Introducing containers to the microservice architecture

The microservice architecture is another approach to developing a distributed application. This approach is suitable for the agility, scale, and reliability requirements of modern cloud applications. As we know, a microservice application is decomposed into separate components independently to work together to achieve the whole system.

In microservice architecture, you can scale out independently on the specific functionality rather than unnecessarily scaling out other areas of the application. So, you can scale the resources, such as processing power or network bandwidth, for a specific microservice. But what about sharing infrastructures with another microservice? In this chapter, we will discuss this challenge. Containerization comes into the picture to solve the problem of sharing infrastructure between microservices and allowing microservices to be more autonomous.

Containerization allows you to run your microservices in a completely isolated environment. So, according to the containerization approach, a container is an artifact in which a microservice and its versioned set of dependencies, plus its environment configuration, are abstracted as deployment manifest files. The container contains all infrastructure-related dependencies, environment variables, and configurations. It is packaged together as a container image. And this image is tested as a unit and deployed to a host operating system.

Containerization is nothing but it is a different approach to development and deployment of the microservices. The container is an isolated and runnable instance of an image. That image contains everything required to run an application. In the container, an application can run without using the resources of another container or host machine. You also have full control over a container to create, delete, move, start, and stop this container using a CLI, such as the Docker client. Containers can be connected to each other using a network. A container acts like a separate, independent, and isolated physical or virtual machine.

Although a container looks like a physical or virtual machine, the containers use the technology and concepts very differently from virtual machines. Although a container runs an operating system, it has a file system, and it can be accessed over a network, just like a virtual machine. Let's see the following diagram on virtual machine:

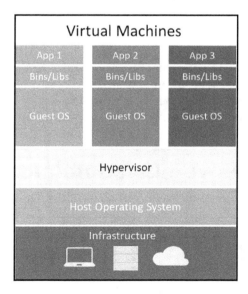

As you can see in the preceding diagram, **Virtual Machines** include the application, the required dependencies, and a full guest operating system. **Hypervisor** is a computer software that shares and manages hardware. Let's see the following diagram about **Containers**:

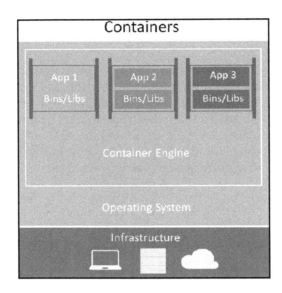

As you can see in the preceding diagram, **Containers** include the application and its required dependencies. Unlike virtual machines, **Containers** share the **Operating System** and underlying **Infrastructure** with other containers. These are running as an isolated process on the host operating system. Because **Containers** share resources, they require fewer resources than virtual machines.

Virtual machines versus containers

Let's see the following differences between virtual machines and containers:

Virtual machines	Containers
Virtual machines include the applications, the required dependencies, and a full guest operating system	Containers include the applications and the required dependencies, and share operating systems and underlying infrastructure

Each virtual machine has its own guest operating system; because of this, it requires more resources	Because containers share resources, they require fewer resource, the minimal kernel of the operating system present for each container
The hypervisor manages VMs, environments	The container engine manages containers
You have to add specific resources for scaling	You can scale out containers by creating another container of an image
Fewer virtual machines can be created for the same hardware and resources	More containers can be created for the same hardware and resources
Virtual machines are virtualizing the underlying hardware	Containers are virtualizing the underlying operating system
A VM can take up several GB depending on guest OS	Containers don't require that many GB, because they share resources, they merely use dozens of MB
Virtual machines are generally more suitable for monolithic applications with high-security concerns	Containers are generally more suitable for microservice-based applications, or other cloud-native applications, where security is not the major concern

As we have seen in the previous table, VMs and containers cannot replace each other. So, we can choose according to application requirements and application architecture.

Benefits of a container-oriented approach

The following are the advantages of a container-oriented development and deployment approach:

- A container-oriented approach eliminates the challenges that arise from inconsistent environment setups.
- You can do fast application scale-up by instancing new containers as required.
- Requires minimal usage of kernels on the operating system.
- You can create the number of containers for a microservice, depending on application requirements.
- You can easily allocate resources to processes and run your application in various environments.
- Containerization decreases the time of development, testing, and deployment of applications and services.

- Bug fixing and tracking are also less complicated as there is no difference between running your application, testing, and production.
- It is a very cost-effective solution.
- It is a great option for microservice-based applications, such as DevOps, and continuous deployment.
- Container images are reusable artifacts in similar situations.
- Containers are popular choices for cloud-based elastic applications because of their scalability. Container images are very small, don't require booting of the OS, and take little time to start and shut down.

We have seen some benefits of a container-oriented approach to application development and deployment. There are some key limitations of containers. Let's see some drawbacks or challenges to this approach.

Drawbacks of a container-oriented approach

The following are the drawbacks or challenges of the container-oriented approach to application development and deployment:

- Containers can only run Linux-based operating systems.
- The containerization approach requires some extra configurations at the time of deployment and networking. So, maintaining an adequate network connection can be tricky.
- Security is one the major problems of the container-oriented approach, because containers share the kernel and host operating system, and have root access.

So, we have seen the drawbacks of the container-oriented approach for application development and deployment. Let's see the key concepts of the container-oriented approach.

Key concepts of the containers-oriented approach

The container-oriented approach has the following key concepts:

- **Container Host**: The Container Host is like an engine for containers and it can run multiple containers. And it can configure the virtual machine to host containers.
- **Container**: It is a runtime instance of an image.

- **Container image**: An application needs several resources to run, such as layered filesystems, OS, and configurations. The container image consists of everything an application requires. The container image is immutable in nature. It cannot change its state as it's deployed to different environments.
- **Container OS image**: The container OS image is created from several other container images to make up a container. It also can't be modified.
- **Container repository**: It is used to store the container image and its related dependencies. It can be local repository used each time a container image is created. You can reuse these images many times on the container host. Docker Hub is an example of a container repository. They can be used across different container hosts.

As you can see, the preceding list outlined key concepts and approaches for using a container-based infrastructure for your microservices-based application. This is a very popular approach and adopted by several companies in distributed application development and deployment. Docker is an example and implementation of this approach. Let's discuss Docker as a container in the next section.

Getting started with Docker

In the previous section, we discussed the container-oriented approach of an application's development and deployment, and its benefits. Docker is one of the container-implementation and software platforms for containerization. Due to the popularity of Docker, sometimes containerization is referred to as **Dockerization**. Docker is an open-source computer program designed to assist with creating, deploying, and running applications using containers. Containers allow the developers to partition all the different parts of an application, such as libraries, dependencies, and exceptions, and then store it in the form of a package. This process of containerization assures the developer that the application will execute on any Linux machine, despite the change in settings between the machine the application was made on and the machine it is supposed to be tested on.

Due to being open source, Docker can also be manipulated to meet the needs of any particular user. And anyone can contribute to it, making it more and more suitable for use, improving its condition, and adding different useful features to it.

Docker was originally developed for the Linux operating system, making use of the isolating features of the Linux Kernel, for example, groups and namespaces of the kernels. The filing systems available in Linux, such as OverlayFS, allow different containers to run in a single Linux instance instead of bearing the overhead of the setup, installation, and maintenance of virtual machines. Docker can somewhat be perceived as a virtual machine but, unlike a VM, Docker does not create a whole virtual operating system. In fact, it lets the applications use the machine's kernel, only supplying the application requirements that are not already in the machine. While providing the application a perfect environment to execute, it also provides a significant performance boost and reduces the memory space taken up by the application.

Docker is a software tool that is not only useful for developers, but also for system administrators, which makes it part of the DevOps toolchain. Docker allows developers to concentrate on their coding rather than being worried about whether the code will run on certain systems or not, and the system administrators can rest easy about not having to be worried about system specifications because Docker allows the application to run on any system. Docker also provides flexibility and reduces the number of systems required, due to its small footprints and even lower overhead.

Docker provides security to the applications executing in the shared environment, but containers are not able to replace proper security measures required by any application. However, if Docker is not run on a system shared by multiple parties, and the machine is running good security practices for the containers, Docker security does not remain your concern. Some people also confuse Docker as an alternative to virtual machines, but it is really not that simple.

Installing Docker

As we have seen, the Docker software platform is used to build, ship, and run lightweight containers. These containers are based on Linux kernels, so Docker has a default support for Linux platforms. But Docker also has support for macOS and Windows using Docker Toolbox, which runs on top of VirtualBox.

Docker also supports cloud platforms, such as **Amazon Web Service** (**AWS**), Microsoft Azure, and IBM Cloud. Amazon **EC2 Container Service** (**ECS**) has out-of-the-box support for Docker on AWS EC2 instances. We will discuss cloud deployment in `Chapter 14`, *Deploying in Cloud (AWS)*.

Installing Docker on Linux

To install the latest Docker version on a Linux machine, perform the following steps:

1. Update your `apt` packages index by using the following command:

   ```
   $ sudo apt-get update
   ```

2. After updating `apt` package, let's start the `docker-engine` installation by using the following command:

   ```
   $ sudo apt-get install docker-engine
   ```

3. The preceding command will install Docker on your Linux machine. Now let's start the Docker daemon by using the following command:

   ```
   $ sudo service docker start
   ```

4. You can test Docker on your machine by using the following command:

   ```
   $ sudo docker run hello-world
   ```

The preceding command verifies that Docker is installed correctly by running the `hello-world` image; this command downloads a test image and runs it in a container. The following output will be displayed after executing the preceding command:

```
$ docker run hello-world

Hello from Docker!
This message shows that your installation appears to be working correctly.

To generate this message, Docker took the following steps:
 1. The Docker client contacted the Docker daemon.
 2. The Docker daemon pulled the "hello-world" image from the Docker Hub.
    (amd64)
 3. The Docker daemon created a new container from that image which runs the
    executable that produces the output you are currently reading.
 4. The Docker daemon streamed that output to the Docker client, which sent it
    to your terminal.

To try something more ambitious, you can run an Ubuntu container with:
 $ docker run -it ubuntu bash
```

Installing Docker on Windows

Let's see how to install Docker on your Windows-based machine. First, you have to download it from `https://download.docker.com/win/stable/Docker%20for%20Windows%20Installer.exe`; it is available for Windows 10. If you have old Windows (8), then you have to download Docker Toolbox from `https://download.docker.com/win/stable/DockerToolbox.exe` and then install it by double-clicking on the installer. After Docker Toolbox is installed, it will add Docker Toolbox, VirtualBox, and Kinematic to your applications folder. Let's start Docker Toolbox and run a simple Docker command. You will see the following icons on your desktop after successfully installing Docker Toolbox:

The three icons are verifying proper installation of Docker Toolbox. Click on the **Docker QuickStart** icon to launch a preconfigured Docker Toolbox terminal. Once opened, you will see Docker configured and launched. You will get an interactive shell for Docker, as follows:

```
Select MINGW64:/c/Users/Dinesh.Rajput
Starting "default"...
(default) Check network to re-create if needed...
(default) Windows might ask for the permission to configure a dhcp server. Somet
imes, such confirmation window is minimized in the taskbar.
(default) Waiting for an IP...
Machine "default" was started.
Waiting for SSH to be available...
Detecting the provisioner...
Started machines may have new IP addresses. You may need to re-run the `docker-m
achine env` command.
Regenerate TLS machine certs?  Warning: this is irreversible. (y/n): Regeneratin
g TLS certificates
Waiting for SSH to be available...
Detecting the provisioner...
Copying certs to the local machine directory...
Copying certs to the remote machine...
Setting Docker configuration on the remote daemon...


               ##         .
         ## ## ##        ==
      ## ## ## ## ##    ===
  /"""""""""""""""""\___/ ===
 {                       /  ===-
  _____ o           __/
    \    \         __/
     _____/


docker is configured to use the default machine with IP 192.168.99.100
For help getting started, check out the docs at https://docs.docker.com

Start interactive shell

Dinesh.Rajput@MRNDTHTMOBL0002 MINGW64 ~
$
```

Let's test the preceding terminal and type the $ `docker version` command to check the version of Docker:

```
Dinesh.Rajput@MRNDTHTMOBL0002 MINGW64 ~
$ docker version
Client:
 Version:       17.10.0-ce
 API version:   1.33
 Go version:    go1.8.3
 Git commit:    f4ffd25
 Built:         Tue Oct 17 19:00:02 2017
 OS/Arch:       windows/amd64

Server:
 Version:       17.11.0-ce
 API version:   1.34 (minimum version 1.12)
 Go version:    go1.8.5
 Git commit:    1caf76c
 Built:         Mon Nov 20 18:39:28 2017
 OS/Arch:       linux/amd64
 Experimental:  false
```

Docker commands

The following Docker commands are frequently used:

Command	Description
docker ps	This command will be used to list all running containers with information such as ID, name, base image name, and port forwarding.
docker build	This command will be used to create a definition for the container. You can create new container definitions by using this command with the Docker build file.
docker pull [image name]	You can use this command to pull Docker images from the Docker repository, either the remote or local repository.
docker run	This command is responsible for starting a Docker container either from the local or remote container definition.
docker push	This command will be used to publish your application's Docker container to the Docker repository, such as DockerHub.

Container-specific commands

These container-specific commands take either a container ID or container name as a parameter:

Command	Description
`docker stats [container name/ID] [container name/ID]`	You can use this command to show the load status, such as CPU percentage, memory usage, and network traffic, for each container.
`docker logs [-f] [container name/ID]`	This command will be responsible for showing log output from the container. You can also use the `-f` option as like tail the `-f` command.
`docker inspect [container name/ID]`	You can use this command to dump all of the configuration information on the container in JSON format.
`docker port [container name/ID]`	This command will be used to display all available forwarding ports between the container host and the container.
`docker exec [-i] [-t] [container name/ID]`	You can use this command to execute a command to the target container.

Docker architecture

Docker is based on a client-server architecture. Docker has three main components to its architecture:

- Docker client
- Docker daemon
- Docker registries

Let's see the following diagram of the Docker architecture:

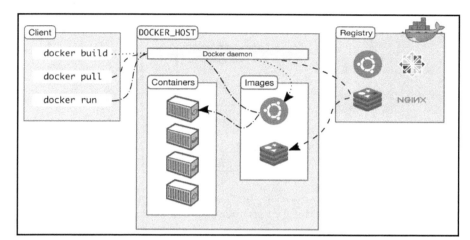

- **Docker client**: It is an interface (CLI) to run the Docker commands, such as build, run, and stop. The Docker client interacts with the Docker daemon server. You can also connect the Docker client with the remote Docker daemon. It uses REST APIs to build communication between the Docker client and the Docker daemon server using Unix sockets or a network interface.

- **Docker daemon**: It is a process running in the background. It can listen for all requests of the Docker API and it can manage Docker objects, such as images, containers, networks, and volumes.

- **Docker registries**: This component is used to store Docker images either publicly or privately. Docker Hub and Docker Cloud are examples of the public Docker registry; anyone can use this type of registry. **Docker Datacenter** (**DDC**) and **Docker Trusted Registry** (**DTR**) are examples of private Docker registries.

- **Docker Host**: It is the complete Docker environment required to run your application. Docker Host provides Docker images, containers, and the Docker daemon server.

- **Docker image**: It is an immutable Docker object and it cannot be changed once created. Docker images are one of the key components of the Docker architecture. It contains all required resources for running your application, such as operating system and libraries. It can be run from any Docker platform after creation.

For example, in a Spring Boot microservice, the accumulated package of operating systems, such as Ubuntu, Alpine, JRE, and the Spring Boot application JAR file, is a Docker image. Let's see the following diagram of the Docker image:

As you can see, it contains Spring Boot application JAR, **Java Runtime** (JRE), and operating systems, such as Ubuntu. It is a runnable artifact and can be run on any Docker machine.

To see the list of images that are available locally, use the docker images command. Let's see the output of this command:

```
Dinesh.Rajput@MRNDTHTMOBL0002 MINGW64 ~
$ docker images
REPOSITORY                      TAG            IMAGE ID          CREATED          SIZE
mongo                           latest         5b1317f8158f      3 weeks ago      366MB
doj/customer                    latest         220e0dcb7f19      3 months ago     780MB
<none>                          <none>         abb1e42e0404      3 months ago     780MB
<none>                          <none>         57c71085177f      3 months ago     780MB
doj/webclient                   latest         38faba59c677      3 months ago     144MB
<none>                          <none>         480369ab01ae      3 months ago     144MB
<none>                          <none>         c7d612c2795d      3 months ago     144MB
doj/accounts-microservice       latest         32892103e1a0      3 months ago     141MB
doj/discovery                   latest         48e2f0407814      3 months ago     144MB
```

The preceding screenshot displays a list of Docker images containing information such as REPOSITORY, TAG, Image ID, CREATED time, and SIZE. REPOSITORY refers to the local repository name for a Docker image. TAG means the version of a Docker image and IMAGE ID represents a unique identifier for a Docker image. Let's see another component of the Docker architecture.

Docker Engine

Docker Engine is a client-server application that has the following major components:

- A daemon process, which is a server and long-running process in the background

- A REST service interface, which used to talk to the daemon process and instruct it what to do
- A **command-line interface** (**CLI**) client

Let's see the following diagram about Docker Engine:

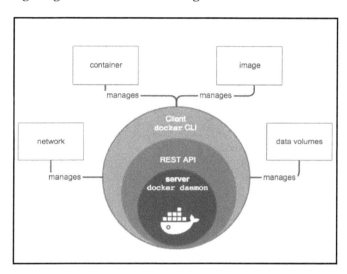

As you can see, the Docker CLI is the client that manages **container**, **image**, **network**, and **data volumes**. The Docker client uses the REST API to interact with the server, which is a **docker daemon** process.

Docker container

The Docker containers are running instances of a Docker image. Docker provides CLI commands to run, start, stop, move, or delete a container. You can set environment variables and provide configuration for the network from a container. The containers will get their own network configuration and filesystem. Each container process has its own isolated process space using kernel features that are ensured by Docker at runtime. The Docker containers use the kernel of the host operating system at runtime. They share the host kernel with other containers running on the same operating system host. Even the containers are initiated from the same Docker image and they have own specific resource allocation, such as memory and CPU.

Let's see the following diagram about the Docker container:

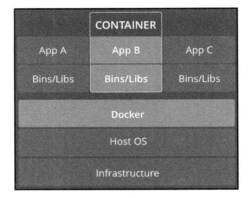

As you can see, Docker Engine manages the Docker containers, and a Docker container is nothing but a running instance of a Docker image that has an application and associated library dependencies.

Let's see how to create a Docker container from a Docker image using the following command:

```
$ docker run hello-world
```

The preceding command has three parts:

- `docker`: It is Docker Engine and used to run a Docker program. It tells to the operating system that you are running for the docker program.
- `run`: It is used to create and run a docker container.
- `hello-world`: It is the name of an image. You need to specify the name of an image that is to load into the container.

So, we have discussed that each container has its own copy of resources, such kernel of host operating system, RAM, and file system. How are we going to do that? We can do that by using `Dockerfile`. Let's discuss how to create `Dockerfile` in the next section.

Writing Dockerfile

`Dockerfile` is sometimes called the `Docker build` file. It is a simple text file that has a set of commands that the Docker client calls at the time of image creation. `Dockerfile` automates the Docker image creation process. The `Dockerfile` commands are almost identical to their equivalent Linux commands. So, there is no special syntax required for this build file, you can easily create your own `Dockerfile` to build Docker containers.

Docker uses `Dockerfile` to build a Docker image, and you can define all required dependencies and steps to run the Docker image inside your container. How to access resources, such as storage and network interfaces, can be defined in this `Dockerfile`. You can also virtualize disk drives inside this environment using `Dockerfile`. All resources that you have defined inside this `Dockerfile` will be isolated from the outside of your container. But you can define the application port to use it the outside world.

After the creation of `Dockerfile`, put this file in the application directory. Let's start creating a new blank file in our text editor and save it into the application directory. The following are the steps to write `Dockerfile`:

Create a file using the `vim` command and save it as `Dockerfile`. Note that the filename must be `Dockerfile` with a capital `D`.

Let's write the `Dockerfile` instructions into your `Dockerfile`:

```
#This is a Dockerfile for a microservice application

# Use an official Java 8 runtime as a parent image
FROM openjdk:8-jdk-alpine

#Set maintainer email id
MAINTAINER admin@dineshonjava.com

# Set the working directory to /app
WORKDIR /app

# Copy the current directory contents into the container at /app
ADD . /app

# Install any needed packages libraries
RUN mvn clean install

# Build and create jar using maven command
RUN mvn package
```

```
# Make port 80 available to the world outside this container
EXPOSE 80

# Define environment variable
ENV JAVA_OPTS=""

# Run accounts-microservice.jar when the container launches
CMD ["java $JAVA_OPTS -Djava.security.egd=file:/dev/./urandom -jar
accounts-microservice.jar", "accounts-microservice.jar"]
```

As you can see, the preceding Dockerfile has some instructions to create a Docker image and container. The following points need to be noted from the Dockerfile:

- The instructions in Dockerfile are case-insensitive; that means it is not necessary to write commands in a particular case, but you must follow conventions that recommend using uppercase.
- Docker follows the top-to-bottom order to run instructions of Dockerfile. Each Dockerfile must have the first instruction as FROM in order to specify the base image. In our example, we are creating an image from the openjdk:8-jdk-alpine image.
- In the preceding Dockerfile, a statement beginning with # is treated as a comment, such as #This is a Dockerfile for a microservice application. Other instructions, such as RUN, CMD, FROM, EXPOSE, and ENV can be used in our Dockerfile.
- The next command is the person who is going to maintain this image. Here you specify the MAINTAINER keyword and just mention the email ID.
- You can use the WORKDIR command to set the working directory for any RUN, CMD, and COPY instruction that follows it in Dockerfile. If the working directory does not exist, it will be created by default. This command can be used multiple times in Dockerfile.
- The ADD command is used to copy the current directory contents into the container at /app.

- The RUN command is used to run instructions against the image. In our case, the first RUN command is used to run the mvn command install and clean any needed packages libraries in our microservice application. The second RUN command creates a JAR file by running the mvn package maven command.
- The EXPOSE command of Dockerfile is used to make port 80 available to the world outside this container.
- The ENV command can be used to define the environment variables for our microservice application.
- The last CMD command is used to execute the microservice application by the image.
- Save Dockerfile and in the next section, we will discuss how to build the image using Spring Boot application.

As we have created Dockerfile with some instructions, there are more instructions available for Dockerfile as per as your application requirements. Because all instruction commands are very simple and easy to write, I am not going to explain them. The docker build command looks up the Dockerfile for instructions for building. Let's move to create a Spring Boot application and dockerize it.

Dockerizing any Spring Boot application

In this section, I'll focus on how to dockerize a Spring Boot application (Account-Service) to run in an isolated environment, which is a container. In the previous chapters, we have created some microservices, such as Account-Service and Customer-Service. Now I will describe the process of migrating a Spring Boot Account-Service to Docker. We will start by modifying a build file, then we will create Dockerfile so it can be run locally.

So let's go ahead and create Dockerfile in our Spring Boot project:

```
#This is a Dockerfile for a microservice application

# Use an official Java 8 runtime as a parent image
FROM maven:3.5-jdk-8-alpine

VOLUME /tmp

#Set maintainer email id
MAINTAINER admin@dineshonjava.com

# Set the working directory to /app
```

```
WORKDIR /app

# Copy the current directory contents into the container at /app
ADD . /app

# Build and create jar using maven command
#RUN mvn package -DskipTests=true -Ddir=app

# Copy the current directory contents into the container at /app
ADD target/account-service-0.0.1-SNAPSHOT.jar accounts-microservice.jar

# Make port 80 available to the world outside this container
EXPOSE 80

# Define environment variable
ENV JAVA_OPTS=""

# Run accounts-microservice.jar when the container launches
ENTRYPOINT [ "sh", "-c", "java $JAVA_OPTS -
Djava.security.egd=file:/dev/./urandom -jar accounts-microservice.jar" ]
```

The preceding `Dockerfile` is very simple, but that file has all you need to run a Spring Boot application and create a JAR file using the `maven` command `mvn` package. The project JAR file is added to the container as `accounts-microservice.jar` and then executed in `ENTRYPOINT`.

Let's see the following screenshot of this application directory structure:

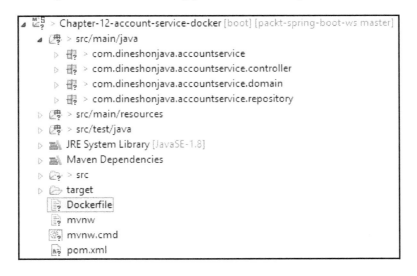

As you can see, `Dockerfile` has placed the application on a directory parallel to the `pom.xml` file. Now, let's create a Docker image by using the following command:

```
$ docker build -t spring-boot-app .
```

`spring-boot-app` is the name of the image. We can give our Docker image any name. The preceding command will build the image from `Dockerfile`, we need to specify the `Dockerfile` path. In the previous command, we mentioned "." at end of the command, its means Dockerfile is located in the current working directory.

The `-t` option is for tagging, it tags the new image followed by the version:

```
$ docker build -t spring-boot-app:1.0.1 .
```

Let's see the following screenshot of the output of preceding command:

```
Dinesh.Rajput@MRNDTHTMOBL0002 MINGW64 /d/packt-spring-boot-ws/Chapter-12-account-service-docker
$ docker build -t spring-boot-app .
Sending build context to Docker daemon  52.62MB
Step 1/9 : FROM maven:3.5-jdk-8-alpine
 ---> 08790c3343de
Step 2/9 : VOLUME /tmp
 ---> Using cache
 ---> f547d7ee9e0e
Step 3/9 : MAINTAINER admin@dineshonjava.com
 ---> Using cache
 ---> 173eae5492f2
Step 4/9 : WORKDIR /app
 ---> Using cache
 ---> 265ece0a5d47
Step 5/9 : ADD . /app
 ---> 313b940e276e
Step 6/9 : ADD target/account-service-0.0.1-SNAPSHOT.jar accounts-microservice.jar
 ---> 777351309215
Step 7/9 : EXPOSE 80
 ---> Running in 403e55725e4a
Removing intermediate container 403e55725e4a
 ---> 25c4ee521eb5
Step 8/9 : ENV JAVA_OPTS=""
 ---> Running in 4c8d0a102449
Removing intermediate container 4c8d0a102449
 ---> fe716b2607ad
Step 9/9 : ENTRYPOINT [ "sh", "-c", "java $JAVA_OPTS -Djava.security.egd=file:/dev/./urandom -j
 ---> Running in 335806d93dc2
Removing intermediate container 335806d93dc2
 ---> d51f03786940
Successfully built d51f03786940
Successfully tagged spring-boot-app:latest
```

As you can see, the Docker image has been created successfully. Now, we can run our Docker image using the `docker run` command. The following command is used to run `spring-boot-app`:

```
$ docker run -p 8080:8080 spring-boot-app:latest
```

Let's see the following screenshot of the preceding `docker run` command to run the container of the created `spring-boot-app` Docker image:

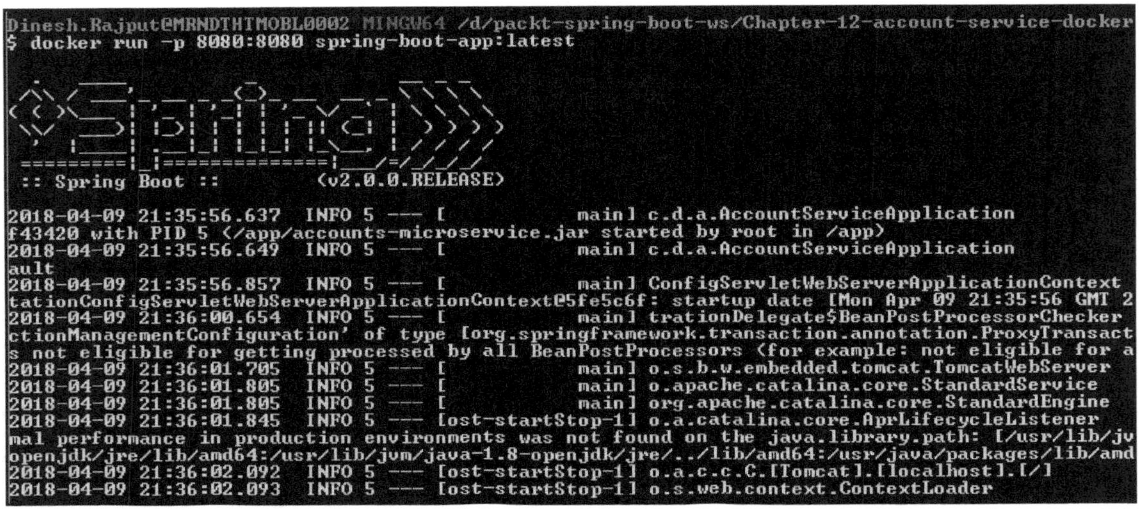

As you can see, our `Account-Service` has been run successfully. Now, we can see that after running `spring-boot-app`, it produced on the browser by accessing the following URL:

```
http://192.168.99.100:8080/account
```

As you can see in the preceding screenshot, it is rendering data access from the H2 DB, as we discussed in previous chapters. Now, our ACCOUNT-SERVICE microservice has been dockerized and is running as a Docker container. http://192.168.99.100 is the IP of the container to access it outside, and 8080 is the port of this particular container.

So far, we have created a microservice and built it as a Docker image by using the docker build command. We can also create a Docker image by using Maven or Gradle. Let's see the following section.

Creating a Docker image using Maven

If you have used Maven to resolve dependencies but the Maven provides support to create a build by adding some plugins to the Maven configuration file pom.xml. So, if you want to create a Docker image by using the Maven commands, you have to add a new plugin in the Maven pom.xml file. Consider the following:

```
<properties>
    ...
    <docker.image.prefix>doj</docker.image.prefix>
</properties>

<build>
    <plugins>
        <plugin>
            <groupId>com.spotify</groupId>
            <artifactId>dockerfile-maven-plugin</artifactId>
            <version>1.3.4</version>
            <configuration>
<repository>${docker.image.prefix}/${project.artifactId}</repository>
                <buildArgs>
<JAR_FILE>target/${project.build.finalName}.jar</JAR_FILE>
                </buildArgs>
            </configuration>
        </plugin>
        ...
    </plugins>
</build>
```

As you can see in the preceding Maven pom.xml file, we have configured a new plugin with groupId com.spotify and artifactId dockerfile-maven-plugin with the following two configurations:

- The repository with the image name, which will end up here as doj/account-account-service
- The name of the JAR file, exposing the maven configuration as a build argument for Docker

Now you can use the following Maven command to build a Docker image:

```
$ ./mvnw install dockerfile:build
```

You can also push this Docker image to Docker Hub using the following command:

```
./mvnw dockerfile:push
```

Similarly, you can use Gradle to build a Docker image using the Gradle build command.

Now let's move on and discuss Docker Compose in the next section.

Getting started with Docker Compose

Docker Compose is a Docker tool that is used to run multiple containers as a single service. For example, we have an application that requires ACCOUNT-SERVICE and CUSTOMER-SERVICE, so, you could create only one file, which will be used to start and stop the containers as a single service without the need to start and stop individually.

In this section, we will discuss Docker Compose and see how to get started with it. Then, we will look at how to get a single service with ACCOUNT-SERVICE and CUSTOMER-SERVICE up and running using Docker Compose.

As we have seen, each individual container has its own Docker command and particular Dockerfile. This Dockerfile is suitable for creating individual containers. But an enterprise system is not about a single container; it must have multiple containers to operate on a network of isolated applications, or the container management quickly becomes cluttered.

Docker Compose comes into the picture to solve that with its own build file in YAML format, which is better suited to managing multiple containers. For example, it is able to start or stop a composite of services in one command or merge logging output of multiple services together into one pseudo-tty. It is a great tool for development, testing, and staging environments. Let's see how to install Docker Compose on your machine.

Installing Docker Compose

OrchardUp launched a tool, called Fig, to make isolated development environments work with Docker. Currently, this tool is known as **Docker Compose** because when Fig was gaining popularity in the industry, it was acquired by Docker Inc. and rebranded as Docker Compose. It is available to install for macOS, Windows, and Linux.

On Windows and Mac, Docker Toolbox already includes Compose along with other Docker apps. So, you don't need to install Docker Compose separately.

On Linux, let's download the Docker Compose binary from the Compose repository release page on GitHub. Follow the instructions from the link, which involve running the `curl` command on the command line to download the binaries. Then follow these step-by-step instructions:

Run the following command to download the latest version of Docker Compose:

```
sudo curl -L
https://github.com/docker/compose/releases/download/1.21.0/docker-compose-$
(uname -s)-$(uname -m) -o /usr/local/bin/docker-compose
```

Apply executable permissions to the binary:

```
sudo chmod +x /usr/local/bin/docker-compose
```

Test the installation, as follows:

```
$ docker-compose --version
docker-compose version 1.16.1, build 6d1ac219
```

Now that we have Docker Compose installed, we can jump to the next step, that is, how to use Docker Compose and how to write the `docker-compose.yml` file.

Let's create an example of two microservice applications running in different Docker containers. These services will communicate with each other and be presented as a single application unit to the host system. So, we will create `Account` and `Customer` services here, as you can see in the following screenshot:

```
Dinesh.Rajput@MRNDTHTMOBL0002 MINGW64 /d/packt-spring-boot-ws/Chapter-12-customer-service-docker (master)
$ docker ps
CONTAINER ID    IMAGE                 PORTS                            NAMES
8d26fd170e4e    doj/customer-service  8181/tcp, 0.0.0.0:8282->6060/tcp dreamy_einstein
8206caf99fba    doj/account-service   8080/tcp, 0.0.0.0:8181->6060/tcp cocky_thompson
1f97ede49f98    doj/eureka-server     0.0.0.0:8080->8761/tcp           ecstatic_jepsen
```

There are three containers running currently image name as `doj/account-service`, `doj/constomer-service`, and `doj/eureka-server`. Let's see how to use Docker Compose. You can find the complete code for all these services on GitHub at https://github.com/PacktPublishing/Mastering-Spring-Boot-2.0.

Our target is to run these services as a single isolated system rather than individually running three separate containers. Using Docker Compose provides support to run these services as a single isolated system using a single command. Let's see in the following section how to use Docker Compose.

Using Docker Compose

Docker Compose is very easy to use; basically, it has a three-step process:

1. Define the environment of your services with Dockerfile so it can be recreated anywhere.
2. After defining the microservices that will be used as a single application in the `docker-compose.yml` file. By using this `docker-compose.yml` file, you can run these services together in an isolated environment.
3. Run `docker-compose up` and Compose will start and run your entire app.

We have seen three steps to use Docker Compose in an isolated application; let's see how to write a Docker Compose file.

Writing a docker-compose file

The Docker Compose file is a simple YAML-format file that contains instructions about an isolated system with links to multiple containers. We can also define the environment of each individual container. It is able to start or stop a composite of services with one command. A typical `docker-compose.yml` file looks like the following:

```
version: "2"
services:
  eureka:
    image: doj/eureka-server
    ports:
      - "8080:8761"
  account:
    image: doj/account-service
    ports:
      - "8181:6060"
    links:
      - eureka
  customer:
    image: doj/customer-service
    ports:
      - "8282:6060"
    links:
      - eureka
      - account
```

As you can see in the preceding `docker-compose.yml` file, it is very easy and has a simple `yml` syntax. Let's take a close look and what the file means:

- At the parent level, the `version` key defines the format of the Docker Compose file. This field is mandatory.
- At the same level, the `services` key defines the names of our services, such as `account`, `customer`, and `eureka`.
- Each service requires an image to run the Docker container, so we have added additional `image` parameters.
- The `image` keyword is used to specify the image from Docker Hub for `eureka`, `account`, and `customer` services:
    - For `eureka`, we just refer to the `doj/eureka-server` image available on Docker Hub
    - For `account`, we refer to the `doj/account-service` image available on Docker Hub
    - For `customer`, we refer to the `doj/customer-service` image available on Docker Hub
- The `ports` keyword mentions the ports that need to be exposed to `eureka`, `account`, and `customer` services:
    - For `eureka`, we have exposed ports to `8080:8761` to access it outside
    - For `account`, we have exposed ports to `8181:6060` to access it outside
    - For `customer`, we have exposed ports to `8282:6060` to access it outside
- We also specify the `links` variables for `account` and `customer`, which are required to create an internal network link between these services and the listed services:
    - The `account` service links with the `eureka` service
    - The `customer` service links with `eureka` and `account` services

Now we need to clear out our old running containers with a new version; let's use the `docker stop <container ID>` command to stop old running containers:

```
$ docker stop 8d26fd170e4e 8206caf99fba 1f97ede49f98
8d26fd170e4e
8206caf99fba
1f97ede49f98
```

As we have stopped all old running containers, you can check it with the following command:

```
$ docker ps
```

The following output will be displayed:

```
$ docker ps
CONTAINER ID        IMAGE               COMMAND             CREATED             STATUS              PORTS
```

In an enterprise application, running three services very few, this could be tens or hundreds, so managing these containers and ensuring that all of the various command-line parameters link up to these containers can be a little frustrating. Docker Compose comes and organizes a fleet of containers and makes this work easy.

This process is also known as orchestrating or running the containers. Let's see the following section about orchestration using `docker-compose` and build a Docker Compose example.

Orchestration using a docker-compose file

In the Docker Compose file, you can define it to compose a set of containers. This is a YAML configuration file. `docker-compose` manages runtime configuration of the containers with the right options and configuration. We have created a `docker-compose.yml` file in the preceding section. Let's test the configuration of this file for syntax errors by using the following command:

```
$ docker-compose config
```

You can see the following output:

```
$ docker-compose config
ERROR: yaml.parser.ParserError: while parsing a block mapping
  in ".\docker-compose.yml", line 1, column 1
expected <block end>, but found '-'
  in ".\docker-compose.yml", line 18, column 1
```

In the case of a syntax error, it renders as the following:

```
$ docker-compose config
services:
  account:
    image: doj/account-service
    links:
    - eureka
    ports:
    - 8181:6060/tcp
  customer:
    image: doj/customer-service
    links:
    - eureka
    - account
    ports:
    - 8282:6060/tcp
  eureka:
    image: doj/eureka-server
    ports:
    - 8080:8761/tcp
version: '2.0'
```

You must be inside the directory with the `docker-compose.yml` file in order to execute most Compose commands.

Finally, we can start it with one command:

```
$ docker-compose up -d
```

Let's see the output of the preceding command:

```
$ docker-compose up -d
Creating network "dockercompose_default" with the default driver
Creating dockercompose_eureka_1 ...
Creating dockercompose_eureka_1 ... done
Creating dockercompose_account_1 ...
Creating dockercompose_account_1 ... done
Creating dockercompose_customer_1 ...
Creating dockercompose_customer_1 ... done
```

The preceding command is running containers in the detached mode because of the -d option. Let's check the container's status using the following command:

```
$ docker-compose ps
```

It renders the following output:

```
$ docker-compose ps
            Name                     Command              State              Ports
------------------------------------------------------------------------------------------------
dockercompose_account_1     sh -c java $JAVA_OPTS -Dja ...   Up      0.0.0.0:8181->6060/tcp, 8080/tcp
dockercompose_customer_1    sh -c java $JAVA_OPTS -Dja ...   Up      0.0.0.0:8282->6060/tcp, 8181/tcp
dockercompose_eureka_1      sh -c java $JAVA_OPTS -Dja ...   Up      0.0.0.0:8080->8761/tcp
```

As you can see, the service containers are running successfully; we can test it by accessing the following URLs in the browser.

Let's first test account-service by using the http://192.168.99.100:8181/account/101 URL. It renders data as follows:

```
{
    accountId: 101,
    balance: 3502.92,
    customerId: 1001,
    accountType: "SAVING",
    branchCode: "ICICI001",
    bank: "ICICI"
}
```

Let's test the `customer-service` by using
the `http://192.168.99.100:8282/customer/1001` URL. It renders data as follows:

Let's stop the services from running by using the following command:

```
$ docker-compose down
```

Let's see the following output:

As you can see, all containers have been stopped.

Scaling containers using docker-compose and load balancing

You can use the following command to scale the container of a particular service:

```
$ docker-compose scale [compose container name]=3
```

Consider the following example:

```
$ docker-compose scale account=3
```

Let's see the following output:

```
Dinesh.Rajput@MRNDTHTMOBL0002 MINGW64 /d/packt-spring-boot-ws/docker-compose (master)
$ docker-compose scale account=3
WARNING: The scale command is deprecated. Use the up command with the --scale flag instead.
Starting dockercompose_account_1 ... done
Creating dockercompose_account_2 ...
Creating dockercompose_account_3 ...
Creating dockercompose_account_2 ... done
Creating dockercompose_account_3 ... done

Dinesh.Rajput@MRNDTHTMOBL0002 MINGW64 /d/packt-spring-boot-ws/docker-compose (master)
$ docker-compose ps
          Name                        Command              State              Ports
dockercompose_account_1    sh -c java $JAVA_OPTS -Dja ...   Up      8080/tcp
dockercompose_account_2    sh -c java $JAVA_OPTS -Dja ...   Up      8080/tcp
dockercompose_account_3    sh -c java $JAVA_OPTS -Dja ...   Up      8080/tcp
dockercompose_customer_1   sh -c java $JAVA_OPTS -Dja ...   Up      0.0.0.0:8282->6060/tcp, 8181/tcp
dockercompose_eureka_1     sh -c java $JAVA_OPTS -Dja ...   Up      0.0.0.0:8080->8761/tcp
```

As you can see, our account container now has three instances. But there is a problem here: how will a client call an instance of `account-service` since their ports have changed?

There are some solutions available to solve this issue, such as Kubernetes and AWSs' ECS. We'll discuss Kubernetes in the next section, and deployment with AWSs' ECS in `Chapter 14`, *Deploying in Cloud (AWS)*.

Here I am going to use a very easy solution provided by a company named Tutum. They provide an extension of HAProxy. This proxy can auto-configure itself based on linked containers, and it can be used as a load balancer for our multiple containers. Let's update our `docker-compose.yml` by adding the following configuration related to the `tutum/haproxy` image:

```
version: "2"
services:
  eureka:
```

```
    image: doj/eureka-server
    ports:
      - "8080:8761"
account:
    image: doj/account-service
    links:
      - eureka
customer:
    image: doj/customer-service
    ports:
      - "8282:6060"
    links:
      - eureka
      - account
ha_account:
    image: tutum/haproxy
    links:
      - account
    ports:
      - "8181:80"
```

We have removed the static port configuration for the account service because if we have the static port then it doesn't allow us to create multiple instances of `account-service` with the same static port. The HAProxy Docker container works as a load balancer by default using the **round-robin** (**RR**) algorithm across the three running instances.

Let's discuss another tool for orchestrating Docker containers, Kubernetes. Let's see it in the next section.

Introducing Kubernetes

Kubernetes is a portable and open source platform used for the management of containerized applications and services. It is used to facilitate the configuration and automation of applications. Kubernetes is growing fast, and its support, services, and tools are available to the masses.

Kubernetes is a Google project that was made open source in 2014, and hence it is developed with the decades of Google's experience of handling large-scale workloads, integrated with the best ideas and practices contributed by the community.

Kubernetes works with a lot of different tools, including Docker, to provide the containerized applications a platform for the purposes of scaling, operations, and automation of deployment.

Joe Beda, Brendan Burns, and Craig McLuckie first developed Kubernetes. Different engineers at Google, such as Brian Grant and Tim Hockin, soon joined them. The Borg system of Google has been a heavy influence on the design and development of Kubernetes, as many of the top contributors first worked on the Borg project.

In 2015, Google released Kubernetes v1.0, partnered with Linux Foundation, and went on to form **Cloud Native Computing Foundation (CNCF)**.

Some of the features of Kubernetes are as follows:

- A container platform
- A microservice platform
- A portable cloud platform

The theme of the Kubernetes platform is to support container-related management environments. Kubernetes provides portability, simplicity, and flexibility over different infrastructures, mimicking **Platform as a Service (PaaS)** and **Infrastructure as a Service (IaaS)** on some levels. Kubernetes offers a lot of functionalities, however, the open source nature of this platform enables constant improvement and added features to the system. This regular update system is exactly why Kubernetes was envisioned as a platform so that it builds an ecosystem of components and tools that would assist in the deployment, scaling, and management of the application, making it all easier to handle.

The design of Kubernetes has allowed a number of different systems to be built upon it. Labels allow the users to organize the resources per their desire, and annotations offer them a chance to customize the resources and information to suit their workflow and manage their tools.

The APIs on which the Kubernetes control plane is built are also available to developers and users, and hence, users can build their own customized controls and APIs. They can also be easily targeted by any general CLI tool and manipulated as per the requirements of the developer.

Despite its many awesome functionalities, Kubernetes is still not an alternative to a PaaS system. It can be perceived as such because of its many similarities, such as providing a platform for applications to be deployed, scaled, logged, and monitored. Kubernetes is aimed to support a variety of diverse applications with their workloads and data processing. However, only containerized applications will perform well on the Kubernetes platform.

Summary

As we have learned in this chapter, a container is isolated in nature and portable. You can run a container on any Docker platform. The container-based approach has been adopted by many enterprises and its popularity is increasing every day.

Container-based virtualization is a much better solution for the microservice architectural style, where application features are divided into small, well-defined, distinctive services. Containers and VMs are not independent of each other; they can be viewed as complementary solutions. An excellent example of this is the Netflix Cloud, where containers are running on virtual machines.

This concludes our tour of Docker Compose. With Docker Compose, you can pause your services, run a one-off command on a container, and even scale the number of containers.

In the next chapter, we will explore and implement a Swagger and KONG API manager.

13
API Management

This chapter will explore the need for API Manager in distributed systems, set up the KONG open source API Manager, configure the API endpoints built in the previous chapters in KONG API Manager, introduce you to Swagger for API standards, and end by demonstrating rate limiting and logging using KONG.

In the previous chapters, we learned about the container architecture and its advantages and challenges. We also created Docker containers and deployed the `Account` and `Customer` microservices on the Docker containers. Now we will discuss API management and the tools used for it, such as Swagger and KONG. I will use an example of the microservices system using Spring, Spring Boot, and Spring Cloud.

By the end of this chapter, you will have a better understanding of KONG and Swagger, and how to use these tools to manage and document the REST API.

This chapter will cover the following points:

- API Management
- Rate limiting
- KONG
- Swagger

Let's look at these topics in detail.

API Management

API Management is a mechanism to manage APIs from the outside clients, such as controlling an API's access through throttling or rate limiting. Rate limiting is a mechanism to control access for a specific consumer of an API. For example, you want to give access to a customer to use a specific API with only 100 requests per day. You can monetize your APIs using API Management tools by restricting the access to an API using rate limiting.

API Management tools help to manage the administrative complexities of APIs. As we know, API usage is increasing in the market. A lot of businesses depend on APIs. So, the API Management process is also important for API providers. The API development process is totally different from the API Management process.

If you want to use APIs properly, then strong documentation of them is also very important. Other parameters of API Management, such as increased levels of security, comprehensive testing, routine versioning, and high reliability, are important to have for your APIs. The API Management tools and software provide all these functionalities for API requirements.

Advantages of using API Management software tools

These are the advantages provided by the API Management tools:

- Can monitor traffic coming from individual apps
- Can control connections between an API and the apps that are using the API
- Manages API consistency with its versions
- Provides a caching mechanism and memory management process to improve application performance
- Provides security and protects APIs from outside threats

Now let's see the number of API Management solution providers.

API Management tools

There are many API Management tools available; let's see some of the popular API Management tools:

- Kong
- 3scale API Management
- Akana platform
- Apigee
- Azure API Management
- TIBCO Mashery
- MuleSoft
- WSO2
- Amazon Web Services API Gateway

Let's see one of the functionalities of the API Management platform, which is very important from a security and business point of view.

Rate limiting

Rate limiting is a pattern for a special counter that is used to limit the rate at which an operation can be performed. The classic materialization of this pattern involves limiting the number of requests that can be performed against a public API.

The API provider has a silver bullet for these issues—rate limiting. Rate limiting is the process by which an API rejects requests for a variety of reasons, ranging from having too many concurrent connections, to the requester forming a poor request for high amounts of data. By implementing rate limiting, the developer essentially installs a spigot that can be relaxed to allow for greater flow or tightened to reduce the flow within the system. Another one of the reasons to implement rate limiting is to defend applications against **Denial of Service (DoS)** attacks.

In a safety context, the developer needs to consider the limitations of a system, so as to prevent overflowing. Just like, packed road results in congestion and accidents so do an over-limited logical connection.

From a business context, API providers can implement rate limiting as a profit-and-cost-negation technique. By requiring high-volume users to pay for premium plans, the increased operating expense can be negated and turned instead into a revenue stream.

Implementing rate limiting

There are so many simple and direct ways you can implement rate limiting. One of the most common and easy ways to do so is to use internal caching on the server.

Another implementation we can use is Redis, which utilizes rate limit patterns as follows:

```
FUNCTION LIMIT_API_CALL(ip)
ts = CURRENT_UNIX_TIME()
keyname = ip+":"+ts
current = GET(keyname)
IF current != NULL AND current > 10 THEN
    ERROR "too many requests per second"
ELSE
    MULTI
        INCR(keyname,1)
        EXPIRE(keyname,10)
    EXEC
    PERFORM_API_CALL()
END
```

Basically, we have a counter for every IP, for every seconds. But these counters are always incremented, setting an expiry time of 10 seconds, so that they'll be removed by Redis automatically when the current second changes.

You can also use the interceptor to implement rate limiting for APIs in your microservice project. There are many algorithms available for implementing rate limiting, either for fixed or distributed systems. You can also use the Kong API to quickly set up rate limiting for APIs.

Let's see the KONG API Management tool in the following section.

Learning about KONG

In this section, we will discuss about the KONG, let's see the following quote about the KONG:

> *"Kong allows developers to reduce complexity and deployment times in implementing an API solution on the NGINX platform."*
>
> *– Owen Garrett, head of products at NGINX*

Kong is an open source and scalable API layer, running in front of RESTful APIs that have been extended through plugins. This way, Kong provides extra functionality and services that are way beyond the services provided by the core platform.

The original purpose of building KONG at Mashape was to secure, manage, and extend the APIs and microservices that are above 15,000, for the purposes of marketplace related to APIs. This method generates huge numbers, going into the billions, of requests over a month for more than 2,00,000 developers. Now KONG APIs are used for the deployment of critical missions in various organizations of different scales, small or large.

As we have said, KONG is an API gateway, which is a filter that sits in front of your RESTful API. This gateway will provide the following functionality:

- **Access control**: Only allows authenticated and authorized traffic
- **Rate limiting**: Restricts how much traffic is sent to your API
- **Analytics, metrics, and logging**: Tracks how your API is used
- **Security filtering**: Makes sure the incoming traffic is not an attack
- **Redirection**: Sends traffic to a different endpoint.

Any client makes a call to your REST API by going through KONG. It will send proxy client requests to the REST API. It executes all common functionalities that you have set up for your REST API, such as the rate limit plugin installed. KONG will check and make sure the request doesn't exceed the specified limits before calling your API. Let's see the following diagram:

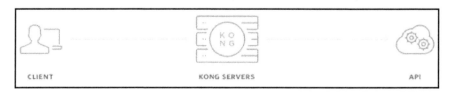

As you can see, the client will call the API through the KONG server. KONG orchestrates common functionality, such as rate limiting, access control, and logging.

Microservice REST APIs with the KONG architecture

Let's see the following diagram about KONG's architectural flow:

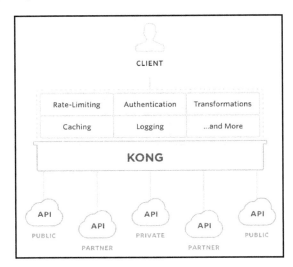

As you can see, **KONG** provides centralized and unified functionality in one place. The KONG architecture is distributed and ready to scale and expand functionality from one place with a simple command. You can configure KONG very easily at the server side without doing any modification at the microservice application level. Developers don't need to worry about API Management mechanisms; just focus on the product, Kong does the REST.

Using APIs without the KONG architecture

The KONG tool provides a centralized solution for the API Management mechanism; if you don't have KONG configuration at the server level for APIs, then you have to implement common functionalities of API Management across your multiple microservices. This means code duplicity will be increased and it will be difficult to maintain and expand without impacting other microservices. The systems tend to be monolithic, as you can see in the following diagram about these common functionalities without the KONG configuration:

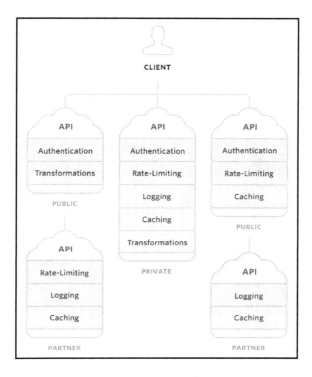

Common functionality codes are distributed across the APIs. It is very difficult to manage, and developers are responsible for API Management, apart from the business code. Let's see in the following section how to install KONG on your system.

Installing KONG

Kong is available to install in multiple operating environments and for containers such as Docker. We will go through the installation process using Docker.

Before installing KONG, you will need to know about Docker; please read through Chapter 12, *Containerizing Microservice*.

Here, I am going to use the `DockerHub` repository to find the Docker image of KONG. In the following example, I will link a KONG Docker container to a Cassandra Docker container. Perform the following steps:

1. Use the Cassandra container to store information related to the KONG API. Use the following command:

```
Dinesh.Rajput@MRNDTHTMOBL0002 MINGW64 ~
$ docker run -d --name kong-database \
>                    -p 9042:9042 \
>                    cassandra:3
```

2. Migrate the Cassandra database with the KONG container by using the following command:

```
Dinesh.Rajput@MRNDTHTMOBL0002 MINGW64 ~
$ docker run --rm \
>     --link kong-database:kong-database \
>     -e "KONG_DATABASE=cassandra" \
>     -e "KONG_PG_HOST=kong-database" \
>     -e "KONG_CASSANDRA_CONTACT_POINTS=kong-database" \
>     kong:latest kong migrations up
```

3. Start KONG:

```
Dinesh.Rajput@MRNDTHTMOBL0002 MINGW64 ~
$ docker run -d --name kong \
>     --link kong-database:kong-database \
>     -e "KONG_DATABASE=cassandra" \
>     -e "KONG_PG_HOST=kong-database" \
>     -e "KONG_CASSANDRA_CONTACT_POINTS=kong-database" \
>     -e "KONG_PROXY_ACCESS_LOG=/dev/stdout" \
>     -e "KONG_ADMIN_ACCESS_LOG=/dev/stdout" \
>     -e "KONG_PROXY_ERROR_LOG=/dev/stderr" \
>     -e "KONG_ADMIN_ERROR_LOG=/dev/stderr" \
>     -e "KONG_ADMIN_LISTEN=0.0.0.0:8001" \
>     -e "KONG_ADMIN_LISTEN_SSL=0.0.0.0:8444" \
>     -p 8000:8000 \
>     -p 8443:8443 \
>     -p 8001:8001 \
>     -p 8444:8444 \
>     kong:latest
```

I have used port `8000` for a non-SSL API call, and port `8443` is used for an SSL-enabled API call. The port `8001` is used to administrate your KONG installation through the RESTful Admin API.

4. Verify the KONG installation:

```
Dinesh.Rajput@MRNDIHTMOBL0002 MINGW64 ~
$ curl -i http://192.168.99.100:8001/
HTTP/1.1 200 OK
Date: Fri, 20 Apr 2018 09:24:32 GMT
Content-Type: application/json; charset=utf-8
Transfer-Encoding: chunked
Connection: keep-alive
Access-Control-Allow-Origin: *
Server: kong/0.13.0
```

I have accessed `http://192.168.99.100:8001/`. It returns data in JSON format from the KONG API.

Using the KONG API

We have installed KONG in Docker, now let's use the KONG API and configure your REST API that we are going to expose to consumers. Perform the following steps:

1. Configure a service in Kong. After installing and starting Kong, use the Admin API on port `8001` to add a new service. Services represent your upstream servers exposing APIs/microservices; let's see the following command:

```
$ curl -i -X POST    --url http://192.168.99.100:8001/services/    --
data 'name=account'    --data
'url=http://192.168.99.100:8181/account/'
```

Let's see this command on the console as following screenshot:

```
Dinesh.Rajput@MRNDIHTMOBL0002 MINGW64 ~
$ curl -i -X POST    --url http://192.168.99.100:8001/services/    --data 'name=account'    --data 'url=http://192.168.99.100:8181/account/'
HTTP/1.1 201 Created
Date: Fri, 20 Apr 2018 09:56:01 GMT
Content-Type: application/json; charset=utf-8
Transfer-Encoding: chunked
Connection: keep-alive
Access-Control-Allow-Origin: *
Server: kong/0.13.0
```

The preceding screenshot rendered the response to the preceding command. Let's
see the following output in the browser, at
`http://192.168.99.100:8001/services`:

```
{
    next: null,
  - data: [
      - {
            host: "192.168.99.100",
            created_at: 1524218160,
            connect_timeout: 60000,
            id: "ac443bb1-4865-4f7a-acde-1eb892357979",
            protocol: "http",
            name: "account",
            read_timeout: 60000,
            port: 8181,
            path: "/account/",
            updated_at: 1524218160,
            retries: 5,
            write_timeout: 60000
        }
    ]
}
```

2. Add a route to expose the service. Once you have a service, expose it to the
   clients by adding one (or many) routes for it. Routes control how client requests
   are matched and proxied to services; let's see the following command:

```
curl -i -X POST    --url
http://192.168.99.100:8001/services/account/routes/    --data
'host=dineshonjava.com'
```

We have run the preceding command to add a route to expose the service.

After adding a proxy route, let's see this setting in the browser by accessing
`http://192.168.99.100:8001/services/account/routes/`:

```
{
    next: null,
  - data: [
      - {
            created_at: 1524219554,
            strip_path: true,
          - hosts: [
                "dineshonjava.com"
            ],
            preserve_host: false,
            regex_priority: 0,
            id: "cdc35db1-6c90-413b-97de-838373b7b377",
            paths: null,
          - service: {
                id: "ac443bb1-4865-4f7a-acde-1eb892357979"
            },
            methods: null,
          - protocols: [
                "http",
                "https"
            ],
            updated_at: 1524219554
        }
    ]
}
```

The preceding screenshot has information about the added service to KONG.

3. Configure plugins. Add extra functionality by using KONG plugins. You can also create your own plugins. Let's see the following command:

```
curl -i -X POST    --url http://192.168.99.100:8001/plugins/   --
data 'name=rate-limiting'    --data 'service_id=ac443bb1-4865-4f7a-
acde-1eb892357979'    --data 'config.minute=100'
```

We used `service_id` as we have generated in the first step of usage of KONG. Let's see the following screenshot:

```
Dinesh.Rajput@MRNDTHTMOBL0002 MINGW64 ~
$ curl -i -X POST \
>    --url http://192.168.99.100:8001/plugins/ \
>    --data 'name=rate-limiting' \
>    --data 'service_id=ac443bb1-4865-4f7a-acde-1eb892357979' \
>    --data 'config.minute=100'
HTTP/1.1 201 Created
Date: Fri, 20 Apr 2018 10:12:13 GMT
Content-Type: application/json; charset=utf-8
Transfer-Encoding: chunked
Connection: keep-alive
Access-Control-Allow-Origin: *
Server: kong/0.13.0
```

You can check the settings of the rate-limiting plugin after this command by accessing `http://192.168.99.100:8001/plugins/` on the browser:

```
{
    total: 1,
  - data: [
      - {
            created_at: 1524219133155,
          - config: {
                hide_client_headers: false,
                minute: 100,
                policy: "cluster",
                redis_database: 0,
                redis_timeout: 2000,
                redis_port: 6379,
                limit_by: "consumer",
                fault_tolerant: true
            },
            id: "5aa8996b-ba50-42a1-ab4b-c50daf19bf7a",
            service_id: "ac443bb1-4865-4f7a-acde-1eb892357979",
            name: "rate-limiting",
            enabled: true
        }
    ]
}
```

Rate limiting has been enabled for the API with the service_id: `ac443bb1-4865-4f7a-acde-1eb892357979`.

4. Proxy a request. Clients can now consume your upstream API/microservice through KONG's proxy server, running on port `8000` by default. Let's see the following command:

```
curl -i -X GET  --url http://192.168.99.100:8000/  --header 'Host:
dineshonjava.com'
```

Let's see the following screenshot for this command with a response:

It returns an account service response using the KONG proxy route. Similarly, you can use multiple plugins on the KONG API for this account service; let's add another key authentication plugin, as follows:

```
curl -i -X POST    --url http://192.168.99.100:8001/plugins/    --
data 'name=key-auth'    --data 'service_id=ac443bb1-4865-4f7a-
acde-1eb892357979'
```

In the following screenshot, we have created authentication key to use for the service:

```
Dinesh.Rajput@MRNDTHTMOBL0002 MINGW64 ~
$ curl -i http://192.168.99.100:8001/
HTTP/1.1 200 OK
Date: Fri, 20 Apr 2018 09:24:32 GMT
Content-Type: application/json; charset=utf-8
Transfer-Encoding: chunked
Connection: keep-alive
Access-Control-Allow-Origin: *
Server: kong/0.13.0
```

Now, the `key-auth` plugin has been added to the KONG API; you can check it in your browser at `http://192.168.99.100:8001/plugins/`:

```
{
    total: 2,
 -  data: [
    - {
            created_at: 1524221934673,
        - config: {
                key_in_body: false,
                run_on_preflight: true,
                anonymous: "",
                hide_credentials: false,
            - key_names: [
                    "apikey"
                ]
            },
            id: "4533fda9-84ae-4722-9cfe-858a63ede90f",
            service_id: "ac443bb1-4865-4f7a-acde-1eb892357979",
            name: "key-auth",
            enabled: true
        },
      + {...}
    ]
}
```

Now, let's access the service again using the KONG proxy, it prevents to call service because of authentication key:

```
Dinesh.Rajput@MRNDTHTMOBL0002 MINGW64 ~
$ curl -i -X GET    --url http://192.168.99.100:8000/    --header 'Host: dineshonjava.com'
HTTP/1.1 401 Unauthorized
Date: Fri, 20 Apr 2018 11:04:41 GMT
Content-Type: application/json; charset=utf-8
Transfer-Encoding: chunked
Connection: keep-alive
WWW-Authenticate: Key realm="kong"
Server: kong/0.13.0

{"message":"No API key found in request"}
```

Note that we now get a `401` response: `HTTP/1.1 401 Unauthorized`.

5. Adding consumers. Let's add a consumer; in order to use the API now, we will need to create a consumer and add a key:

```
curl -X POST http://192.168.99.100:8001/consumers    --data
"username=dineshonjava"    --data "custom_id=1234"
```

Let's see the following screenshot for adding service consumer:

```
Dinesh.Rajput@MRNDTHTMOBL0002 MINGW64 ~
$ curl -X POST http://192.168.99.100:8001/consumers --data "username=dineshonjava" --data "custom_id=1234"
{"custom_id":"1234","created_at":1524222402197,"username":"dineshonjava","id":"97c87134-9389-4ca1-8648-f11a3f21bb11"}
```

You can check added consumers to this service in the browser by accessing the `http://192.168.99.100:8001/consumers` URL:

```
{
    total: 1,
  - data: [
     - {
            custom_id: "1234",
            created_at: 1524222402197,
            username: "dineshonjava",
            id: "97c87134-9389-4ca1-8648-f11a3f21bb11"
        }
    ]
}
```

I have added one consumer with the `dineshonjava` username and its custom ID as `1234`. After adding a consumer, let's create an authentication key for this consumer. Let's use service with `key-auth`:

```
$ curl -X POST
http://192.168.99.100:8001/consumers/dineshonjava/key-auth --data
" "
```

Let's check the authentication key by using
`http://192.168.99.100:8001/consumers/dineshonjava/key-auth`:

```
{
    total: 1,
  - data: [
      - {
            id: "0249169c-73d6-45c8-95f2-5436c4ca333e",
            created_at: 1524223092893,
            key: "yyBFOR5LDfaAb4ksT9IqfHWwLOpVYbtG",
            consumer_id: "97c87134-9389-4ca1-8648-f11a3f21bb11"
        }
    ]
}
```

The plugin auto-generated a key for us. The value of key will be used in order to call the API. You can pass this key in the body of the request.

Let's access this API again and make sure this consumer is now able to access this API using their API key generated from the preceding screenshot code. We need to pass in a new apikey header with the key, as follows:

```
curl -i -X GET    --url http://192.168.99.100:8000/    --header 'Host:
dineshonjava.com'    --header 'apikey: yyBFOR5LDfaAb4ksT9IqfHWwLOpVYbtG'
```

Let's see the following screen shot where we have used apikey to access the secure API:

```
Dinesh.Rajput@MRNDTHTMOBL0002 MINGW64 ~
$ curl -i -X GET \
>    --url http://192.168.99.100:8000/ \
>    --header 'Host: dineshonjava.com' \
>    --header 'apikey: yyBFOR5LDfaAb4ksT9IqfHWwLOpVYbtG'
HTTP/1.1 200
Content-Type: application/json;charset=UTF-8
Transfer-Encoding: chunked
Connection: keep-alive
X-RateLimit-Limit-minute: 100
X-RateLimit-Remaining-minute: 99
Date: Fri, 20 Apr 2018 11:27:23 GMT
X-Kong-Upstream-Latency: 18
X-Kong-Proxy-Latency: 155
Via: kong/0.13.0

[{"accountId":100,"balance":3502.92,"customerId":1000,"ac
01,"accountType":"SAVING","branchCode":"ICICI001","bank":
,"bank":"HDFC"},{"accountId":201,"balance":3122.05,"custo
43,"customerId":1002,"accountType":"SAVING","branchCode":
Code":"ICICI003","bank":"ICICI"}]
```

Now the consumer is able to access the restricted API by using the API key as an authentication Key. So, we have seen that KONG is a great framework for API Management. It provides a lot of extensible functionality for your REST APIs by putting your services behind Kong and adding powerful functionality through Kong plugins, all in one command. Look at the following diagram:

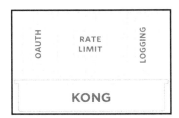

KONG is placed on the bottom to provide API Management functionalities to your REST APIs. Let's see the important features of the KONG API in the next section.

Features of the KONG API

Some features of the KONG API include:

- **Scalability**: You can increase the scalability of the KONG API very easily; all you have to do is increase the number of machines horizontally. Scalability offers you an advantage of being able to handle any load while keeping the latency of the system low.
- **Modularity**: KONG allows you to divide your API into different portions so that it can handle the workload easily. The KONG API can be modulated by adding additional plugins to the API. These plugins can be easily configured by the source of the RESTful API relating to the admin.
- **Runnable on any infrastructure**: You can deploy KONG almost anywhere, on any infrastructure. Be it cloud or local, KONG is ready-made to run per your instructions. This also includes data centers, with either single or multiple setups for all kinds of APIs, whether they are public, private, or invite-only.

The client requests the workflow provided by KONG for the APIs. KONG servers are provided the requested APIs and serve as a platform for the APIs. After the setup is completed, all the requests that will be made to the API will go to the KONG server first, who will then forward it to the final API. Between the time of request sent and the response received, KONG decides to execute a plugin that you are prompted to download. Should you decide to download it, the installed plugin will then empower your API further. This way, the KONG server will become the main point of entry for all incoming API requests.

KONG helps us to micromanage the APIs more easily and much faster than ever before. The technology companies, e-commerce innovators, major bank firms, and even a lot of government agencies, prefer to get KONG as the main server for all their web-related workloads. This also increases the popularity of the KONG platform among developers around the globe, who then actively contribute to the innovations done over the KONG platform. The company of KONG platforms focuses on customer satisfaction and technological advancements, building a platform worthy of international fame. Not only do they develop the APIs, but also help customers realize the importance of the infrastructure with microservices for security, agility, and scalability.

Let's see how to create REST API documentation in your Spring Boot microservice project in the next section.

Swagger

Swagger is an open source platform that provides a variety of tools for developers to assist them in designing, building, documenting, and consuming RESTful web services. Although Swagger is generally known for its user interface tools, it also provides the user with other tools, such as automation and test cases.

At first, the popularity of the Swagger API was limited to the reach of small-scale organizations and individual developers. Most of the time, mechanisms that support machine readability are not available with RESTful APIs, but the Swagger API provided an easy and simple way of doing so. However, soon enough, with the help of an open source license from Apache 2.0, products and online services started offering Swagger as a part of their toolkit. This soon led to global companies, such as Apigee, Intuit, Microsoft, and IBM, to start endorsing the Swagger project publicly.

Let's see the usage of the Swagger for the REST APIs in the next section.

Usage of Swagger

These are some of the important usages of the Swagger API toolkit:

- **Developing APIs**: The Swagger toolkit for API development can be utilized to automatically create an Open API document related to the code. The informal word used for it would be the code-first or bottom-up development of an API. Using another tool provided by the Swagger API, called *Swagger Codegen*, coders can decouple the open API documentation, and the client-side and server-side code can then be directly generated from it.
- **Interaction with APIs**: Swagger Codegen allows the end users to generate the SDK code exactly from the Open API Doc, and hence abate the requirement for the code for clients generated by humans. As of 2017, the Swagger Codegen project now supports more than 50 formats and languages for the code generated for the SDK Client.
- **Documentation**: According to the Open API Document, this API is an open source toolkit that can be utilized to directly interact with this API through Swagger UI. Connections to the APIs are also allowed by the project directly via an HTML-based interactive user interface.

Let's see the implementation of Swagger for a REST API for the `Account` microservice.

Using Swagger in a microservice

Let's see the example of creating a REST API for `Account` microservice as we have used this example in this book, any REST API must have good documentation with usage.

Managing and creating documentation is a tedious job, so, we have to move with automation of the process. Such that every change in the API should be simultaneously described in the reference documentation. Swagger comes into the picture to automate the documentation process of a REST API.

In this section, we will discuss the usage with examples of Swagger 2 for a Spring REST web service. We will use the SpringFox implementation of the Swagger 2 specification in this example.

We will explore some examples of the `Account` microservice of the previous chapters, so, let's start by adding Maven dependencies for the SpringFox implementation of Swagger 2 in the `pom.xml` file of the `Account` microservice example.

Adding a Maven dependency

There is a Maven dependency required to have the SpringFox implementation of the Swagger 2 specification in your `Account` microservice project:

```
<dependency>
    <groupId>io.springfox</groupId>
    <artifactId>springfox-swagger2</artifactId>
    <version>${swagger.version}</version>
</dependency>
```

In the preceding Maven dependency, we have added the SpringFox Maven dependency for Swagger 2 with groupId `io.springfox` and the `springfox-swagger2` artifact ID. Let's configure Swagger using the following configuration:

```
<properties>
    ...
    <swagger.version>2.7.0</swagger.version>
</properties>
```

After adding the Swagger 2 dependency with our example of the `Account` microservice, let's integrate the Swagger 2 configuration.

Configuring Swagger 2 in your project

Let's configure Swagger 2 in your `Account` microservice project using Java-based configuration:

```
package com.dineshonjava.accountservice.config;

import org.springframework.context.annotation.Bean;
import org.springframework.context.annotation.Configuration;

import springfox.documentation.builders.PathSelectors;
import springfox.documentation.builders.RequestHandlerSelectors;
import springfox.documentation.spi.DocumentationType;
import springfox.documentation.spring.web.plugins.Docket;
import springfox.documentation.swagger2.annotations.EnableSwagger2;

@Configuration
@EnableSwagger2
public class SwaggerConfig {
    @Bean
    public Docket api() {
        return new Docket(DocumentationType.SWAGGER_2)
```

```
                .select()
                .apis(RequestHandlerSelectors.any())
                .paths(PathSelectors.any())
                .build();
    }
}
```

We have used two annotations, @Configuration and @EnableSwagger2, at the top of our configuration class; here this configuration class mainly centers on the Docket bean. The @Configuration annotation is used to make this class a configuration class for this project. The @EnableSwagger2 annotation is used to enable the Swagger 2 functionality into your project.

In the preceding configuration, we defined a bean Docket. This Docket bean of DocumentationType.SWAGGER_2 will be created by this bean definition. As you can see in the configuration code, the select() method will return an instance of ApiSelectorBuilder. ApiSelectorBuilder will provide a way to control the endpoints exposed by Swagger. Another method, paths(), will return an instance of a predicate. And the predicate will provide a way to select RequestHandlers. RequestHandlers can be configured by using RequestHandlerSelectors and PathSelectors.

Finally, PathSelectors's any() method will prepare documentation for your entire APIs, available through Swagger. This configuration is enough to integrate Swagger 2 into the existing Spring Boot project for the Account microservice. Let's run this project and verify that SpringFox is working.

Open the following URL in your favorite browser and see the output at

http://localhost:6060/v2/api-docs. This URL will render as JSON data of the documentation of the REST API. Let's see the following screenshot:

```
{
    swagger: "2.0",
  - info: {
        description: "Api Documentation",
        version: "1.0",
        title: "Api Documentation",
        termsOfService: "urn:tos",
        contact: { },
      - license: {
            name: "Apache 2.0",
            url: "http://www.apache.org/licenses/LICENSE-2.0"
        }
    },
    host: "localhost:6060",
    basePath: "/",
  - tags: [
      - {
            name: "account-controller",
            description: "Account Controller"
        },
      - {
            name: "basic-error-controller",
            description: "Basic Error Controller"
        }
    ],
  - paths: {
      - /account: {
          - get: {
              - tags: [
                    "account-controller"
                ],
                summary: "all",
                ...
                ...
```

The result is a JSON response with a large number of key-value pairs (the screenshot displays some of the output only). This response is not very human-readable. Swagger also provides Swagger UI for the REST API documentation by adding another maven dependency in your `Account` microservice Spring Boot project. Let's see the next section.

Configuring Swagger UI in your project

You can easily configure Swagger UI in your microservice project by using a built-in solution in the Swagger 2 library, which creates Swagger UI with the Swagger-generated API documentation. Let's configure another Maven dependency for the Swagger UI:

```
<dependency>
    <groupId>io.springfox</groupId>
    <artifactId>springfox-swagger-ui</artifactId>
    <version>${swagger.version}</version>
</dependency>
```

We have added a dependency with groupId io.springfix and the springfox-swagger-ui artifact ID with the given version. This is enough to configure Swagger UI in your project to see API documentation. All required HTML pages will be rendered by this library only, we don't need to place any HTML for the Swagger UI.

Let's run your Spring Boot Account microservice project again and you can test it in your favorite browser by accessing following URL:

```
http://localhost:6060/swagger-ui.html#/
```

It renders Swagger UI as follows:

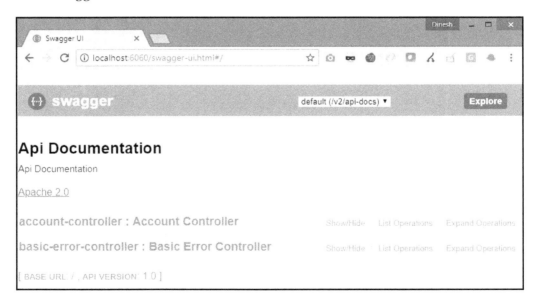

It renders Swagger UI for your Spring Boot project's `Account` microservice. It displays a list of controllers because Swagger scans your project code and exposes the documentation for all controllers. The client can use this URL and Swagger UI to learn how to use your REST APIs. It displays all HTTP methods to call for each URL and also displays input documents to send and the status code to expect.

In the preceding screenshot of Swagger UI, let's click on any controller from the rendered list. It will render a list of HTTP methods, such as `DELETE`, `GET`, `HEAD`, `OPTIONS`, `PATCH`, `POST`, and `PUT`. Click on any method in Swagger UI and it will render additional details, such as content type, response status, and parameters. You can test this method using a **Try it Out** button on Swagger UI.

As you can see the following screenshot, when I clicked on the account controller link in Swagger UI, it expands with available methods of the account controller (as you can see, `delete()` with HTTP `DELETE`, `all()` with HTTP `GET`, `save()` with HTTP `POST`, and `update()` with HTTP `PUT`):

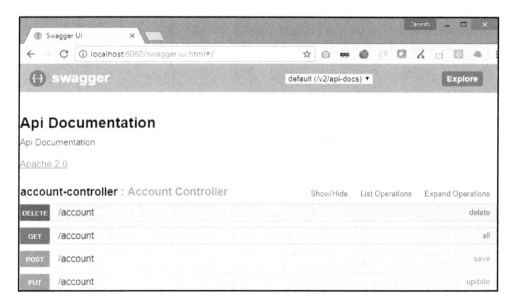

In the preceding screenshot, click on any of the `delete()`, `all()`, `save()`, or `update()` methods and Swagger UI will display the following UI:

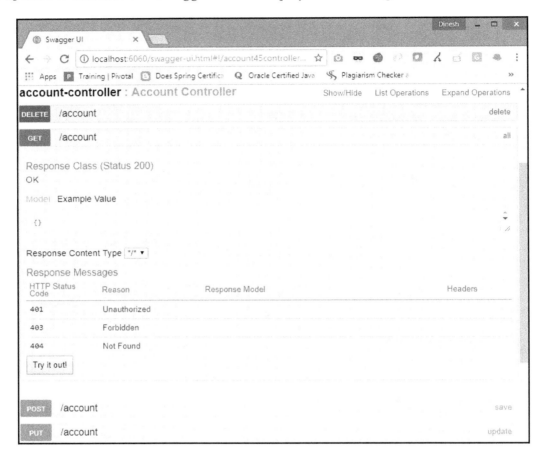

It has displayed the details such as **Response Status**, **Input Parameters**, **Response Content Type**, and **HTTP Status Code**. You can also use the **Try it out** button to test this API method.

So far, we have created API documentation for only one controller, `AccountController`, Swagger can easily synchronize with your code base if you add another controller, `CustomerController`, to the same application. Let's add the following controller:

```
@RestController
public class CustomerController {
    @GetMapping("/customer/name")
```

```
    public String customerName(){
        return "Arnav Rajput";
    }
    @PostMapping("/customer/name")
    public String addCustomerName(){
        return "Aashi Rajput";
    }
}
```

After adding the controller and refreshing your browser with Swagger UI, it will display a list of controllers, including `CustomerController`:

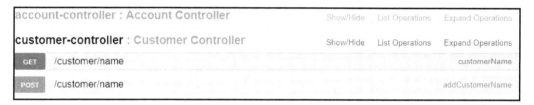

You have seen the default meta-configuration provided by the Swagger, you can also customize this meta-configuration according to your application parameters by using the Docket bean. Let's see how to add extra configuration in your Spring Boot project with Swagger.

Customizing the Swagger UI meta-configuration

You can customize the Docket bean configuration in your application to give it more control over the REST API documentation generation. Let's see how to filter some APIs for Swagger response.

Filtering an API from Swagger's documentation

Let's see the following updated Docket bean configuration:

```
@Bean
public Docket api() {
    return new Docket(DocumentationType.SWAGGER_2)
            .select()
.apis(RequestHandlerSelectors.basePackage("com.dineshonjava.accountservice.
controller"))            .paths(PathSelectors.ant("/customer/*"))
            .build();
}
```

In the preceding configuration of the Docket bean, we have filtered some APIs from the documentation. Sometimes, we don't want to expose the documentation of some APIs. You can pass parameters to the `apis()` and `paths()` methods of the `Docket` class to restrict Swagger's response. The `RequestHandlerSelectors` class allows you to use the any or none predicates. You can use `RequestHandlerSelectors` to filter the API according to the base package (`com.dineshonjava.accountservice.controller`), class annotation, and method annotations.

Swagger also allows you to filter using predicates. The `paths()` method takes the `PathSelectors` class as a parameter to provide additional filtering. The `PathSelectors` class has several methods, such as `any()`, `none()`, `regex()`, or `ant()`, to scan the request paths of your application.

In the preceding example, Swagger will include only the `com.dineshonjava.accountservice.controller` package with a specific path that contains `/customer/*` in the URL, using the `ant()` predicate. Let's refresh the browser of Swagger UI:

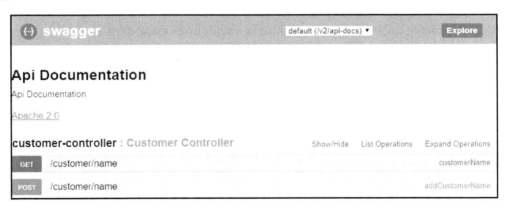

Swagger has created the documentation only for those REST APIs that contains the `/customer/*` URL pattern. In the preceding screenshot, you can see other information, such as API version, **API Documentation**, and **Created by Contact Email**. You can also change this API information in your application.

Let's see the following example to add custom API information, you can use the `apiInfo(ApiInfo apiInfo)` method to change the API information, such as API version, API documentation, and created by contact email:

```
@Bean
public Docket api() {
    return new Docket(DocumentationType.SWAGGER_2)
        .select()
.apis(RequestHandlerSelectors.basePackage("com.dineshonjava.accountservice.
controller"))
        .paths(PathSelectors.ant("/customer/*"))
        .build()
        .apiInfo(apiInfo());
}
private ApiInfo apiInfo() {
    return new ApiInfo(
        "Customer Microservice REST API",
        "These are customer service APIs.",
        "API 2.0",
        "https://www.dineshonjava.com/Termsofservice",
        new Contact("Dinesh Rajput", "https://www.dineshonjava.com",
"admin@dineshonjava.com"),
        "License of API", "https://www.dineshonjava.com/license",
Collections.emptyList());
}
```

As you can see in the preceding configurations, the Docket bean has been configured with the `apiInfo()` method. The `apiInfo()` method provides the API with information such as API documentation name, API version, API description, contact information, and terms of service URL. Let's refresh Swagger UI in the browser:

It renders the API information, such as API version, API documentation, and created by contact email, to Swagger UI. Swagger also allows us to customize the messages for response methods. Let's see in the following example:

For customizing messages for response methods, let's see the following updated Docket bean configuration:

```
@Bean
public Docket api() {
    return new Docket(DocumentationType.SWAGGER_2)
                .select()
.apis(RequestHandlerSelectors.basePackage("com.dineshonjava.accountservice.
controller"))
                .paths(PathSelectors.ant("/customer/*"))
                .build()
                .apiInfo(apiInfo())
                .useDefaultResponseMessages(false)
                .globalResponseMessage(RequestMethod.GET,
                    newArrayList(
                            new ResponseMessageBuilder()
                            .code(500)
                            .message("500 : Internal Server Error into
                             customer microservice")
                            .responseModel(new ModelRef("Error"))
                            .build(),
                            new ResponseMessageBuilder()
                                .code(403)
                                .message("API Request Forbidden!")
                                .build(),
                            new ResponseMessageBuilder()
                                .code(404)
                                .message("Request API Not Found!")
                                .build()
                                ));
}
```

As you can see in the preceding configuration for the Docket API bean, we have set the default response message to false to instruct Swagger not to use default response messages, and we have overridden global response messages of HTTP methods through Docket's globalResponseMessage() method. In our example, I have overridden three response messages with the 500, 403, and 404 codes for all methods of the Customer microservice.

Let's see the following screenshot after refreshing the browser:

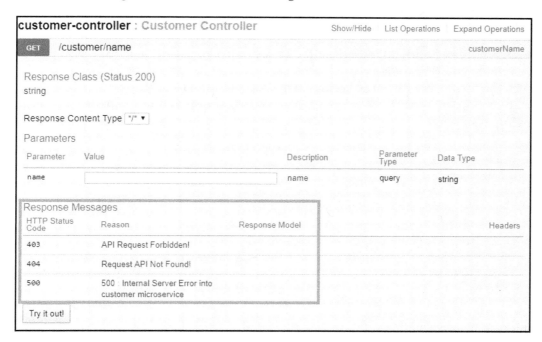

We have overridden the default response messages of HTTP status, code such as 403, 404, and 500. Apart from the Docket bean configuration, Swagger also allows us to customize API documentation by using Swagger annotations. Let's see, in the next sub section.

Customizing with Swagger annotations

Swagger provides some additional annotations required on top of existing Spring MVC annotations. Let's see the following example using these annotations.

In the microservice application, each REST controller that is supposed to be documented should be annotated with the @Api annotation:

```
@Api( value = "/customer", description = "Manage Customer" )
public class CustomerController {
    // ...
}
```

The `CustomerController` class has been annotated with the `@Api` annotation with the value and `description` attributes. The `@Api` annotation narrates the description about the responsibilities of the controller.

Next, each request handler methods of the Rest Controller class that is supposed to be documented should be annotated with the `@ApiOperation` annotation. This annotation narrates the responsibility of the specific method. You can also use another Swagger annotation, `@ApiResponses`/`@ApiResponse`, with request handler methods. Let's see the following example:

```
@ApiOperation(value = "Returns Customer Name")
@ApiResponses(
    value = {
  @ApiResponse(code = 100, message = "100 is the message"),
  @ApiResponse(code = 200, message = "Successful Return Customer Name")
      }
)
@GetMapping("/name")
public String customerName(@ApiParam(name="name", value="Customer Name")
String name){
    return "Arnav Rajput";
}
```

The request handler method of `CustomerController` has annotated with the `@ApiOperation` and `@ApiResponse`/`@ApiResponses`.

If the request handler method accepts parameters, those should be annotated with the `@ApiParam` annotation. As you can see in the preceding example, the `@ApiOperation` annotation narrates the responsibility of the specific method.

Similarly, you can also document your model classes to provide the model schema, which helps with documenting the request-response structure using the specific annotation, such as using the `@ApiModel` annotations. The REST resource classes or model classes require special annotations—`@ApiModel` and `@ApiModelProperty`. Let's see the following `Customer` model class:

```
@ApiModel( value = "Customer", description = "Customer resource
representation" )
public class Customer {
@ApiModelProperty(notes = "Name of the Customer") String name;
@ApiModelProperty(notes = "Email of the Customer") String email;
@ApiModelProperty(notes = "Mobile of the Customer") String mobile;
@ApiModelProperty(notes = "Address of the Customer") String address; //...
}
```

Let's run your Spring Boot microservice project and refresh the browser:

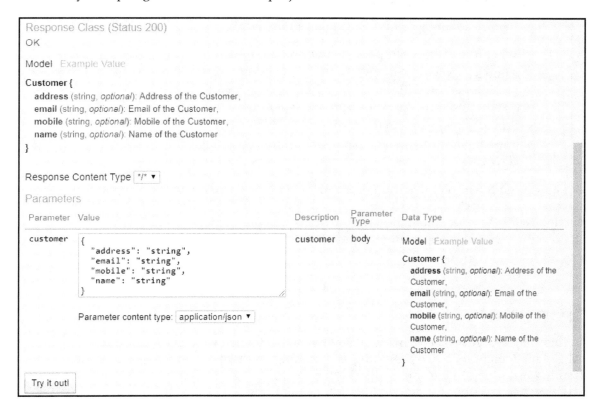

It has rendered the details about the model of the customer class. Now, Swagger provided more descriptive API documentation. So, you can easily customize the API documentation using Swagger annotations.

Swagger enables the REST API service producer to update the API documentation in real time. The client and API documentation system are creating at the same pace as the server. Swagger is maintaining the synchronization in APIs and its documentation with the methods, parameters, and models described in the server code.

Advantages of Swagger

The following are advantages of the Swagger Framework:

- Synchronizes the API documentation with the server and client at the same pace.
- Allows us to generate REST API documentation and interact with the REST API. The interaction with the REST API using the Swagger UI Framework gives clear insight into how the API responds to parameters.
- Provides responses in the format of JSON and XML.
- Implementations are available for various technologies, such as Scala, Java, and HTML5.

We have seen the implementation of the Swagger Framework in our Spring Boot microservice project to expose `Account` and `Customer` REST APIs. In this example, we created REST API documentation for the `Account` and `Customer` REST APIs. You can find the complete code for this example on GitHub at `https://github.com/PacktPublishing/Mastering-Spring-Boot-2.0`.

Summary

In this chapter, we learned how to manage your API when we expose to the consumers. API Management includes providing rate limiting, authentication, and logging. Rate limiting is nothing but a simple algorithm to restrict consumption of the API due to business needs, either for monetizing or for safety from DOS attacks.

We saw how to run KONG using Docker. We also created a use case to manage using the KONG management API. KONG plugins offer a lot of flexibility and customization for your APIs.

Finally, we set up Swagger 2 to generate documentation for a Spring REST API. We also explored the Swagger UI Framework to visualize and customize Swagger's output.

In the next chapter, we will explore how to deploy your microservice to the AWS cloud.

Deploying in Cloud (AWS) 14

This chapter will explore manually deploying microservices in AWS EC2 instances and using CloudFormation scripts. You will learn here how to run a Docker-enabled Spring Boot microservice application on the Amazon **Elastic Compute Cloud** (**EC2**) instances.

In previous chapters, we have discussed different aspects of the microservices architecture and its benefits, such as it is highly scalable, fault-tolerant, and so on. However, there are many challenges with the microservices architecture, such as managing the deployment of microservices and infrastructure dependencies for distributed applications. Containerization comes with a solution for these problems. Docker provides a containerization approach to develop and deploy microservices without infrastructure dependencies. We have already discussed Docker in `Chapter 12`, *Containerizing Microservice*. We can easily deploy Docker containers to **Amazon Web Services** (**AWS**), Azure, Pivotal Cloud Foundry, and so on.

This chapter will cover the following topics:

- Spinning up an AWS EC2 instance
- Microservices architecture on AWS
- Publishing microservices to the Docker Hub
- Installing Docker on AWS EC2
- Running microservices on AWS EC2

At the end of this chapter, you will have a better understanding of how to manually deploy microservices and Docker containers to AWS EC2 instances and use CloudFormation scripts.

Spinning up an AWS EC2 instance

Amazon Web Services (AWS) provides lots of platforms for cloud computing solutions. You can use AWS to build and deploy applications. Amazon EC2 is a service that provides resizable computing capacity in the cloud and makes web-scale cloud computing easier for developers.

Another platform is the AWS Elastic Container Service. It is used to deploy microservices using Docker. Microservices can be deployed to Amazon ECS by creating a Docker image of your application. You can easily push this Docker image to the Amazon **Elastic Container Registry (ECR)**.

In this chapter, I will deploy a microservice using a Docker image of your application to the Amazon EC2. I will use the Docker registry to the Docker Hub to push a Docker image. Let's see how to set up an Amazon EC2 instance:

1. First of all, we need to have an Amazon account. You can create an Amazon Free Tier account at `https://aws.amazon.com/free/`:

2. Log in to the AWS Management Console. After a successful login, you should see the following screen:

The preceding screenshot displays all the available AWS services. You can use any service by just clicking and configuring it accordingly.

3. Click on the EC2 service on the Amazon AWS dashboard, as shown in the following screenshot:

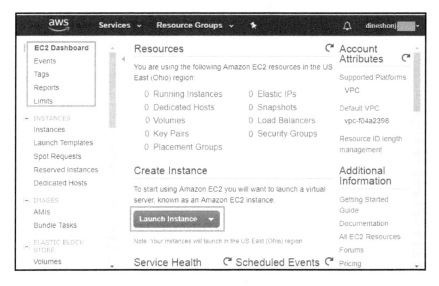

In the preceding screenshot, the EC2 dashboard displays all the available options for the EC2 instance.

4. To create an EC2 instance, click on the **Launch Instance** button. It will render options to choose an **Amazon Machine Image** (**AMI**), as shown in the following screenshot:

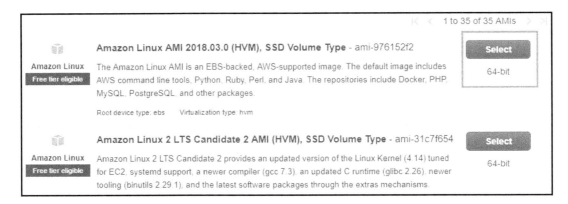

As you can see in the preceding screenshot, you can select any AMI according to your application and business requirements. AWS has more than 35 AMIs, depending on your application requirements and usage. They have multiple platforms, such as Linux, Windows, and more.

5. Select any AMI. We are going to use a Linux-based AMI and SSD volume type with 64-bit OS. The following screenshot illustrates how to select an instance type of this AMI:

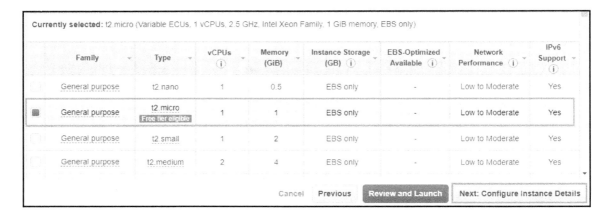

The preceding screenshot has displayed all the available options to choose an instance type. Here, I have chosen the **t2.micro** instance. Amazon EC2 provides lots of instance types according to different use cases. Instances are used to run applications as virtual machines. They have different capacities with various combinations of CPU, memory, storage, and networking capacity. This gives you the flexibility to choose the appropriate mix of resources for your applications.

6. AWS also allows you to configure EC2 instances to suit your requirements. Let's click on the **Configure Instance Details** button, as shown in the preceding screenshot:

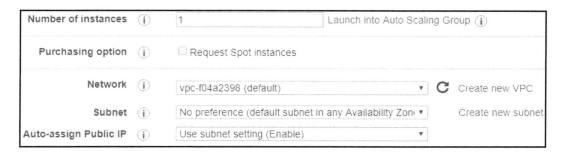

As you can see in the preceding screenshot, you can launch multiple instances from the same AMI, and other options are also included.

7. Also, you can add additional EBS volumes and instance store volumes to your instance as per as your application requirement, as shown in the following screenshot:

8. After attaching additional storage, let's add a tag to this instance to help you manage your instances, images, and other Amazon EC2 resources. As shown in the following screenshot, you can see I have added the key `Name` and value of this key, `AccountService`:

9. You can also configure the security group for this instance to protect it and make it secure. It is very simple to configure the security group to this instance by clicking the **Configure Security Group** button in the preceding screenshot. There are a lot of security groups available for several requirements, such as firewall rules that control the traffic for your instance, as shown in the following screenshot:

10. After configuring the security group, let's click on the **Review and Launch** button, shown in the preceding screenshot. It will ask you to create a key pair, as shown in the following screenshot:

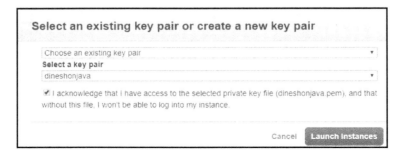

In the preceding screenshot, I have created a key pair with the name `dineshonjava` and saved it to the local drive. We will use this `dineshonjava.pem` file to access this instance using SSH.

Next, you can also configure a key pair to access this instance from clients such as PuTTY or FileZilla. If you have an existing key pair, then just use it for this instance, or you can create a new key pair. A key pair consists of a public key that AWS stores, and a private key file that you store.

11. Let's launch this **t2.micro** instance of the AWS EC2 service. It will display the following message:

As you can see in the preceding screenshot, we have successfully launched an EC2 service instance. Let's click on the generated instance ID to see this running instance, as shown in the following screenshot:

You have seen how to configure and launch the EC2 service instance (**t2.micro**). We have named the instance `AccountService`.

The AWS EC2 instance is very simple to configure and launch. It is very easy to use and it has several benefits, including the following:

- Elastic web-scale computing
- Completely controlled
- Flexible cloud hosting services
- Integrated
- Reliable
- Secure
- Inexpensive
- Easy to start

Now that you have seen the benefits of the AWS EC2 instance, let's look at the microservices architecture on AWS in the next section.

Microservices architecture on AWS

We have discussed the microservices architecture and its benefits in previous chapters of this book. In this section, we will discuss the microservices architecture on AWS and how to use several Amazon services to provide better cloud-native solutions to a microservice-based distributed application. The following diagram illustrates the simple microservice architecture on AWS:

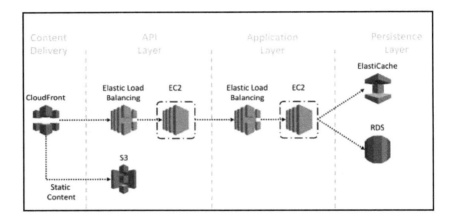

In the preceding diagram, the microservices-based application architecture is designed with four layers, **Content Delivery**, **API Layer**, **Application Layer**, and **Persistence Layer**.

AWS provides several services for each aspect of the application, such as the frontend (user interface), and the backend, such as the service layer and persistence layer. In the frontend layer of the application, services are required to manage static content, such as scripts, images, CSS, and so on, and dynamic content, such as rendering web pages. Services such as **Amazon Simple Storage Service** (**Amazon S3**) and Amazon CloudFront are used to serve static web content.

 AWS CloudFront is an AWS service used to manage content for your websites and APIs, such as video content and other web assets. It is a global **content delivery network** (**CDN**) service used to accelerate static content delivery.

AWS services such as Amazon S3 and Amazon CloudFront provide solutions for static and dynamic content and are used to accelerate the delivery of content. The Amazon S3 service is used to store static content, such as images, CSS, JS, and so on. And Amazon CloudFront delivers this static content. The REST API uses microservices to serve dynamic content for the frontend. To reduce the latency of networks, we can use other caching mechanisms.

The API layer is an abstract layer for the application layer. This layer hides application logic from the content layer. This layer serves all requests coming from the content layer using the HTTP REST API. Amazon Elastic Load Balancing has used it to manage and distribute traffic. This API layer is also responsible for client request routing, filtering, caching, authentication, and authorization.

> Amazon ELB is used to manage and distribute incoming application traffic across multiple Amazon EC2 instances.

At the persistence layer, you can configure data storage, such as caching (Memcached or Redis), NoSQL DB, or SQL DB. AWS also provides Relation DB support, such as Amazon RDS. The Amazon ElastiCache service is used to manage caching mechanisms. The application layer has actual business logic to connect the persistence layer and caching, and this layer is also used by ELB to scale EC2 instances and manage incoming traffic from the API layer.

Let's look at another typical microservice architecture on AWS. In the previous architecture, we have used different layers, such as the content delivery layer, API layer, application layer, and persistence layer. In the microservice architecture, we divide an application into separate verticals based on the specific functionality rather than technological layers. The following diagram illustrates another aspect of a microservices application on AWS:

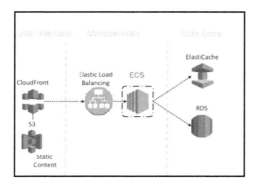

So, as you can see in the preceding diagram, the **User interface** is very similar to the content delivery layer in the previous diagram. It serves static content using the Amazon S3 service.

In this architecture, I have used Amazon ECS (EC2 Container Service) to run the application using containers. This service supports Docker containers and allows you to easily run applications on a managed cluster of Amazon EC2 instances.

You can also scale the Amazon ECS depending on incoming traffic from the client. Amazon ELB can be used to manage the incoming traffic across these containers, and it distributes the traffic to Amazon ECS container instances running REST APIs.

Amazon ECS eliminates the specific requirement for the infrastructure of your application in this architecture of AWS. You can use container-based approach technologies, such as Docker, for deploying the services. We have discussed several benefits in `Chapter 12`, *Containerizing Microservice*.

Similar to the persistence layer in the previous diagram, we can use several data stores, such as Amazon RDS and Amazon ElastiCache, to persist data needed by the microservices. Amazon ElastiCache is used to optimize application performance by using an in-memory data store or cache in the cloud. It is easy to deploy, operate, and scale.

Publishing microservices to the Docker Hub

The Docker Hub is a central repository to store all Docker images. The Docker Hub allows you to create either a public or private repository to store these Docker images. The steps to publish microservices to the Docker Hub are described next.

Let's follow these steps to set up and run a local registry:

1. Create an account on the Docker Hub at `https://hub.docker.com/`.
2. Create a repository (private or public) for the Docker images, as shown in the following screenshot:

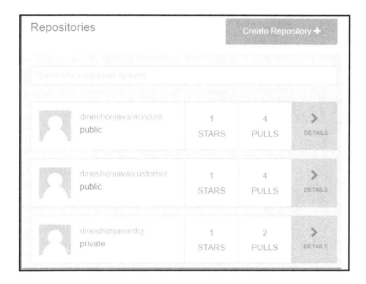

As you can see in the preceding screenshot, we have created three repositories named `dineshonjava/account`, `dineshonjava/customer`, and `dineshonjava/doj`. Of the three, one repository is `private` and the other two are `public`.

3. Log in to the Docker cloud using the Docker login command:

```
Dinesh.Rajput@MRNDTHTMOBL0002 MINGW64 ~
$ docker login
Login with your Docker ID to push and pull images from Docker Hub. If you don't
have a Docker ID, head over to https://hub.docker.com to create one.
Username (dineshonjava): dineshonjava
Password:
Login Succeeded
```

4. Tag your Docker image using the Docker tag:

```
Dinesh.Rajput@MRNDTHTMOBL0002 MINGW64 ~
$ docker tag account-service dineshonjava/account:1.0
```

5. Push your image to the Docker Hub using `docker push`:

```
Dinesh.Rajput@MRNDTHTMOBL0002 MINGW64 ~
$ docker push dineshonjava/account:1.0
The push refers to repository [docker.io/dineshonjava/account]
```

6. Check that the image you just pushed appears in the Docker cloud at `https://hub.docker.com/r/dineshonjava/account/tags/`:

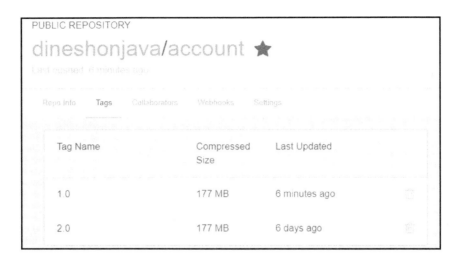

As you can see in the preceding screenshot, I have pushed two tags of the Account microservice.

We have seen in this section how to set up and use the Docker Hub to publish the Docker images. We can globally access the Docker images by this convenient mechanism. We have published three Docker images to the Docker Hub from the local machine. Let's look at how to download and run these images to the AWS EC2 instances. But first, we have to install Docker on the AWS EC2 instance.

Installing Docker on AWS EC2

You can easily install Docker on the AWS EC2 instance. Let's connect the EC2 instance using PuTTY. In this section, we will install Docker on the EC2 instance. Follow these steps to install Docker:

1. Let's run the EC2 instance and generate a private key using PuTTYgen. You have to load the `dineshonjava.pem` file that we generated in the previous section. It will generate the `dineshonjava.ppk` file. It will be used to connect the EC2 instance using Putty.

2. Open Putty and connect to the EC2 instance. In **Host Name**, use `Public DNS` to connect this EC2 instance and port `22`. Also, load the private key file for authentication. In the **category** section, go to **Connection | SSH | Auth** and upload the private key file for authentication, as shown in the following screenshot:

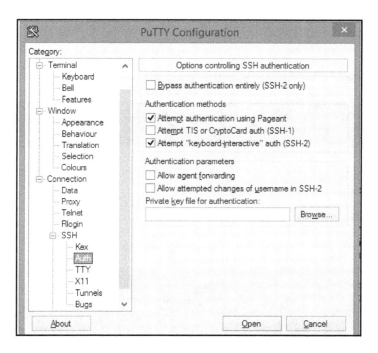

3. Upload a private key file, `dineshonjava.ppk`, and click on the **Open** button. It will connect to the AWS EC2 instance, as shown in the following screenshot:

```
Using username "ec2-user".
Authenticating with public key "imported-openssh-key"

       _|  _|_  )
      _|  (     /     Amazon Linux AMI
       _|\___|___|

https://aws.amazon.com/amazon-linux-ami/2018.03-release-notes/
1 package(s) needed for security, out of 5 available
Run "sudo yum update" to apply all updates.
[ec2-user@ip-172-31-21-186 ~]$ ▮
```

As you can see in the preceding screenshot, we have connected to the AWS EC2 instance using Putty. Now you can easily install Docker on the EC2 instance.

4. Install Docker, using the following command:

```
$ sudo yum install docker
```

5. Start the Docker service, using the following command:

```
$ sudo service docker start
```

Let's see the following screenshot about the preceding command:

```
[ec2-user@ip-172-31-21-186 ~]$ sudo service docker start
Starting cgconfig service:                                    [  OK  ]
Starting docker:               .                              [  OK  ]
```

6. The preceding command will install Docker on the EC2 instance. Verify the installation with the following command:

```
$ sudo docker version
```

Let's see the following screenshot about the preceding command:

```
[ec2-user@ip-172-31-21-186 ~]$ sudo docker version
Client:
 Version:      17.12.1-ce
 API version:  1.35
 Go version:   go1.9.4
 Git commit:   3dfb8343b139d6342acfd9975d7f1068b5b1c3d3
 Built: Tue Apr  3 23:37:44 2018
 OS/Arch:      linux/amd64
```

As you can see in the preceding screenshot, we have successfully installed Docker on the AWS EC2 instance. Let's see in the next section how to run the microservice on the AWS EC2 instance using Docker images.

Running microservices on AWS EC2

In this section, we will set up account and customer microservices on the EC2 instance. We are using Spring Boot 2.0 in this example:

1. We have to install Java 8 as well our EC2 instance using the following command:

    ```
    wget -c --header "Cookie: oraclelicense=accept-securebackup-cookie
    ```

    You can also refer to the following link:

    ```
    http://download.oracle.com/otn-pub/java/jdk/8u131-b11/
    d54c1d3a095b4ff2b6607d096fa80163/jdk-8u131-linux-x64.tar.gz
    ```

    The preceding command will download a `jdk-8u131-linux-x64.tar.gz` file. We extract this file using the following command:

    ```
    $ sudo tar -xvf jdk-8u131-linux-x64.tar.gz
    ```

2. After `untar`, let's set up the `JAVA_HOME` and `PATH` environment variables, as follows:

    ```
    $ JAVA_HOME=/home/ec2-user/jdk1.8.0_131
    $ PATH=/home/ec2-user/jdk1.8.0_131/bin:$PATH
    $ export JAVA_HOME PATH
    ```

    Let's check the Java version, using the following command:

    ```
    [ec2-user@ip-172-31-21-186 ~]$ java -version
    java version "1.8.0_131"
    Java(TM) SE Runtime Environment (build 1.8.0_131-b11)
    Java HotSpot(TM) 64-Bit Server VM (build 25.131-b11, mixed mode)
    ```

3. As you can see, we have set up Java 8 in the EC2 instance. Let's run a microservice on this EC2 instance.

    Execute the following commands in sequence:

    ```
    $ sudo docker run -p 80:8761 dineshonjava/doj:1.0
    $ sudo docker run -p 8181:6060 dineshonjava/account:1.0
    $ sudo docker run -p 8282:6060 dineshonjava/customer:1.0
    ```

4. Let's validate that all the services are working by opening the following URL in the browser:

```
http://ec2-18-219-255-59.us-east-2.compute.amazonaws.com/
```

Note that we will be using the public IP or public DNS of the EC2 instance. This URL will open the Eureka dashboard, as shown in the following screenshot:

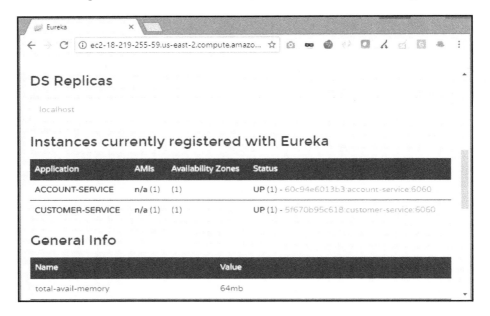

As you can see in the preceding screenshot, we have registered two microservices, Account and Customer, with the Eureka server running on the AWS EC2 instance.

5. Let's deploy the customer microservice to AWS EC2 using the Docker image with the following command:

```
$ sudo docker run -p 80:6060 dineshonjava/customer:1.0
```

6. Let's test this microservice using the browser by navigating to the following URL:

```
http://ec2-18-219-255-59.us-east-2.compute.amazonaws.com/customer/1001
```

It will render the details of a customer with the customer ID `1001`, as shown in the following screenshot:

```
┌────────────────────────────────────────────────────────┐
│  🌐 ec2-18-219-255-59.us-e  ×                            │
├────────────────────────────────────────────────────────┤
│  ←  →  C   ① ec2-18-219-255-59.us-east-2.compute.amazonaws.com/customer/1001 │
│                                                          │
│  {                                                       │
│      customerId: 1001,                                   │
│      customerName: "Arnav Rajput",                       │
│      mobile: "54312XX223",                               │
│      email: "arnavxxx@mail.com",                         │
│      city: "Noida",                                      │
│    - account: [                                          │
│       - {                                                │
│             accountId: 0,                                │
│             balance: 1,                                  │
│             customerId: 0,                               │
│             accountType: "UNKNOWN ACCOUNT TYPE",         │
│             branchCode: "UNK",                           │
│             bank: "FALLBACK BANK"                        │
│         }                                                │
│      ]                                                   │
│  }                                                       │
└────────────────────────────────────────────────────────┘
```

Summary

In this chapter, we have learned about several AWS services. We have discussed the microservices architecture on AWS. We have set up AWS EC2 instances and also installed Java 8 and Docker on the EC2 instances. The Docker Hub provides an easy solution to register Docker images of your microservices to a registry server. We have registered three microservices in this chapter to the Docker Hub.

Finally, we have installed Docker on the AWS EC2 instance and pulled all Docker images from the Docker Hub and deployed these images to the EC2 instances.

In the next chapter, `Chapter 15`, *Production Ready Service Monitoring and Best Practices*, we will explore how to monitor logs of the distributed system.

15
Production Ready Service Monitoring and Best Practices

Monitoring and logging are very important for any enterprise application, especially when we are dealing with a microservices-based distributed application with the involvement of several technologies. But logging and monitoring for individual microservices-based applications are very challenging due to the distributed behavior of the application's deployment. In a distributed application, several microservices are running together on several machines, so logs generated by different microservices are very difficult to trace end-to-end transactions.

In this chapter, we will elaborate on some of the best practices in building distributed systems and on performance monitoring for production-ready services. We will introduce log aggregation using the Elasticsearch/Logstash/Kibana stack for distributed applications.

By the end of this chapter, you will have a better understanding of how to monitor a distributed system and how to aggregate distributed logs generated by individual microservices of a distributed application.

This chapter will cover the following topic:

- Monitoring containers
- Logging challenges in the microservices architecture
- Centralized logging for microservices
- Log aggregation using the ELK stack
- Request tracing using Sleuth
- Request tracing using Zipkin

Monitoring containers

Container monitoring is the activity of monitoring the performance of microservice containers in different environments. Monitoring is the first step toward optimizing and improving performance.

Logging challenges for the microservices architecture

As we know, logging is very important for any application to debug and audit business metrics, because logs contain important information to analyze. So, logging is a process to write a file, and logs are streams of events coming from running applications on a server. There are a number of frameworks are available to implement logging on your application, such as Log4j, Logback, and SLF4J. There are very popular logging frameworks used in J2EE traditional applications.

In a J2EE application, most logs are written into the console or in a filesystem on your disk space, so, we have to take care with the disk space and we have to implement a shell script to recycle the log files after a particular amount of time to avoid logs filling up all the disk space. So, a best practice of log-handling for your application is to avoid unnecessary log writing in the production environment, because of the cost of disk I/O. The disk I/O can slow down your application and also fill all the disk space; it can be cause of to down or stop your application on the production server.

Logging frameworks, such as Log4j, Logback, and SLF4J, provide log levels (INFO, DEBUG, ERROR) to control logging at runtime and also restrict what has to be printed. These logging frameworks allow you to change the logging level and configuration at runtime to control the logging in your application. Sometimes, we can't restrict some log entries because they are required for business analysis and to understand the application's behavior.

In a traditional J2EE monolithic application, we can avoid the problem of disk space and also scale hardware for logging easily, but what happens when we move from the traditional J2EE monolithic application to cloud-based distributed application? A cloud-based deployment doesn't bind with a predefined machine. A distributed cloud-based system can be deployed over multiple virtual machines and containers.

As we discussed in `Chapter 12`, *Containerizing Microservice*, containers, such as Docker, are short-lived. So, we can't rely on the container and its persistent state of the disk, because as a container is stopped or restarted, it will lose all logs written to the desk.

In the microservices architecture, a distributed application will be running on several isolated machines, either virtual or physical, which means log files will be generated in all machines separately. So, it is impossible to trace these files' end-to-end transactions, because they are processed by multiple microservices. Let's see the following diagram:

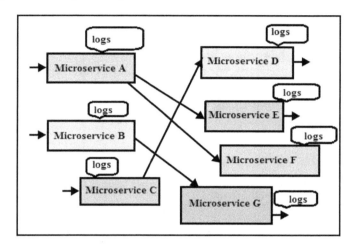

As you can see, microservices are running on separate infrastructure and machines, and each microservice emits logs to that local machine. Suppose one task calls **Microservice A** followed by calling **Microservice E** and **Microservice F**. So, **Microservice A**, **Microservice E**, and **Microservice F** are running different machines and each service writes a log for this task on different log files on different machines. This makes it harder to debug and analyze logs for a particular end-to-end task in the microservice-based application. So, we have to set up a tool for log aggregation at the service level. Let's see in the next section how to achieve a centralized logging solution for the microservices-based distributed application.

Centralized logging solution for the microservices architecture

Logging frameworks, such as Log4j, Logback, and SLF4J, provide logging functionality for each microservice application. Now we need a tool that can aggregate all logs coming from multiple microservices to a central location from local virtual machines and running analytics on top of the log messages. This solution must provide the logging to track end-to-end transactions. The centralized logging solution can eliminate dependency on the local disk space and keep logs for a long time for analysis in the future.

According to the centralized logging solution, all log messages must be stored in a central location rather than on each local machine of each microservice. This solution provides a separation of concerns between log storage and the service execution environments. We can use any big data technology, such as HDFS, to store a large number of log messages. So, actual logs are written into the local machine shipped from the execution environment to a central big data store.

Let's see the following diagram, which elaborates on the centralized logging solution for the microservices-distributed application:

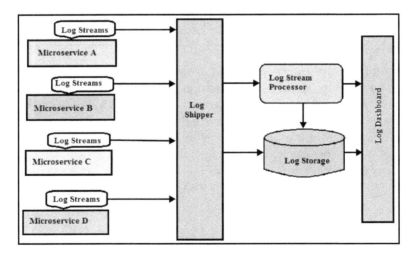

There are a number of components working together for the centralized logging solution, as follows:

- **Log streams**: These are logging messages generated by the microservices. In a microservice, we can use any logging framework to generate log streams, such as Log4j, Logback, and SLF4J.
- **Log shippers**: This component has a responsibility to collect all log streams generated by several microservices from different machines. The log shippers ship these log messages to the central storage such as a database, pushing to a dashboard, or to any stream-processing units for analysis in real time.

Logstash is one of the very popular log shipper solutions for centralized logging; this tool can be used for collecting and shipping log files from multiple distributed microservices. Logstash works as a broker, it accepts log streams from multiple endpoints and sinks these log streams to other destinations (Elasticsearch, HDFS, or any other database).

The logging framework, such as Log4j and Logback, can be used to send log messages to Logstash from Spring Boot microservices using its appenders. After that, Logstash will send these log message to the connected log storage. We will discuss Logstash with examples in the next section of this chapter.

The other tools, such as Fluentd and Logspout, are very similar to Logstash. But these tools can be more appropriate in different environments and infrastructures, such as a Docker-based environment.

- **Log storages**: This is the central place where all log streams will be stored for real-time analysis, such as the NoSQL database and HDFS.

We will discuss log storage, with examples, in the *Elasticsearch* section. Elasticsearch can be used to store real-time log messages. Elasticsearch is a text-based search technology that a client can query by using text-based indexes.

HDFS can be used to store archive log messages, and other metadata, such as transaction counts, can be stored in either MongoDB or Cassandra. Finally, we can use the Hadoop map-reduce programs for this offline log processing.

- **Log stream processor**: It is a log-analysis engine in real-time for making quick decisions. It can send information to the log dashboard. And also it can process to send alerts and take action to resolve the problems in case of self-healing system.

Sometimes we need a real-time-based system that can analyze the log streams on the fly and can also make decisions for critical situations to self-healing and to be handled as soon as possible. So, the log stream processor can be used optionally in a situation of self-healing and be analyzing log messages in real time on the fly.

We can use a combination of Flume and Kafka for stream processing with Storm or Spark Streaming. The log stream processors (Storm or Spark) process, on the fly, all log messages coming from Kafka and then send them to Elasticsearch or other log storages. We can use the Log4j logging framework, it has Flume appenders to collect log messages and send them into distributed Kafka message queues.

There are many other solutions for log streaming processes provided by the Spring Framework, such as Spring Cloud Stream, Spring Cloud Stream modules, and Spring Cloud Data Flow.

- **Log dashboard**: This is a log visualization component of the central logging solution, it displays log analysis reports in the form of graphs and charts. The log dashboard is useful for decision makers in business teams.

There are several logging dashboard solutions to display log analysis reports, such as Kibana, Graphite, and Grafana. Kibana is one of the logging dashboards that can be used for log analysis on top of an Elasticsearch data store.

As we have seen, this centralized approach for logging implementation into distributed microservice-based applications doesn't force us to write logs into the local machine's disk space.

In the centralized logging approach, we have to follow a standard for log messages, the log message must have a context, message, and correlation ID. The context information will be the IP address, user information, process details, timestamp, and log type. The message will be a simple bit of text, and the correlation ID will be used for linking end-to-end tracing for a specific task across microservices.

There are a number solutions available for the centralized logging approach, based on different application architectures and technologies. There are many prebuilt tools available to provide end-to-end centralized logging solutions, such as *Graylog* and *Splunk*. Graylog is an open source log management tool and it uses Elasticsearch for log storage, and GELF libraries for Log4j log streaming. Splunk is another commercial log management tool.

There are a number of cloud logging services available as SaaS solutions. Loggly, AWS CloudTrail, Papertrail, Logsene, Sumo Logic, Google Cloud Logging, and Logentries are examples of other cloud-based logging solutions.

Let's see how to implement a centralized custom logging solution using Elasticsearch/Logstash/Kibana in the next section.

Log aggregation using the ELK stack

As we have seen about the centralized logging approach for the distributed microservices based application. The components, such as Log streams, Log shippers, Log storage, and Log Dashboard, work together to provide a centralized logging solution for distributed applications, deployed either on the container-based environment or on virtual/physical machines.

Logstash is an open source tool for collecting, parsing, and storing logs for future use. Kibana is a web interface that can be used to search and view the logs that Logstash has indexed. Both of these tools are based on Elasticsearch, which is used for storing logs.

The *Elasticsearch*, *Logstash*, and *Kibana* tools, collectively known as the *ELK* stack, provide an end-to-end logging solution in the distributed application. The ELK is one of the most commonly used architectures for custom logging management. The following diagram shows the centralized log-monitoring architecture:

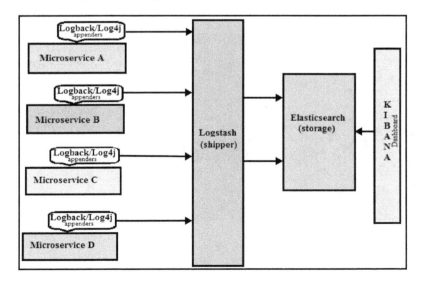

Production Ready Service Monitoring and Best Practices

As you can see in the diagram of ELK stack tools, the multiple microservices, A, B, C, and D, are using Log4j/Logback to emit log streams and Logback appenders to write log streams to the Logstash directly, and Logstash is working as a broker between log streams and log storage, sending log messages to Elasticsearch. The Elasticsearch tool saves the generated logs in the form of text-based indexes. Kibana uses these indexes, it is working as a log dashboard to display log analysis reports.

Let's see the following steps to implement the ELK stack for central custom logging:

Step 1: Install all three components of the centralized logging approach that we have to download and install Elasticsearch, Kibana, and Logstash on a single server, known as the ELK server.

Install Elasticsearch

Elasticsearch is available for all platforms, either Linux or Windows. Download it from `https://www.elastic.co/`, here I am using Window system, so I have downloaded `https://www.elastic.co/guide/en/elasticsearch/reference/current/zip-windows.html`, and unzip Elasticsearch. In the Linux system, you can install Elasticsearch from our package repositories using `apt` or `yum`. After installation, let's test it by running the Elasticsearch service using the following command:

```
.bin/elasticsearch.exe
```

Let's see the following screenshot after executing this command:

```
..
[2018-05-05T01:03:39,808][INFO ][o.e.t.TransportService   ] [_xGM-qp] publish_ad
dress {127.0.0.1:9300}, bound_addresses {127.0.0.1:9300}, {[::1]:9300}
[2018-05-05T01:03:43,064][INFO ][o.e.c.s.MasterService    ] [_xGM-qp] zen-disco-
elected-as-master {[0] nodes joined}, reason: new_master {_xGM-qp}{_xGM-qp3RIC89
nk5TICRGQ}{W0PZvW1GRjW_KPTXNhgewQ}{127.0.0.1}{127.0.0.1:9300}
[2018-05-05T01:03:43,080][INFO ][o.e.c.s.ClusterApplierService] [_xGM-qp] new_ma
ster {_xGM-qp}{_xGM-qp3RIC89nk5TICRGQ}{W0PZvW1GRjW_KPTXNhgewQ}{127.0.0.1}{127.0.
0.1:9300}, reason: apply cluster state {from master [master {_xGM-qp}{_xGM-qp3RI
C89nk5TICRGQ}{W0PZvW1GRjW_KPTXNhgewQ}{127.0.0.1}{127.0.0.1:9300} committed versi
on [1] source [zen-disco-elected-as-master {[0] nodes joined}]]}
[2018-05-05T01:03:43,960][INFO ][o.e.g.GatewayService     ] [_xGM-qp] recovered
[0] indices into cluster_state
[2018-05-05T01:03:44,387][INFO ][o.e.h.n.Netty4HttpServerTransport] [_xGM-qp] pu
blish_address {127.0.0.1:9200}, bound_addresses {127.0.0.1:9200}, {[::1]:9200}
[2018-05-05T01:03:44,387][INFO ][o.e.n.Node               ] [_xGM-qp] started
[2018-05-05T01:11:57,137][INFO ][o.e.c.m.MetaDataCreateIndexService] [_xGM-qp] [
logstash-2018.05.04] creating index, cause [auto(bulk api)], templates [logstash
], shards [5]/[1], mappings [_default_]
```

As you can see in the preceding screenshot, Elasticsearch is running on port 9200; let's access it using the browser by accessing `http://localhost:9200/`:

Your Elasticsearch node is running by sending an HTTP request to port 9200.

Install Logstash

Similar to Elasticsearch, you can download the Logstash archive from `https://www.elastic.co/downloads/logstash`. It is also available for all platforms. As we are using a Windows machine, let's download the ZIP archive for the Windows machine and unzip it. You can run the Logstash service on your machine by using the following command on the CLI:

```
bin/logstash -f logstash.conf
```

Here `logstash.conf` is the configuration file we will see in the example.

Install Kibana

Kibana is also available for all platforms; you can download it from `https://www.elastic.co/downloads/kibana`. If you're using a Windows machine, download the ZIP archive for Windows and unzip it.

If you want to customize the Kibana configuration, open `config/kibana.yml` in an editor and customize the given information according to your application infrastructure. Finally, you can run Kibana by using the following command:

```
bin/kibana
```

Let's see the following screenshot:

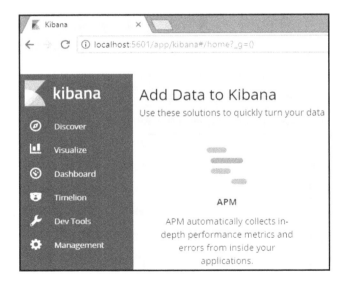

As you can see in the preceding screenshot, Kibana by default is running on port `5601`. Let's access `http://localhost:5601` in the browser:

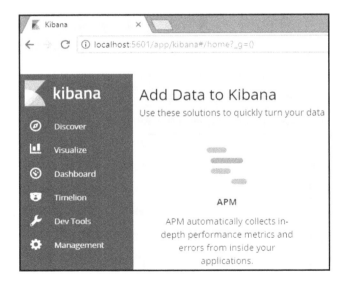

Step 2: Change into our microservices (`eureka`, `account`, and `customer` services) by adding some log statements. We are using `slf4j` to generate log messages; let's add the following logs in the `AccountController` and `CustomerController` controller classes:

```
. . .
import org.slf4j.Logger;
import org.slf4j.LoggerFactory;
. . .
@RestController
public class AccountController {
private static final Logger logger =
LoggerFactory.getLogger(AccountController.class);
. . .
@GetMapping(value = "/account")
public Iterable<Account> all (){
logger.info("Find all accounts information ");
return accountRepository.findAll();
}
. . .
}
```

As you can see in the preceding code snippet, I have added logs to all the request methods of `AccountController`. Similarly, I have added the `CustomerController`:

```
. . .
import org.slf4j.Logger;
import org.slf4j.LoggerFactory;
. . .
@RestController
public class CustomerController {
private static final Logger logger =
LoggerFactory.getLogger(CustomerController.class);
. . .
@GetMapping(value = "/customer/{customerId}")
public Customer findByAccountId (@PathVariable Integer customerId){
Customer customer = customerRepository.findByCustomerId(customerId);
customer.setAccount(accountService.findByCutomer(customerId));
logger.info("Find Customer information by id: "+customerId);
return customer;
}
. . .
}
```

As you can see, we have added a logger with info level in each request method of this `CustomerController`. Let's add the Maven dependency for Logstash.

Step 3: Add the Logstash Maven dependency into Maven configuration file of each microservices:

```
<dependency>
<groupId>net.logstash.logback</groupId>
<artifactId>logstash-logback-encoder</artifactId>
<version>5.0</version>
</dependency>
```

As you can see in the preceding code snippet, we have added the Logstash dependency to integrate logback to Logstash in all microservices using the pom.xml file.

Step 4: We have to override the default logback configuration because we have to add appenders for logstash. You can add a new logback.xml under src/main/resources. Let's see the following logback.xml file be added to each microservices:

```
<?xml version="1.0" encoding="UTF-8"?>
<configuration>
<include resource="org/springframework/boot/logging/logback/defaults.xml"/>
<include resource="org/springframework/boot/logging/logback/console-appender.xml" />
<appender name="stash"
class="net.logstash.logback.appender.LogstashTcpSocketAppender">
<destination>localhost:4567</destination>
<!-- encoder is required -->
<encoder class="net.logstash.logback.encoder.LogstashEncoder" />
</appender>
<root level="INFO">
<appender-ref ref="CONSOLE" />
<appender-ref ref="stash" />
</root>
</configuration>
```

As you can see in the preceding logback configuration file (logback.xml), this file overrides the default logback configuration. The custom logback configuration file has a new TCP socket appender. This appender streams all log messages to the Logstash service, which is running on port 4567. We have to configure this port into a Logstash configuration file. We can see in **step 5**. It is important to add an encoder, as mentioned in the preceding configuration.

Step 5: Create a Logstash configuration file:

```
input {
tcp {
port => 4567
host => localhost
```

```
}
}
output {
elasticsearch {
hosts => ["localhost:9200"]
}
stdout {
codec => rubydebug
}
}
```

As you can see in the preceding `logstash.conf` file, we have configured the input and output. Logstash will use port `4567` to take input from the socket and also configure output, Elasticsearch will be used at port `9200`. `stdout` is optional and set for debugging. We can place this file anywhere and run the `Logstash` service.

Step 6: Run all services, Elasticsearch, Logstash, and Kibana, from their respective installation folders:

```
./bin/elasticsearch
./bin/kibana
./bin/logstash -f logstash.conf
```

Step 7: Run all microservices of the example, such as the `Account` microservice and the `Customer` service. The Access customer microservice will print logs into Logstash.

Step 8: Open the Kibana dashboard in the browser at `http://localhost:5601` and go to the settings to create an index pattern:

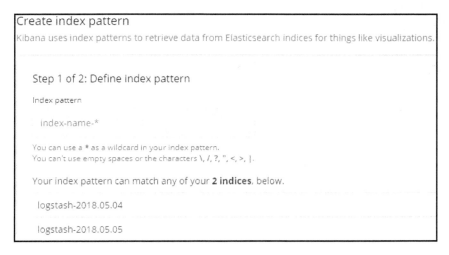

As you can see in the preceding screenshot, we have set up indexes, `logstash-*`.

Step 9: Click on the **Discover** option on the menu. It will render the log dashboard:

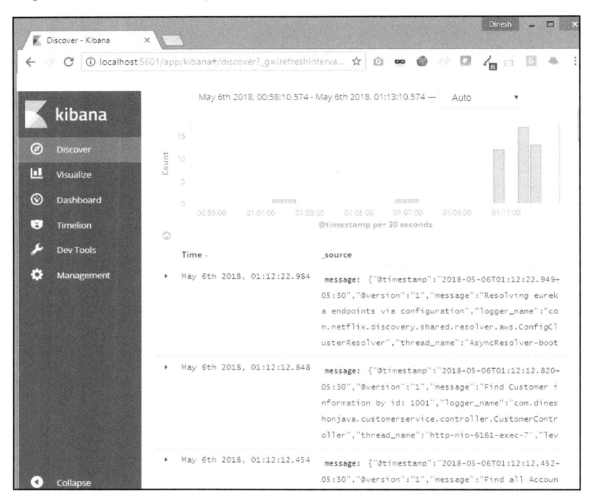

As you can see in the preceding screenshot of the Kibana UI, on the Kibana dashboard, the log messages are displayed. Kibana provides out-of-the-box features to build summary charts and graphs using log messages.

Requesting tracing using Sleuth

We have seen how to get solutions for the distributed and fragmented logging to the centralized logging architecture. So, with this approach, we have solved the problems related to the distributed logging into separate local machines, now we have to aggregate all the logs in central storage. But how do we trace these logs for a single request for end-to-end transactions? All transactions are spreading across microservices, so in order to track them from end to end, we need a correlation ID. We need a solution that can focus on tracking how a request travels through the microservices, especially when you may not have any insight into the implementation of the microservice you are calling.

Spring Cloud provides a library, Spring Cloud Sleuth, to help with this exact problem. Spring Cloud Sleuth provides unique IDs to each log message, and this unique ID will be consistent across micsroservice calls for a single request. By using this unique ID, you can find all log messages generated for a transaction. Twitter's Zipkin, Cloudera's HTrace, and Google's Dapper are examples of distributed tracing systems.

Spring Cloud Sleuth has two key concepts, Span and Trace, and it works based on these two concepts. It creates IDs for these two concepts, which are Span ID and Trace ID. Span means a basic unit of a task and Span ID represents a unit of a task, such as an HTTP call to a resource. Trace means a set of tasks or set of spans, which means a Trace ID denotes a set of Span IDs generated for end-to-end transactions. So, for a specific task, the trace ID will be the same across the microservices calls. You can use the trace ID to track a call from end to end:

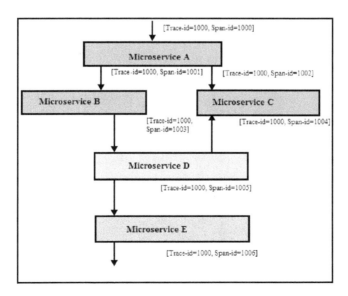

As you can see in the preceding diagram, there are multiple microservices running on different nodes. So, **Microservice A** calls **B** and **C**, and **B** calls **D**, **D** calls **E**, and so on. In this case, as you can see in the diagram, the trace ID will be passed across all microservices and this trace ID will be used for tracking end-to-end log transactions.

Let's update our previous example of the `Account` and `Customer` microservices. A new Maven dependency will be added for the Spring Cloud Sleuth library. These are the steps to create an example using Spring Cloud Sleuth in your distributed application:

1. Add another Maven dependency for Spring Cloud Sleuth in your distributed application:

```
<dependency>
<groupId>org.springframework.cloud</groupId>
<artifactId>spring-cloud-starter-sleuth</artifactId>
</dependency>
```

2. The `Logstash` dependency will be same as we have added in previous examples for implementing centralized logging.

3. You can set the application name by setting a `spring.application.name` property in either `application.yml` or `bootstrap.yml`. But you can also add this application name into the Logback configuration file of each microservice:

```
<property name="spring.application.name" value="account-service"/>
<property name="spring.application.name" value="customer-service"/>
```

The preceding given application name will show up as part of the tracing produced by Spring Cloud Sleuth.

4. Add log messages if you don't have any, and also ensure one service can call another service to check log tracing in this distributed application. I have added one request method to demonstrate the propagation of the trace ID across multiple microservices. This method in the `customer` service will call the `account` service to fetch account information of a customer using `RestTemplate` and also added log messages on these methods of both services.

In the `CustomerController` class:

```
@GetMapping(value = "/customer/{customerId}")
public Customer findByAccountId (@PathVariable Integer customerId){
Customer customer =
customerRepository.findByCustomerId(customerId);
logger.info("Customer's account information by calling account-
service ");
```

```
List<Account> list =
restTemplate.getForObject("http://localhost:6060/account/customer/"
+customerId, List.class, customer);
customer.setAccount(list);
logger.info("Find Customer information by id with fetched account
info: "+customerId);
return customer;
}
```

In the `AccountController` class:

```
@GetMapping(value = "/account/customer/{customer}")
public List<Account> findByCutomer (@PathVariable Integer
customer){
logger.info("Find all Accounts information by customer:
"+customer);
return accountRepository.findAllByCustomerId(customer);
}
```

5. Run both services `Customer` and `Account`, and hit the following endpoint in the browser: `http://localhost:6161/customer/1001`.

6. Let's look at the log messages on the console logs to see the trace ID and span IDs printed.

   The `Customer` microservice console logs:

```
2018-05-09 00:51:00.639 INFO [customer-service,9a562435c0fb488a,
9a562435c0fb488a,false] Customer's account information by calling
account-service
2018-05-09 00:51:00.766 INFO [customer-service,9a562435c0fb488a,
9a562435c0fb488a,false] Find Customer information by id with
fetched account info: 1001
```

As you can see in the preceding log statement, Sleuth adds [customer-service,9a562435c0fb488a, 9a562435c0fb488a, false]. The first part (customer-service) is the application name, the second part is the trace ID, the third part is the span ID, and the last part indicates whether the span should be exported to Zipkin.

The `Account` microservice console logs:

```
2018-05-09 00:51:00.741 INFO [account-service, 9a562435c0fb488a,
72a6bb245fccafd9,false] Find all Accounts information by customer:
1001
2018-05-09 00:53:38.109 INFO [account-service,, ] Resolving eureka
endpoints via configuration
```

You can see in the preceding logs of both services, the trace IDs are the same but the span IDs are different.

You can also check the same thing on the Kibana dashboard:

May 9th 2018, 00:51:00.845   message: {"@timestamp":"2018-05-08T19:21:00.766+00:00","severity":"INFO","service":"customer-service","trace":"9a562435c0fb488a","span":"9a562435c0fb488a","parent":"","exportable":"false","pid":"12224","thread":"http-nio-6161-exec-4","class":"c.d.c.controller.CustomerController","rest":"Find Customer information by id with fetched account info: 1001"} @version: 1 port: 63,324 host: 127.0.0.1 @timestamp: May 9th 2018, 00:51:00.845   id: oOQzQWMBscxd1tLHJWOc

May 9th 2018, 00:51:00.744   message: {"@timestamp":"2018-05-08T19:21:00.741+00:00","severity":"INFO","service":"account-service","trace":"72a6bb245fccafd9","span":"72a6bb245fccafd9","parent":"","exportable":"false","pid":"12120","thread":"http-nio-6060-exec-4","class":"c.d.a.controller.AccountController","rest":"Find all Accounts information by customer: 1001"} @version: 1 port: 63,314 host: 127.0.0.1 @timestamp: May 9th 2018, 00:51:00.744   id: f-QzQWMBscxd1tLHJWOc   type: doc   index: logstas

May 9th 2018, 00:51:00.671   message: {"@timestamp":"2018-05-08T19:21:00.639+00:00","severity":"INFO","service":"customer-service","trace":"9a562435c0fb488a","span":"9a562435c0fb488a","parent":"","exportable":"false","pid":"12224","thread":"http-nio-6161-exec-4","class":"c.d.c.controller.CustomerController","rest":"Customer's account information by calling account-service "} @version: 1 port: 63,324 host: 127.0.0.1 @timestamp: May 9th 2018, 00:51:00.671   id: fuQzQWMBscxd1tLHJG1v   type: do

We have discussed the Sleuth library to store the log messages. Let's see how Zipkin helps to analyze the latency of the service calls.

Requesting tracing with Zipkin

Spring Cloud also provides integration to the Zipkin library. We will discuss how to add Zipkin to our microservices-based application. Zipkin provides a mechanism for log-message tracing into your application, such as sending, receiving, storing, and visualizing traces. Zipkin also allows us to trace log activity across servers and gives a much clearer picture of your application and what is happening in our microservices.

As we have discussed in the previous section about Spring Cloud Sleuth, by using it, you can easily trace the log messages in your distributed application. Any library could provide the additional information in your log messages, which would be great for your application. So, we have used ELK, which helps to collect and analyze log messages for your microservices, and it can be helpful for your application monitoring. We can use the trace ID to search all log message across all microservices and provide a picture of how the request passed from one microservice to the next. But sometimes we want more information in our log messages, such as timing information to calculate how long a request took to get from one microservice to the next microservice. To solve this problem, Spring Cloud supports the Zipkin library and provides the Spring Cloud Sleuth Zipkin module. You can add this module by adding the `Spring-cloud-sleuth-Zipkin` Maven dependency in your project.

Spring Cloud Sleuth will send tracing information to the Zipkin server where you point it. By default, Zipkin is running at `http://localhost:9411`. You can customize it by setting the `spring.zipkin.baseUrl` property in your application's properties. Let's enable our application to use Spring Cloud Sleuth Zipkin and send tracing information to the Zipkin server. Let's see the following Maven dependency:

```
<dependency>
<groupId>org.springframework.cloud</groupId>
<artifactId>spring-cloud-sleuth-zipkin</artifactId>
</dependency>
```

By default, if you add `spring-cloud-starter-zipkin` as a dependency to your project when the span is closed, it is sent to Zipkin over HTTP. The communication is asynchronous. You can configure the URL by setting the `spring.zipkin.baseUrl` property, as follows:

```
spring.zipkin.baseUrl: http://localhost:9411/
```

Adding the Zipkin server to your machine

Let's add the Zipkin server to your machine, you can create the Zipkin server application by using the following Maven Zipkin dependencies:

```
<dependency>
    <groupId>io.zipkin.java</groupId>
    <artifactId>zipkin-server</artifactId>
</dependency>
<dependency>
    <groupId>io.zipkin.java</groupId>
    <artifactId>zipkin-autoconfigure-ui</artifactId>
    <scope>runtime</scope>
</dependency>
```

The preceding Maven dependencies have the Zipkin server and Zipkin UI application, but you have to enable it by using an annotation.

It will be a Spring Boot application and enable the Zipkin server by using the @EnableZipkinServer annotation in the main application class:

```
@SpringBootApplication
@EnableZipkinServer
public class ZipkinServerApplication {
            . . .
}
```

By default, the Zipkin server will run at http://localhost:9411. The @EnableZipkinServer annotation will use it to listen for incoming spans and the http://localhost:9411 URL UI for querying.

But it doesn't need to create a Zipkin server application, you can use the built-up Zipkin application. Zipkin has a Docker image and an executable JAR of this application at https://zipkin.io/pages/quickstart.html. You just download it to your machine and run it by using the following command:

```
$ java -jar zipkin-server-2.8.3-exec.jar
```

Let's see the following screenshot after running the Zipkin application on the machine:

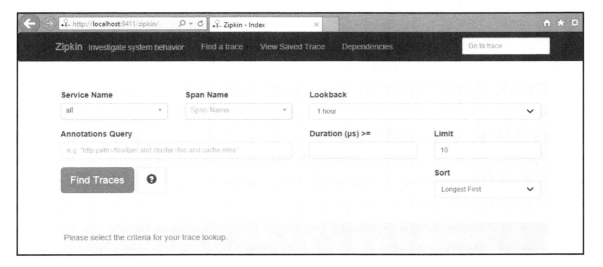

As you can see in the preceding screenshot, the Zipkin server is started, you can access it by navigating to `http://localhost:9411` in your favorite browser:

As you can see, the Zipkin UI can be used to find traces and spans.

After adding and starting the Zipkin server, let's add the Spring Cloud Sleuth Zipkin dependency to your microservices, such as the `Account` and `Customer` services, by adding the following Maven dependency to each microservice:

```
<dependency>
    <groupId>org.springframework.cloud</groupId>
    <artifactId>spring-cloud-starter-zipkin</artifactId>
</dependency>
```

The preceding Zipkin starter dependency will also include the Spring Cloud Sleuth library (`spring-cloud-starter-sleuth`), so it doesn't require you to add it separately.

We have already discussed the Sleuth tool, it is used to generate the trace IDs and span IDs. Sleuth adds information, such as trace IDs and span IDs, to the service calls in the headers, so that the Zipkin tool and ELK can use this information.

So far, we have integrated Zipkin and Sleuth in our microservices applications. So, whenever we call customer service endpoints, Sleuth works automatically and sends this service call information to the attached Zipkin server. And Zipkin will calculate the service call latency along with some other information.

Let's see the following diagram, when we call the `Customer` service:

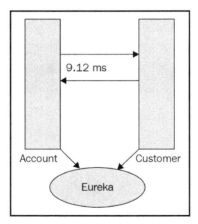

As you can see in the preceding diagram, Zipkin will store this latency information. Let's open the Zipkin dashboard after calling the `customer` service in the browser, as follows:

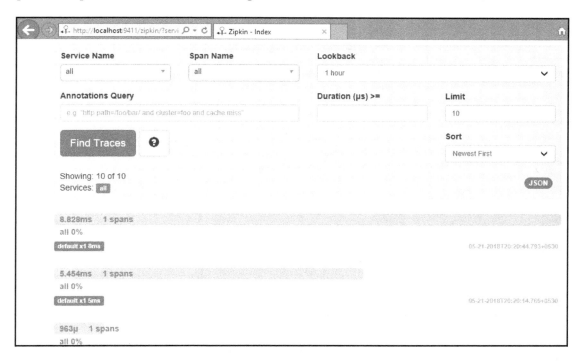

As you can see in the preceding screenshot, it has included the latency of service calls with span IDs. Let's click on the trace ID in the dashboard. It will render information regarding the trace ID:

As you can see, the preceding screenshot has information about a particular trace ID, which means a particular end-to-end transaction. You can also see the details of the trace, including all span IDs, by clicking on this row, and it will be displayed as in the following screenshot:

The preceding screenshot has more details about the trace ID for a particular end-to-end transaction of the microservices.

I hope you have learned to use the Zipkin library to analyze the latency of the service calls across the microservices in a distributed system. Sleuth passes the API call information to Zipkin.

Summary

We discussed the importance of monitoring microservices and containers; we also created a central logging approach to solve the problems of traditional logging systems using ELK.

The Spring Cloud Sleuth API provides a log-tracing mechanism and end-to-end log tracing of a transaction in a distributed microservices-based application. Zipkin also provides log-tracing techniques with timestamps. So, the Zipkin library is very useful for distributed applications.

Other Books You May Enjoy

If you enjoyed this book, you may be interested in these other books by Packt:

Spring Boot 2.0 Cookbook - Second Edition
Alex Antonov

ISBN: 978-1-78712-982-5

- Get to know Spring Boot Starters and create custom auto-configurations
- Work with custom annotations that enable bean activation
- Use DevTools to easily develop and debug applications
- Learn the effective testing techniques by integrating Cucumber and Spock
- Observe an eternal application configuration using Consul
- Move your existing Spring Boot applications to the cloud
- Use Hashicorp Consul and Netflix Eureka for dynamic Service Discovery
- Understand the various mechanisms that Spring Boot provides to examine an application's health

Spring: Microservices with Spring Boot
Ranga Rao Karanam

ISBN: 978-1-78913-258-8

- Use Spring Initializr to create a basic spring project
- Build a basic microservice with Spring Boot
- Implement caching and exception handling
- Secure your microservice with Spring security and OAuth2
- Deploy microservices using self-contained HTTP server
- Monitor your microservices with Spring Boot actuator
- Learn to develop more effectively with developer tools

Leave a review - let other readers know what you think

Please share your thoughts on this book with others by leaving a review on the site that you bought it from. If you purchased the book from Amazon, please leave us an honest review on this book's Amazon page. This is vital so that other potential readers can see and use your unbiased opinion to make purchasing decisions, we can understand what our customers think about our products, and our authors can see your feedback on the title that they have worked with Packt to create. It will only take a few minutes of your time, but is valuable to other potential customers, our authors, and Packt. Thank you!

Index

Z

Zipkin
  server, adding to machine 358, 360, 362
  used, for tracing request 357
Zuul service proxy

enabling 157
Zuul
  filters, adding 161
  filters, registering 162
  including, with Maven dependency 156
  properties, configuring 157, 161

www.ingramcontent.com/pod-product-compliance
Lightning Source LLC
LaVergne TN
LVHW081513050326
832903LV00025B/1468